Black Social Capital

STUDIES IN GOVERNMENT
AND PUBLIC POLICY

Black Social Capital:
The Politics of School Reform
in Baltimore, 1986–1998

Marion Orr

 University Press of Kansas

Published by the University Press of Kansas (Lawrence, Kansas 66049), which was
organized by the Kansas Board of Regents and is operated and funded by Emporia
State University, Fort Hays State University, Kansas State University, Pittsburg State
University, the University of Kansas, and Wichita State University

Library of Congress Cataloging-in-Publication Data

Orr, Marion, 1962–
    Black social capital : the politics of school reform in Baltimore,
    1986–1998 / Marion Orr.
        p.   cm. — (Studies in government and public policy)
    Includes bibliographical references and index.
    ISBN 0-7006-0981-4 (cloth : alk. paper). — ISBN 0-7006-0982-2
    (pbk. : alk. paper)
        1. Afro-Americans—Education—Maryland—Baltimore—History—20th
    century.   2. Educational change—Political aspects—Maryland—
    Baltimore Case studies.   I. Title.   II. Series.
    LC2803.B35077   1999
    371.829'60730752'6—dc21   99-22219

British Library Cataloguing in Publication Data is available.

10 9 8 7 6 5 4 3 2

The paper used in this publication meets the minimum requirements of the American
National Standard for Permanence of Paper for Printed Library Materials Z39.48-1984.

To my parents, Delores B. Orr and Robert L. Orr,
for all their love and support

Contents

Tables and Illustrations

TABLES

ILLUSTRATIONS

Preface and Acknowledgments

For more than forty years, the top priority on the agenda of many U.S. cities has been the rearrangement of land-use patterns to make way for office towers, hotels, convention centers, festival markets, and transportation networks. In many big cities, dominant business interests, financial institutions, newspapers, public officials, and large property holders have been actively involved in downtown redevelopment. Given the emphasis of local leaders on physical redevelopment, it is little wonder that Paul Peterson, in his influential *City Limits* (Chicago: University of Chicago Press, 1981), would assert that "urban politics is above all the politics of land use" (p. 25).

The issue of education is not directly linked to physical redevelopment and land use, nor is it of immediate concern to growth coalitions. Thus, it is easy to see why education and related issues are often accorded low priority. Quality education is very much a public good, the kind that rational choice theorists see as susceptible to the free-rider problem. Moreover, because education offers no quick results, it has little appeal to issue entrepreneurs. My work therefore is concerned with the capacity of local leaders to forge coalitions devoted to school reform. It confirms that for a policy to have a high priority, it needs the support of major sectors of the community. And for education and school reform, a coalition with the strength comparable to downtown growth machines is necessary.

My attention to urban school reform is driven by a concern for the growing economic polarization taking place in the United States. I view education and school reform as meaningful policy arenas that can serve to improve the life chances and expand the opportunities of disadvantaged urban residents, especially children and youth.

In conducting research for an earlier study, a comparative analysis of Baltimore and Detroit, I was aided by a mountain of journal articles, dissertations, and books on Detroit. The dearth of published materials on Baltimore was a considerable handicap. To be sure, a handful of solid studies on the city exist, but compared to Detroit, Chicago, Philadelphia, Atlanta, and New York, cities most frequently subjected to scholarly inquiry, Baltimore, I discovered, is almost totally unstudied.

Such a paucity of material is surprising. As Maryland's only central city, and one of the largest U.S. cities south of the Mason-Dixon line, Baltimore has a rich and interesting political history. Its long tradition of machine-style politics provides the perfect venue for an analysis of party politics and local elections. Baltimore has long been an important center of African-American social and political life. Situated in a context of southern segregation and racial polarization, the city offers an ideal setting for an examination of racial politics and African-American political mobilization. In short, Baltimore is fertile ground for the study of urban politics. It provided me a wonderful opportunity to cut my academic teeth.

Over the years I have benefited from many people who have aided my scholarly development. I owe a large debt of thanks to my professors at Savannah State College, a small college in my hometown where I earned my undergraduate degree in political science. Primarily, I would like to express my gratitude to Hanes Walton Jr., an important early influence. In his classes, Hanes made political science come alive. His lectures were always stimulating, and the personal attention he gave me and the other small number of political science majors left an indelible imprint. In my sophomore year I discovered that Hanes was more than a teacher; he is also a research scholar and arguably the nation's leading authority on African-American politics. We were fortunate to have Professor Walton at Savannah State. He continues to be my mentor, colleague, and friend. Much of what I have accomplished in the discipline I owe to Hanes Walton Jr. To him I offer my greatest appreciation and thanks.

Among the other professors at Savannah State who started me on my way are Annette K. Brock, the late Thomas Byers, Marilyn Stewart-Gaulden, Otis S. Johnson, Isaiah McIver, Luetta C. Milledge, John Simpson, and Steven R. Smith. These women and men became my professional role models, and I thank them.

I am further indebted to the scholars who taught me in graduate school. At Atlanta University (now Clark Atlanta University), Robert Holmes guided me through the process of writing a master's thesis. Mack H. Jones's tough seminar, "Scope and Methods," introduced me to the epistemological foundations of political science, helping me establish a frame of reference that continues to guide my work today.

My adviser at the University of Maryland, Clarence N. Stone, deserves special mention. He introduced me to the study of urban politics. Few people know more about this subject than Clarence Stone. My views on urban politics have been substantially influenced by his *Regime Politics*. Clarence has been a true mentor. Over the years he has unselfishly shared his brilliant insights on urban politics, formally through course work, and informally through my many visits to his home and office and in many hours on the telephone. I also appreciate the confidence he has shown in me over the years. His words of encouragement and sage advice have pulled me through many challenging days. Every newly minted Ph.D. ought to have a mentor like Clarence Stone.

In writing this book, I have received helpful suggestions and comments from colleagues. Richard DeLeon and Dianne Pinderhughes, who reviewed the book for the University Press of Kansas, provided many suggestions and criticisms that improved it. Rich DeLeon, in particular, took a special interest in this project; his detailed and thoughtful comments were instrumental in my revisions. Howell Baum, who has been actively involved in reform programs in the Baltimore schools, read the manuscript and provided thoughtful comments and suggestions. Wilbur C. Rich, whose pioneering book on urban school reform politics has set a standard, offered useful ideas and fine insights. John Brehm provided good feedback on several chapters. I want to give special thanks to Fred Woodward, director of the University Press of Kansas, for his encouragement, patience, and professionalism throughout the completion of this project. Susan K. Schott and other UPK staff treated my manuscript with great care and were a pleasure to work with.

This book was completed while I was at Duke University. Thanks are due to my colleagues in the Department of Political Science who provided a congenial and supportive environment throughout the completion of the book.

Over the years, I have interviewed hundreds of persons in Baltimore City. Many of those interviewed shared their personal letters and correspondence and pointed me to valuable unpublished materials on Baltimore. Although prior agreements concerning confidentiality prevent me from naming them, I thank them for their time and cooperation. Without them this book could not have been completed. Jeff Korman and John Sondheim, research librarians in the Maryland Department of the Enoch Pratt Free Library in Baltimore, provided priceless assistance. Neil Carlson and Jennifer Merola, graduate students at Duke University, prepared the maps and some of the diagrams and tracked down bibliographic sources.

I am also blessed with a cadre of supportive and cheerful friends. Barry B. Brewer, an economist trained at the University of Maryland, finished graduate school with me and remains one of my closest friends. Valerie C. Johnson, another Maryland Ph.D., helped make the graduate school experience enjoyable. The Reverend Barry Wright, a Duke University Divinity School graduate, who now leads a prominent congregation in Columbia, South Carolina, provided spiritual guidance throughout the writing of this book and (unbeknownst to him) aided me as I navigated the waters of academic life at a leading American university. One of the many benefits of marrying an intelligent woman is getting to know her equally bright friends. A special thanks goes to our friend Mélina Brown, whose editorial assistance helped produce a solid first draft.

Finally, I want to thank my family. My wife, Ramona Burton, saw me through the stress and frustration of writing my first book. She listened patiently as I thought aloud about "the book," often challenging me to be clearer. Superbly trained, with a Ph.D. in political science from the University of North Carolina at Chapel Hill, Ramona read the manuscript, offering keen insights and thoughtful suggestions on how it might be improved. Whenever I thought I couldn't pull it off, she was there to ease my anxiety and to reassure me. I am so pleased that Ramona is my partner in life.

To my brother and sister, Robert D. Orr and Rhonda Gale Orr, I offer thanks for their support. My parents, Robert L. Orr and Delores Burns Orr, have been my longest supporters. Their love and hard work provided a caring home, helping me to establish a firm foundation. For all this and more, it is to them that I dedicate this book.

Marion Orr—

1

Social Capital, Urban Regimes, and School Reform

Social capital is productive, making possible the achievement of certain ends that would not be attainable in its absence.
– JAMES S. COLEMAN

If a governing regime is to do more than provide routine services, it must be able to mobilize private as well as public actors. Informally achieved cooperation is therefore vital to the capacity to govern.
– CLARENCE N. STONE

Most objective indicators of educational performance raise serious questions about the capacity of large urban school systems to meet their educational mission.[1] Summary data provided by the Council of Great City Schools report that significantly more than half the students in big-city school systems fall beneath the national norms for standardized testing in math and reading. Issues such as violence against students and staff and problems of infrastructure arise in many large, urban school districts more often than in smaller districts.[2] Instructional equipment, including books, computers, and basic supplies, are often outdated or in limited quantity in these larger districts.[3] Further, there is considerable case study evidence that administrative and financial controls are lacking in many urban school districts.[4]

These problems are of great concern to people living in central cities. Parents worry about the future of their children and wonder whether the schools can prepare them with the skills and knowledge needed in a technologically advanced global economy. Business leaders too are concerned about the quality of their future workforce, complaining that schools are producing graduates who lack basic skills. Ministers, social workers, child advocates, and other community-based

1

leaders believe that a poor educational environment encourages young people to drop out of school, leaving them unprepared for higher education and employment opportunities and unraveling the city's social fabric because of the resultant crime and juvenile delinquency. Further, mayors, city councillors, and other city officials view deteriorating school systems as negative reflections of their city's image.

In Baltimore, the plight of the city's public schools has caused heightened concern among parents, church groups, youth advocacy organizations, business leaders, and city and state elected officials ever since the local Morris Goldseker Foundation commissioned *Baltimore 2000,* a consultant study that assessed the city's economic and social future.[5] Released in 1986, the study was hardly flattering to the Baltimore City Public School System (BCPS), describing it as "ineffective, undisciplined, and dangerous. . . . The fact remains that, on leaving the school system, very few Baltimore students have been pressed to the limit of their intellectual potential, many are unprepared for any but menial employment, and some are unready for jobs of any kind." "Blow it up," one section suggested. "Blow it up, and start all over again."[6] The report concluded that Baltimore faced a bleak future, growing smaller, poorer, and more isolated unless significant steps were taken to improve the city's public education system.

Demographically, Baltimore and its school system do not seem to differ much from other large American cities. In 1990 its population was 736,014, making it the fourteenth largest U.S. city. It is Maryland's only central city. Nearly 60 percent of its total population is African American.[7] Hence, unlike in Atlanta, Detroit, and Washington, DC, for example, white residents remain a sizable component of Baltimore's total population.

Though there is some variation, Baltimore's public school system, to a large extent, does not differ much from other big-city systems. With an enrollment of over 110,000 students, the BCPS ranks as the nation's twentieth largest school district. Its students are primarily African American (82 percent) and poor. In 1995 nearly 70 percent of the students were eligible for the federally assisted school-lunch program. The majority of the school district's professional staff is African American, and since the early 1970s all permanent school superintendents have been also.

Baltimore's civic leadership has devoted a lot of attention to school reform. Shortly after the release of *Baltimore 2000,* Kurt L. Schmoke, pledging to bring about "a renaissance in public education" to Maryland's largest central city, was elected mayor. A wide assortment of organizations and community activists joined Schmoke in the school-reform movement. Since the mid-1980s, the business community, organized under the Greater Baltimore Committee (GBC), has become more active in school affairs, testifying before the state legislature to support increased state funding for the city's schools, forging partnerships with several of them, and training principals to operate schools more like businesses. The Abell Foundation, one of Maryland's largest, has contributed millions of dollars to support school-reform efforts in Baltimore. Educational researchers at Johns Hopkins

University have launched numerous studies and pilot programs in many of the schools. The Citizens Planning and Housing Association (CPHA), a nonprofit organization formed in the 1940s, added education as one of its principal concerns in the late 1980s, helping train and organize parents and community leaders to improve their local schools. Baltimoreans United in Leadership Development (BUILD), an influential organization made up of fifty-five black churches and three labor unions, has been very effective in mobilizing community-based support to improve the quality of public schooling. State officials, especially the State Board of Education and the State Superintendent of Education, have pushed school reform initiatives in Baltimore and throughout Maryland.

However, despite more than a decade of effort, school reform and improved student achievement remain elusive. Baltimore consistently performs far worse than Maryland's other school districts on the Maryland School Performance Program's tests of student achievement. In 1996 over 20 percent of the city's schools were designated "reconstitution eligible" by state education officials, meaning they were eligible for state intervention, such as taking over the school or turning it over to a private company to run. Frustrated with the slow pace of school improvement, in 1997 the Maryland legislature passed measures increasing the role of state officials in the operation of the BCPS. Even Mayor Schmoke recently admitted that the public schools in his city "still have serious problems."[8]

Why is school reform so difficult in Baltimore? What role have business and civic leaders played during the past decade to improve the public schools? How does leadership, especially leadership derived from formal authority (as vested in a city's mayor, a school superintendent, or a principal), mobilize the community and provide essential resources? What has been the impact of race in bringing together and sustaining a coalition of professional educators, parents, ministers, community-based leaders, corporate executives, union officials, and public officeholders to reform Baltimore's schools? I shall apply "social capital" theory to address these questions.

SOCIAL CAPITAL

The concept of social capital was recently developed as a way to understand government and society.[9] Robert Putnam's influential formulation popularized the concept and sparked a vigorous debate in academic and journalistic circles.[10] Putnam defines social capital as "features of social organization, such as trust, norms, and networks, that can improve the efficiency of society by facilitating coordinated actions."[11]

Putnam's book on social capital became one of the most acclaimed recent works in political science. Indeed, he is leading this line of research in the United States.[12] Although much of his analysis remains underdeveloped, Putnam's preliminary finding is that social capital in America is eroding.[13] Analyzing longitudinal national survey data and examining membership records of major civic associations, Putnam concludes that in the last three decades, Americans have experienced a diminished level of civic engagement and social connectedness. Voter turnout is down, trust in government has declined, and membership in church-related activities, labor unions, parent-teacher associations (PTA), civic and fraternal organizations, Boy Scouts, and many other major civic organizations has fallen steadily in the last thirty years.[14] "The weight of the available evidence," Putnam writes, "confirms that Americans today are significantly less engaged with their communities than was true a generation ago."[15] As he puts it, more Americans are "bowling alone."[16]

Putnam laments the erosion of America's stock of social capital, believing that the existence and maintenance of civic engagement and a vibrant associational life can lower the amount of drug use and criminal activity, increase the success of students in schools, enhance economic development, and make government more effective. Just as joblessness, inadequate education, and poor health clearly curtail the life chances of inner-city residents, Putnam asserts, "so do profound deficiencies in social capital."[17] He explains:

> Even those most sympathetic to the plight of America's ghettos are not persuaded that simply reviving the social programs dismantled in the last decade or so will solve the problems [of America's central cities]. The erosion of social capital is an essential and under-appreciated part of the diagnosis. . . . In any comprehensive strategy for improving the plight of America's communities, rebuilding social capital is as important as investing in human and physical capital.[18]

Putnam argues that there is an obvious link between America's social problems and its level of social capital.

Putnam's conception of social capital is based on an exhaustive empirical analysis of different regions in Italy. In 1970 the Italian government established twenty new regional governments with virtually identical constitutional structures and authority but with dramatically different social, economic, and political contexts. Putnam spent two decades comparing the performance of these governments in such matters as regional cabinet stability, bureaucratic responsiveness, creation and implementation of new social programs, and expenditures for housing, day care, health services, and agriculture.[19] Some regional governments were discovered to be "consistently more successful than others—more efficient in their internal operations, more creative in their policy initiatives, more effective in implementing those initiatives."[20] These regional differences were evident even though the planning institutions in both the north and the south were essentially identical.

After testing several explanations that could account for these qualitative differences, Putnam concluded that social capital, a property he found flourishing in the north but at "meager" levels in the south, was key to effective govern-ment. In the "uncivic" regions of the south, he detected "vicious circles" of dis-trust, with negative consequences of economic backwardness and ineffective government.[21] On the other hand, regional governments blessed with a tradition of citizen involvement in guilds, mutual aid societies, cooperatives, unions, sing-ing groups, soccer clubs, literary societies, and birdwatching groups were likely to have effective governments. In these regions, voluntary associations grow and flourish, producing feelings of trust and empowerment.

Most citizens in these regions read eagerly about community affairs in the daily press. They are engaged by public issues, but not by personalistic or patron-client politics. Inhabitants trust one another to act fairly and to obey the law. Leaders in these regions are relatively honest. They believe in popular govern-ment, and they are predisposed to compromise with their political adversaries. Both citizens and leaders here find equality congenial. Social capital and po-litical networks are organized horizontally, not hierarchically. The community values solidarity, civic engagement, cooperation, and honesty. Government works. Small wonder that people in these regions are content![22]

Social capital, Putnam explains, does not simply spring up. "The civic com-munity has deep historical roots," he argues.[23] For example, the Italian regions characterized by civic involvement and high levels of social capital in the late twentieth century, he discovered, "are almost precisely the same regions where cooperatives and cultural associations and mutual aid societies were most abun-dant in the nineteenth century, and where neighborhood associations and religious confraternities and guilds had contributed to the flourishing communal republics of the twelfth century."[24] In other words, social capital has deep roots in political culture, growing at a glacial pace over long periods of history. Social capital wasn't born yesterday, and it doesn't bounce up and down daily like the stock market or public opinion.

RETHINKING SOCIAL CAPITAL

Critics attacked Putnam's formulation on a number of fronts.[25] Margaret Levi reminds us that the capacity to be engaged collectively is not always a good thing.[26] Sheri Berman agrees, arguing that Putnam mistakenly assumes that "collective endeavors and activist skills are good things *in and of themselves*, without regard to the purposes to which they will be directed. . . . Under certain conditions, in fact, civil society organizations may help dissatisfied individuals come together to air and share their grievances, mobilizing them for subversive political activ-ity."[27] As James Coleman argues, "A given form of social capital that is useful facilitating certain actions may be useless or even harmful for others."[28] The rise of the homeowners' movement in Detroit and other large cities during the early 1940s and into the 1960s is an apt example. Variously called "civic associations" and "neighborhood improvement associations," these grassroots organizations offered a unified voice in city politics for homeowners groups that shared "a common bond of whiteness and Americanness" and a collective desire to keep African Americans out of their neighborhoods.[29] The consequence of this type of social capital (or "unsocial capital," to use Levi's term), however, was inequality in housing and access to jobs, the enforcement of the ideology of race held by whites, and the creation of racially divided cities. Where local groups are polarized, social capital within groups is often promoted at the expense of intergroup cooperation. In short, participation in associational life sometimes serves to fragment, rather than to integrate, a society.

Putnam's theoretical analysis also neglects important actors beyond the citizenry, most notably the government. Government institutions (and government officials) may be a source of social capital. Levi contends that "state institutions can, under certain circumstances, lay the basis for generalized trust."[30] Yet government can work to undermine social capital. "Failures of government representatives to uphold policy compacts, to achieve stated ends, or to treat potentially trustworthy citizens as untrustworthy can have disastrous effects" on social capital.[31] Moreover, Putnam does not thoroughly specify the "mechanisms" that produce, maintain, and nurture social capital, misconstruing the "causal chain" between associational involvement and effective governance.[32] Rather, he assumes good government is a result of social capital. In social science parlance, Putnam presupposes that "government institutions are the dependent variable."[33]

Other scholars have followed Levi's line of critique, ascribing to Putnam a "benign view of government."[34] Sidney Tarrow maintains that "lack of a state agency . . . is one of the major flaws of [Putnam's] explanatory model" and asserts that much of the social disintegration and lack of social capital in Italy's southern region resulted from governmental decisions. Yet in Putnam's social capital model, the "character of the state is external to the model, suffering results of the [southern] region's associational incapacity but with no responsibility for producing it."[35] The danger of accepting Putnam's model of social capital as a guide to making policy is that government—and government officials whose decisions help cause anomie and social disintegration—is let off the hook.[36]

Putnam's society-centered analysis, for example, attributes the causes of the urban crisis in U.S. society today to a lack of social capital in cities and in the associational life of inner-city residents. However, such an analysis renders unimportant the federal and state governmental policies and structural factors that could have actively contributed to the malaise in the first place. People concerned about social conditions might do better to focus on making government more responsive and on strengthening governmental institutions rather than focusing on associational life. In critiquing what he sees as a crucial omission by Putnam,

Tarrow asks, "Can we be satisfied interpreting civic capacity as a home-grown product in which the state has played no role?"[37]

Since the publication of *Making Democracy Work*, political scientists and other scholars have applied and adapted the social capital concept. Using national survey data, John Brehm and Wendy Rahn disaggregated the social capital concept, examining individual antecedents and mechanisms of its production.[38] Putnam focused on social capital within communities. Brehm and Rahn remind us that it is people who constitute those communities, demonstrating "the presence of social capital in the form of a tight reciprocal relationship between civic engagement and interpersonal trust."[39] Thus, citizens who participate extensively in their communities are more likely to have high levels of interpersonal trust. Brehm and Rahn also provide evidence that social capital between whites and blacks may be affected by race. Although cautious in interpreting their results, they speculate that "being a member of a minority increases one's chances of being a victim of prejudice or discrimination [and] may lead to heightened self-consciousness, which may contribute to a suspiciousness of one's surroundings and the motives of others."[40] Brehm and Rahn at least hint for the first time at the confounding role of race in social capital formation.

Mark Schneider and his colleagues' research on public school–choice programs in New York and New Jersey provides the first empirical examination of local activities of citizens and social capital.[41] Schneider and his associates sought to assess the degree to which parent's choice of schools increases social capital. Using four measures of social capital—PTA membership, parent volunteerism, school discussions with other parents, and parents' trust in their children's teacher—they found that school-choice programs greatly enhanced social capital among parents. Although the kind of individual-level characteristics identified by Brehm and Rahn affect the formation of social capital, programs and policies promulgated by mayors, city councillors, school board members, and other local public officials also can affect the level of civic engagement in local school affairs. This is consistent with Jeffrey Berry, Kent Portney, and Ken Thomson's research on city government–sponsored neighborhood associations in five large American cities.[42] "Governmental policies can and do affect the level of social capital."[43]

Steven Rathgeb Smith has examined efforts of public and private organizations forming local coalitions to prevent substance abuse.[44] Smith observed that social capital formation through community coalitions is heavily dependent on the fiscal strength of political institutions. His research on local efforts to prevent drug abuse highlights an important point omitted by the work on social capital published in the United States: without adequate public and private financial resources, local organizations and associations are ill-suited to address many of the challenges facing inner-city communities.

BLACK AND INTERGROUP SOCIAL CAPITAL: THE ISSUE OF TRANSFERABILITY

Although the possible decline in the level of social capital in the United States has received considerable attention from scholars, less has been paid to citizens' local activities that help define a nation's stock of social capital.[45] For school activists and other local leaders, social capital theory offers a Tocquevillean policy prescription for addressing the crisis in big-city public schools: establish, nurture, and sustain social capital by reinvigorating inner-city associational life and expanding networks of civic engagement through community-based organizations, PTAs, church groups, and school/business partnerships. Such networks would cultivate reciprocity and generalized trust, allowing local stakeholders to cooperate with each other in order to bring about meaningful urban school reform.

Implicit here is the understanding that school reform involves relationships between the school and its community. If reformers seek to improve urban schools they must institutionalize internal change within the schools and more effectively emphasize the many conceivable alliances that can be developed (and redeveloped) between a school and its community. Those relationships must engage parents, whose cooperation has proven to be indispensable to students' academic success, but they should expand beyond those family members who are immediately concerned with children's learning to reach out to churches, the corporate sector, and public officials such as the police, school board members, and city councillors. By enhancing social capital, local communities can have a direct impact on reforming central-city schools.

Baltimore's experience with school reform, however, demonstrates the need to refine and extend the social capital concept. My aim in this book is to make more explicit the underlying structure of the concept and to see how it might be extended. I attempt this by breaking social capital into two dimensions. The first dimension, *black social capital,* refers to its interpersonal and institutional forms within the African-American community. The second dimension, *intergroup social capital,* refers to cross-sector formations of mutual trust and networks of cooperation that bridge the black-white divide, especially at the elite level of sociopolitical organization.

Baltimore's African-American community developed significant common bonds and important internal institutions to combat racial discrimination. These bonds have deep roots, dating from the antebellum era. African-American church leaders, civil rights organizations, and advocacy groups developed bonds that were characterized by reciprocity, trust, and efficacy based on past experiences, facilitating their capacity to work together, achieve shared goals, and accomplish collective purposes. Throughout the city's history, African-American leaders have drawn on reserves of black social capital to protect their community's interests and to expand black opportunities.

As Putnam's work on Italy makes clear, culture rests on a past, a history, a continuity; it brings together a community that has a shared experience, a collective existence, an overall vision for the future. Black social capital in Baltimore—as represented by the benevolent societies, fraternities, voluntary associations, church congregations, and tightly knit neighborhoods formed in the late nineteenth century and by the black newspapers, historically African-American colleges, and civil rights organizations established in the early decades of the twentieth century—must be understood against a political culture and history of white domination and black exclusion.[46] African Americans formed large reserves of social capital in response to a history of racial exclusion and segregation and to a political culture of white supremacy.

The Baltimore experience, however, demonstrates that social capital within the African-American community does not necessarily translate into the kind of intergroup social capital required to accomplish systemwide school reform. If social capital is confined to individuals of the same ethnic, racial, cultural, religious, or social background, cooperation may be facilitated within particular groups but not necessarily beyond them. The scope of cooperation is narrow. Black social capital may enable African-American leaders to mobilize and cooperate to gain social ends, for example, but it may be promoted at the expense of wider cooperation among other groups.

We can see this limitation in a number of political settings, among an array of groups with a shared social (e.g., racial or religious) identity. In Northern Ireland, for instance, the political mobilization of religious solidarities can build social capital within each religious group but only at the price of exacerbating intergroup conflict and weakening the scant intergroup social capital that now exists. The traditional Orangemen march through Catholic neighborhoods is an important part of Protestant social capital, but it provokes the countermobilization of Catholic solidarity, destroying the foundations for building intergroup social capital and peace. Similarly, the language issue in Montreal, Canada, illustrates that intragroup social capital can be instrumental in mobilizing groups with shared social identities, facilitating the accomplishment of the group members' collected purposes. Though the mobilization of the Francophones in the 1960s, 1970s, and 1980s undoubtedly resulted in a genuine bilingualization of the Montreal economy, expanding the city's French-speaking middle class, in profound ways that mobilization helped erect barriers that inhibited Francophone and Anglophone intergroup social capital, polarizing Quebec and resulting in immobilism.[47]

Mark Granovetter distinguishes between "strong" and "weak" ties.[48] According to him, "ties" are social networks. Our strongest ties are typically within our social group. Strong ties are "generated by intensive, daily contact between people, often of the same tribe, class, or ethnic community."[49] However, Putnam and other social capital theorists maintain that weak ties can promote a prosperous community. "Emphasis on weak ties lends itself to discussion of relations *between* groups."[50] Weak ties are the result of interaction with those people beyond our social network. By putting us in contact with people different from ourselves, weak ties have a greater impact on intergroup social capital. "Weak ties are more likely to link members of *different* small groups than are strong ones, which tend to be concentrated within particular groups."[51] Social capital within groups, as Russell Hardin suggests, "can be a source of great power" while simultaneously encouraging "norms of exclusion" and intergroup conflict.[52] Communitywide collective effort thus is suboptimized (relative to its potential) when social capital is disaggregated and partitioned into separate domains controlled by competing groups.

Eric Uslaner and Richard Conley, in their analysis of trust and social capital in Southern California's Chinese communities, found that intragroup social capital "strengthen[s] group attachments at the expense of civic engagement in the wider society." "Group membership," they argue, "may instill loyalty to others in our circle, but not beyond."[53] Clarence Stone captures the essence of this argument: "*Individuals* accustomed to transacting business with one another can develop habits of reciprocity and a high degree of interpersonal trust. Out of accumulated experience, they may develop feelings of obligation to one another. Yet, take these same individuals and put them in an *intergroup* context, a context in which competitive *group* advantage is salient, and *interpersonal* trust and reciprocity may lose strength."[54]

A major flaw in the social capital argument is that it does not consider the difficulty in transferring intragroup into intergroup social capital. To appreciate the importance of social capital, especially in many of America's central cities, it is necessary to consider it within the context of intergroup competition and the distrusts built up over years of racial divisions and black subordination. An exclusive or excessive emphasis on intragroup social capital can undermine the interpersonal trust and reciprocity that is the basis of intergroup social capital. For instance, if an individual's membership in Group A places demands on loyalty and commitment that reduce the likelihood of benign contact and interaction with individuals in Group B, the formation of interpersonal trust across the boundaries separating Group A and Group B is made more difficult, and intragroup social capital becomes a cage keeping people in rather than a gateway for leading them out.[55]

URBAN REGIMES AND INTERGROUP SOCIAL CAPITAL

Our understanding of urban regimes can help shed light on the significance of intergroup social capital, especially at the local level. Urban regime theory, with Clarence Stone as its foremost interpreter and proposer in recent years, acknowledges that formal structures of local authority are inadequate by themselves to mobilize and coordinate the resources necessary to "produce the capacity to govern and to bring about publicly significant results."[56] Local government is quite limited in what it can do on its own. Because of its limitations and fragmentation, regime theorists emphasize that informal systems of cooperation are indispensable.[57] As Stone writes: "The study of urban regimes is thus a study of who cooperates and how their cooperation is achieved across institutional sectors of community life."[58]

If we think of a regime as the set of arrangements and understandings through which important community decisions are made and carried out, social capital, especially within an intergroup context, becomes an important part of the process of governance. Stone found, for example, that Atlanta's downtown redevelopment regime was strong because the city's corporate elites formed a mode of cooperation among themselves, giving them a powerful voice in major land-use projects. Just as significant, however, were the relationships corporate leaders forged with Atlanta's black community, especially with African-American public officials and prominent black church leaders. Strong regimes, ones capable of concerted action across a range of policy issues, have arrangements and relations enabling cooperation among various community sectors.[59]

Marrying the concepts of regime and social capital accomplishes two theoretical tasks. First, it emphasizes the intergroup dimension of social capital. Regime theory underscores the necessity for cooperation between local public officials, especially mayors, and the array of business groups, voluntary associations, neighborhood groups, religious organizations, labor unions, and other informal associations social capital theorists contend are key to effective governance. Mayors, for instance, are the most visible regime partners. Given their visibility and access to significant resources, their office provides the key institutional arrangement that brings together an array of local actors, including business leaders, community activists, local media, state officials, heads of foundations, and the leaders of neighborhood associations, church-based organizations, and social groups.[60] In sum, urban regimes operate as a cross-sector elite component of intergroup social capital.[61]

Second, linking regimes and social capital brings governmental institutions into the analysis. In Atlanta, for example, Mayors Maynard Jackson and Andrew Young played crucial roles sustaining cooperation between the downtown (largely white) civic elite and the African-American middle-class community.[62] Both mayors were able to produce outcomes by preserving cooperative relations among an array of groups and institutions with shared social identities. Similarly, as Bryan Jones and Lynn Bachelor have observed, Detroit's Mayor Coleman A. Young played a "critical" role convening leaders across institutional lines (labor; religious, business, and neighborhood groups; government) for "peak bargaining" over significant citywide issues.[63] Further, journalist Buzz Bissinger captures the daily activities of Philadelphia's mayor, Edward Rendell, whose formal authority placed him in the pivotal position of sustaining a system of civic cooperation among an array of groups with shared social identities and diverse institutions: leaders of the largely African-American public-housing tenants, representatives of the growing Latino communities, powerful African-American clergy (many representing middle-class church congregations), thousands of municipal labor union members and their leaders, representatives of white-ethnic neighborhood associations, organizations representing small business owners, and managers and chief executive officers of the largest corporations.[64] Clearly, big-city mayors can be the linchpins for intergroup social capital.

The central role played by big-city mayors in urban regimes means that government and elections are not inconsequential. Hence, it is important to stress the more traditional role of electoral mobilization and political incorporation as a political resource.[65] In the 1960s and 1970s, African-American leaders in Baltimore and many other big cities realized the presence of black social capital was not enough to change the direction of city government and black exclusion in the arena of city politics.[66] What was needed was the mobilization of black social capital and its transformation into a force for policy innovation and implementation. Social capital, even robust intergroup social capital combined with financial resources, is not enough without the votes, representation, political incorporation, and political leadership required to back it up and convert it into policy.

Although social capital theorists emphasize the dense and complex networks of churches, clubs, choirs, lodges, and neighborhood associations, the informal ties that promote cooperation, the regime concept suggests that governmental authority can also facilitate cooperation, especially in the case of African-American mayors whose elections tend to alter regime composition, expanding the array of interests that constitute regime partners.[67] In addition to mayors, principals, school superintendents, and state officials, others with legal authority are strategically situated to promote social capital and to facilitate the kind of cooperation "that can bring together people based in different sectors of a community's institutional life."[68]

Figure 1.1 schematizes the principal contours of my study. The pervasiveness of local political culture helps shape the complex relationships between Baltimore's African-American and white communities.[69] The life-patterning social structures and history of race relations embedded in the city's political and civic culture encouraged the formation of a dense network of African-American organizations and voluntary associations. The mobilization of the resultant black social capital ultimately brings about the political incorporation of African-American political and civic elites into the local governing regime, representing the cross-sector elite component of intergroup social capital in which institutional and organizational leaders across community sectors gain a position in a complex set of relationships. At the regime level, political and civic elites work together across institutional lines to assemble the financial resources and programmatic initiatives necessary for the achievement of school reform.

BALTIMORE: A STUDY OF SOCIAL CAPITAL

Use of the social capital concept as a key theoretical construct necessitates several caveats. First, research on social capital is in its infancy; the concept is still

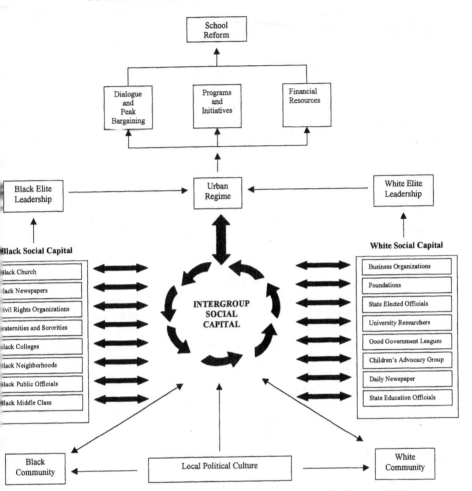

Figure 1.1. The effect of political culture and social capital on school reform in Baltimore

being developed and measured.[70] Hence, social capital does not have a widely understood definition.[71] In this book, social capital is defined as an ability to work together to achieve social ends, based on past experiences and attachments, with minimal reliance on direct payments or coercion.[72] Past experiences and attachments might include community networks, organizations, common bonds, loyalty, and trust and confidence. Social capital can even rest on a sense of efficacy based on past collective accomplishments.

Social capital is conceptually and analytically distinct from cooperation. The latter is the action of working with another or others; the former makes the latter easier. James Coleman describes social capital as social relations "that facilitate action. . . . Social capital consists of relations among persons" that allow the "achievement of goals that could not be achieved in its absence or could be achieved only at a higher cost."[73] Social capital thus enables cooperation.

A second caveat if one seeks to use the theory to explain urban school reform is that the concept must be understood within a context of declining central-city resources. Adjusting for inflation, federal aid to cities was cut by 60 percent between 1980 and 1992. This reduction has put many U.S. cities in a position where their dwindling tax base must serve to pick up costs once covered by the federal government.[74] Many city governments are impoverished, increasingly unable to provide services to their residents. Striking in Putnam's account of the decline of social capital in America is the glaring omission of the fiscal constraints that limit local governments' capacity to address economic and social problems.[75] Social capital in the context of a continuing trend of diminishing financial resources is not enough. As the Baltimore experience attests, even when social capital is present and intentions are good, the best initiatives can crumble without adequate financial support. Despite these caveats, however, the social capital concept offers much to an understanding of urban school reform.

School reform in Baltimore is especially interesting because it has the elements of a broad-based effort, including a mayor who is an education activist. Unlike in most big cities, Baltimore's education department is an agency of city government operated by a nine-member board of school commissioners (until recently) appointed by the mayor. The mayor also has considerable budgetary authority over the education department and is the key political actor in school affairs.

Baltimore has many features of an old frost-belt city, and its economy was built on heavy industry. Job opportunities in the manufacturing plants attracted African Americans and whites from southern Maryland and other southern states, along with Eastern European immigrants. As in many large northeastern cities with sizable racial and ethnic communities, a machine tradition developed in Baltimore's politics. Patronage politics has been prevalent as local party organizations have battled for political hegemony.

Baltimore's economy experienced significant restructuring and decline after World War II. Since 1950 the number of manufacturing jobs has declined by 65 percent. Growth in the economy has occurred primarily in the service sector, much of it centered in the Inner Harbor redevelopment area and downtown. The exodus of middle-class whites (and increasingly middle-class African Americans) and the decline of well-paid jobs, however, have left high concentrations of poverty in the city. In many ways, the social and economic profile of Baltimore and its residents exemplifies the racial isolation and poverty characterizing large American cities.

As a context for social capital, Baltimore plays an important role. Its African-American community is tightly knit and well-networked and has a long history of social capital dating from the late nineteenth century. A key question, however, is how its African-American community relates to the white community and to the larger city leadership.

For many decades, cooperation between its African-American and white leaders centered on patronage politics. Biracial cooperation was based on an exchange of black political support (votes) in return for particular benefits (jobs). In the early 1970s, for example, in response to blacks' demands for a greater role in local decision making, the city's political and civic elites turned over administrative control of the school system to the black middle class. School systems are large enterprises that control substantial benefits in the form of jobs, fringe benefits, and various business and professional opportunities. African Americans were given control of top positions in the school system and the power to determine school policy. Yet the system is a prime example of the dilemma of black social capital. African Americans took control of the school system just as the city was falling apart. Deindustrialization and suburbanization brought tremendous changes to Baltimore and its public schools. The exodus of both affluent residents (largely whites) and jobs left the city with a large proportion of its residents (largely blacks) dependent on government services. The sheer amount and concentration of poverty during the 1980s and 1990s have presented the school system with an unprecedented challenge.

This development puts Baltimore's black leaders in a quandary. The African-American leadership built its social capital on internal solidarity in opposition to white control and domination. Yet as deindustrialization and economic decline set in, black leaders increasingly relied on resources controlled by white corporate elites and white suburban residents for the efficient operation of the schools. Past experiences make the present institutional control of the school system by African Americans especially valued. But Baltimore's black leaders cannot expect Maryland's taxpayers and their representatives to fund an autonomous school system and to impose no conditions. Put bluntly, that black Baltimoreans feel entitled to control the city's schools carries zero weight with white taxpayers.

Racial-group defensiveness, insularity, competition, and whites' insensitivity to past black experiences and the distrust these experiences spawn have hampered cross-sector cooperation, limiting Baltimore's capacity to accomplish large-scale systemwide school reform.[76] Moreover, formation of intergroup social capital depends upon the perception of a common interest. A major barrier to school reform has been suburban voters' and their elected officials' opposition to increasing state educational dollars for the city's schools in their belief that such an increase would mean fewer dollars for their own schools.

RESEARCH STRATEGY

The bulk of my research is based on data collected for an eleven-city study of the politics of urban school reform, "Civic Capacity and Urban Education."[77] I conducted the research and gathered the data on Baltimore, including a wide range of documentary evidence regarding demographic change, school enrollment patterns, governmental expenditures, and school policies. I also conducted extensive interviews with three types of Baltimore respondents. General influentials were individuals who by position or reputation were likely to be important actors in local decision making across a range of policy issues not limited to education. Community-based representatives were those active in children's advocacy groups, minority organizations, neighborhood organizations, religious organizations, and PTAs. Education specialists were persons especially knowledgeable about the implementation of school-system policies and programs. I interviewed fifty-four individuals, a few more than once, from summer 1993 to fall 1996. Thirty-one were African American; twenty-three were white. Eighteen of the respondents were women. Each interview lasted about an hour, although several took nearly two hours. Unless otherwise indicated, direct quotations throughout the book are drawn from the transcripts of the interviews.

Following a long tradition of urban politics literature spanning over four decades, this book is about one case, Baltimore.[78] One of the most favored methods in urban political research, case studies have been, and remain, the building blocks for social science generally and urban research in particular.[79] As Gary King, Robert Keohane, and Sidney Verba observe, "Case studies are essential for description, and are, therefore, fundamental to social science. It is pointless to explain what we have not described with a reasonable degree of precision."[80]

Social capital and its application to urban politics can be more thoroughly investigated by using case study methodology than by relying on a broad overview or survey approach, if theory building is the ultimate purpose of the study. An in-depth case study can analyze the presence of social networks and ferret out the relationships between individuals involved in school reform efforts. Moreover, social capital is a relatively new theoretical force for analyzing American government and society, lacking the range of empirical work surrounding other theoretical frameworks. Further, numerous writers have contended that the concept suffers from a lack of clarity and is generally undertheorized. As Hanes Walton Jr. recently observed, "In a barren and undiscovered intellectual terrain, basic mapping, formal parameters, and useful guideways and promising paths must be fashioned. Case studies permit the establishment of intellectual frontiers."[81] It is my hope that this book can put the social capital concept on the right track.

I have benefited from King, Keohane, and Verba's advice that social scientists should seek to "expand the number of observations" within a single case study. They write: "Although case-study research rarely uses more than a handful of cases, the total number of observations is generally immense."[82] In this book, for instance, one case focuses on school reform efforts at the neighborhood level, examining two communities and movements at the microlevel. Another analysis deals specifically with the role and influence of political, economic, and civic elites. School reform from the broader context of intergovernmental relations is the focus of yet another chapter. One "case" (Baltimore) provides different types of data in distinct contexts and in various units of analysis to provide multiple tests derived from social capital theory.

PLAN OF THE BOOK

In chapter 2 I discuss how Baltimore's early African-American population developed a high level of social capital in the form of extensive social networks and civic organizations. On the eve of the Civil War, the city was home to the largest free black population in the United States. This strong community had enjoyed a measure of integration but found itself politically and physically challenged by segregationist forces. Thus past experiences, collective accomplishments, and opposition to white dominance and black subordination allowed the community to develop extensive social capital through the development of African-American churches, black educational institutions, fraternal and civic associations, and literary and debating societies. These dense networks fostered a common bond among the city's black leadership.

The major focus of chapter 3 is on how Baltimore's patronage culture and machine-politics tradition influenced the nature of black/white cooperation, especially before the 1960s. I argue that despite the relatively high endowments of black social capital, intergroup cooperation centered on personal benefits, particularly jobs. The evolution of patronage culture and pre–civil rights patterns of biracial cooperation led many citizens, particularly the African-American middle class, to view the public school system principally as a major source of jobs and patronage and only secondarily in terms of its educational mission.

In chapter 4 I focus on the demographic and economic changes that transformed the city during the post–World War II period and on how these changes had a particularly damaging impact on living conditions. Drawing on economic and demographic data, I show how the socioeconomic status of Baltimore and its neighborhood populations is closely correlated with the level of financial investment in education and with the school system's success in educating its student population. Historically, the city has been an influential voice in Annapolis, the state capital. Post–World War II demographic trends altered Maryland politics, however, shifting political power away from Baltimore to the state's growing suburban jurisdictions. The city's diminished power in the state legislature makes it increasingly difficult for local leaders to address challenging educational needs.

In chapter 5 the efforts of Baltimore's school leaders and school activists to institute site-based management throughout the school system are examined. Site-based management (SBM) is one of the big reform ideas to catch fire in recent years. The idea behind it is simply to give principals, teachers, parents, and other community members more authority to make management decisions concerning the operation of individual schools. Altering the governance of local school districts, however, is a political process. I stress that limited resources, racial politics, and resistance from teachers and central office administrators hampered efforts to establish site-based management systemwide.

In chapters 6 through 9 I move the analysis outward and upward from the neighborhood to the state level. Two case studies of parents and teachers mobilizing to reform their neighborhood schools are presented in chapter 6. The Barclay School and Stadium School movements are highlighted to illustrate that local leaders with formal authority can mobilize social capital, even in low-income, inner-city communities, and that social capital is no replacement for valuable financial resources if inner-city public schools are to be reformed.

Research on urban regimes suggests that the networks, relationships, connections, and social involvement of corporate officials and other civic elites are crucial components of a city's decision-making process. In chapter 7 I examine black-and white-elite involvement in school reform through a case study of the formation of the Baltimore Commonwealth, a major public-private partnership designed to encourage superior school performance with the promise of jobs, financial assistance to attend college, or both. At stake is the capacity of African-American community leaders and white civic elites to cooperate in order to promote a program designed to improve the quality of the school district's graduates and to place them in meaningful jobs. The Baltimore Commonwealth illustrates the difficulty of transferring black social capital into intergroup social capital. The importance of financial resources, especially private-sector investment, to successful school reform is also revealed.

In chapter 8 I explore Baltimore's decision to hire a private firm to operate nine of the city's public schools. The argument that private management can mobilize social capital by boosting parental involvement, breaking special interests' hold over public schools, improving relations between individual schools and communities, and providing quality education more efficiently is challenged in light of the disrupted social relations that resulted. I also focus on the capacity of African-American leaders to draw on large reserves of black social capital once the private management experiment was perceived as a threat to the community's economic security.

The city/state connection in education between Maryland and Baltimore is examined in chapter 9. Baltimore is home to the largest concentration of the state's African-American residents, and its relationship with the expanding (largely white) suburban jurisdictions involves a volatile mixture of race and class politics and city/suburban division. Part of the story is the battle between a poor central city and wealthier suburbs over school funding, an annual skirmish fought in state capitals across the country. Yet from the perspective of Baltimore's African-American leadership, more than money was at stake: their continued administrative control over the operation and future direction of the city's school system was at risk. Tracing the city/state connection in school reform underscores how the legacies of racial discord, past experiences of African Americans, and the distrust between white and black leaders make it difficult to transfer intragroup social capital into intergroup social capital.

In chapter 10 I summarize the major themes and findings and reflect on their implications for the general understanding of social capital. I also raise several questions about the applicability of the social capital concept to urban politics and big-city school reform.

2
The Formation of Black Social Capital in Baltimore

Baltimore's colored population has created institutions to express ideas, senti-
ments, conventions and customs it deems important. They represent all phases of
Negro life—spiritual, material, social, political, and cultural. All of them serve as
regulators of community activities.
— BALTIMORE URBAN LEAGUE, 1935

Baltimore's African-American community stands out in comparison to those in other cities in its level of sophistication and organization. In 1935, long before the national civil rights movement, a little-known but excellent study commissioned by the Baltimore Urban League observed that "few communities can boast of so many organizations as can the Baltimore colored community."[1] The Cooperative Women's Civic League, the Young Men's Christian Association, and the City-Wide Young People's Forum are among the many black organizations identified by the league's report. The presence of such an elaborately organized African-American community enabled the black leadership to develop a high level of social capital in the form of extensive social networks and civic organizations.

Tracing the roots of black social capital draws us deep into Baltimore's past, beginning with the antebellum period, when the city's large, free black population formed diverse and mass-based civic organizations. The local branch of the National Association for the Advancement of Colored People (NAACP) and the Federated Clubs of Colored Women were created and flourished into the civil rights era of the 1950s and 1960s, when numerous black organizations worked to eliminate racial injustice. To understand how deeply stocks of social capital can affect the way communities address an issue such as school reform, a history and an analysis of the experiences and collective accomplishments that allowed Baltimore's African-American community to develop extensive social capital should be explored. Thus I provide some important background information on the city's economic and social history and examine its industrial growth, the limited role slavery played in its economy, and the rise of its free black population, concluding with a discussion of the formation of black social capital during the nineteenth and twentieth centuries.

THE RISE OF AN INDUSTRIAL CITY

Baltimore has been the center of urban life in Maryland for much of the state's history. Founded in 1729 by a small group of planters seeking to cultivate and market tobacco in and around the Patapsco River, it grew from a village of 200 people in 1752 into the ninth largest town in the British North American colonies by 1776. By 1790 it was the fourth largest city in the new American nation and was impressive enough to be considered as the site for the federal capital.

Though the land could and did grow tobacco, the hilly terrain of the upper reaches of the Chesapeake Bay proved decidedly less favorable to tobacco production than that of southern Maryland. Baltimore benefited from its location in the basin of the Patapsco River, near the Chesapeake, where farmers from southern Pennsylvania and northern Maryland could mill and market their grain to merchants.[2] The key to growth was the enormous expansion of the wheat and flour trades, which began in the 1760s. The shipping and processing and the storage requirements necessitated by this commerce constituted the primary factors responsible for the city's accelerated development.

Baltimore merchants also capitalized on trading with the West Indies during slavery, exporting grain and tobacco there and to Europe and importing sugar and coffee from the Caribbean and Latin America. During the American Revolution, the city became the leading port on the Chesapeake Bay, serving as a re-export center for West Indies' goods and as the chief import center for European goods. It also developed a diversified economy during the war as a result of the proliferation of manufacturing, particularly in flour milling.[3]

In 1820 Baltimore's merchants grew concerned about their ability to compete with Philadelphia and New York, which were closer to important European ports.[4] Private investors, with the aid of public funds from the city and state, embarked on a massive program of improvements: building roads, canals, and railroads. The most important of these was the Baltimore and Ohio Railroad, chartered in 1827 and reaching the Ohio River in 1853.[5] The B&O opened up the trans-Allegheny West to local merchants. Linked by its railroads, the city became a hub for connecting markets in the West and South and a distribution point for the manufactured goods from the Northeast, changes that helped it remain nationally important as a trading center.

In the mid-1800s, Baltimore's economy pushed harder toward manufacturing. Private business groups were formed to encourage new manufacturing interests to come to the city. Between 1820 and 1840, the number of manufacturing workers in Baltimore nearly doubled, but those employed in commerce and agriculture declined.[6] The city became a popular textile center, manufacturing the heavy duck cotton used to make sails, and developing an imposing men's clothing industry.[7] Shipbuilding also became one of Baltimore's largest industries.

Industrial growth continued after the Civil War. Baltimore's blue-collar laborers could find work in the foundries and machine shops, railroad construction and repair shops, and tinware, copperware, and sheet-ironware factories. In 1887 a steel plant was built at Sparrows Point (later Bethlehem Steel) at the mouth of the harbor, just outside the city. A copper plant was also built nearby in Canton, turning Baltimore into a real manufacturing town.

NEITHER NORTH NOR SOUTH

Baltimore's location makes it unique among other large industrial cities. Situated just below the Mason-Dixon line, it has many traditions characteristic of the Deep South. Yet unlike Richmond, Savannah, Charleston, and other Deep South cities, its integrated and variable urban industrial setting made slavery as a widespread economic institution largely impractical.

Baltimore achieved its remarkable growth with only marginal dependence on the institution of slavery. As businesses discovered, market conditions did not favor slave labor. Barbara J. Fields has noted that slavery was fundamentally incompatible with the complexity of Baltimore's urban economy.[8]

> The slave system could never be the center of Baltimore's social existence. By the nature of the city's economic activity, the market for labor was highly seasonal and to a large degree casual. The various services connected with trade . . . obviously depended closely on the rhythm of trades but also on the fortuity of the weather. . . . The internal dynamic of a city like Baltimore excluded slavery as a dominant principle of organization. Though Baltimore in 1860 had a population of over two thousand slaves, it was not then or at any time in its history a slave city. . . . Baltimore was in, but not of, slave society.[9]

Baltimore slaveholders often found themselves in possession of a surplus of domestic slaves. "The problem was not to find work for slaves but to control them when their work was finished."[10] One way was for many of them to hire out their slaves. In the early antebellum period, hotels were among the largest employers of slaves, as were the city's shipyards.

Another unique characteristic of Baltimore's location was that it became a mecca for free African Americans. Maritime occupations and industries there attracted a growing number of both unskilled and skilled free blacks. Before the 1860s African Americans worked along the docks as caulkers, stevedores, draymen, and laborers. Frederick Douglass, the black abolitionist, worked in the Baltimore shipyards as a caulker, a trade virtually monopolized by blacks.[11] Though the largest single occupation was laborer, significant numbers of free blacks also took up such semiskilled trades as carting; draying; sawing; driving hacks, coaches, and stages; whitewashing; brickmaking; baking; cigarmaking; dying; and stonecutting. Moreover, a number of others acquired enough expertise to engage in such highly skilled trades as blacksmithing, barbering, shoemaking, carpentry, and butlering.

Because slavery had little to do with Baltimore's vital economy, the city's black population remained small despite its appeal to free blacks. In 1810 only 22 percent of the city's total population was African American (compared to nearly half the population in southern Maryland), and most of them were free; by 1830 the percentage dropped to 18. In 1860 approximately half of Maryland's black population were slaves, most of whom lived on the Eastern Shore and in southern Maryland. The city offered refuge to former slaves throughout the antebellum era, and as a result, the great majority of free African Americans resided there. Indeed, at the outbreak of the Civil War, Baltimore comprised the largest free black population in the United States.[12] In 1860, 27,898 blacks made up 13 percent of the city's total population and 25,680 (92 percent) of them were free.

These free blacks also comprised a growing number of property owners, especially when compared with the number of free blacks in rural Maryland who owned property. In 1850 the average black owner of real estate in Baltimore held $1,327 worth of real property, but the average free black owner in the Maryland countryside possessed just more than $450 worth. Between 1813 and 1850 the number of black owners of real property in Baltimore had more than doubled. However, when compared to free black populations of other major cities in the nation, Baltimore's free blacks were the least likely to own property.[13] Thus, unlike blacks in Philadelphia, Charleston, Washington, DC, and New Orleans, Baltimore's small number of black propertied elite offered a source of cohesion that few cities shared.

Several factors contributed to Baltimore's large, free black population. Maryland occupied both the geographic and the political middle ground on the issue of slavery and freedom.[14] "Moderate" is the term often used to describe the state, especially its stance on slavery. In 1790 Maryland already had the second-largest free black population in the country (following Virginia) and by 1810 had achieved first rank, which it retained until the final abolition of slavery. Maryland had no legal proscriptions against slave literacy. Marylanders, especially whites in the northernmost part of the state, seemed particularly influenced by the egalitarian principles of the American Revolution. In 1790, as a result of this intellectual climate, Maryland liberalized its manumission law, freeing thousands of slaves.

Revolutionary ideals alone could not account for the wave of manumission that began immediately after the American Revolution. Compelling economic reasons rendered slavery less attractive and too risky for Baltimoreans. "For most

Baltimoreans of the first decades of the nineteenth century, regardless of their occupations, slaveowning was an unaffordable luxury. Simple economics alone ensured that this would remain the case; slaves, no matter what their initial cost, were expensive to maintain."[15] A diversified economy opened alternative means of accumulating capital. More often than not, slave owners allowed slaves to work and buy their freedom, using the funds to invest in other avenues. Further, Maryland's proximity to Pennsylvania (a free state) and the increased threat of slaves escaping no doubt influenced many slaveholders' thinking.

Religious fervor also played a role in the spread of manumission. Quakerism and Methodism had considerable influence in Maryland's northernmost counties, and Christian ethos may have hastened the process in the destruction of slavery in Baltimore. Protests against slavery began early in the city, the first recorded one occurring at the eighth Methodist conference meeting there in April 1780.[16] The first antislavery society in Maryland was formed in Baltimore in September 1788. The Methodists had a particular impact, at least before the final decade of the eighteenth century. Their opposition to slavery was expressed officially in 1743 and later in the rules adopted at a 1784 church conference. This antislavery sentiment was reaffirmed repeatedly on many intervening occasions, and it enhanced significantly Methodism's attractiveness to African Americans, both slaves and free.

No matter how liberal Baltimore might be relative to cities in the Deep South, there existed a color line that legitimized and maintained white hegemony. By maintaining slavery as a legal institution, Maryland ensured white residents social control over not only its slaves but also over free blacks. As a municipality, Baltimore remained under the rule of the large plantation owners who dominated the state legislature and who nurtured fears that the city would become a haven for runaway slaves. Whenever a slave rebellion or disturbance occurred, the legislature considered bills banishing free blacks from the state. The power to remand free blacks to slavery gave white people tacit control over black Marylanders.

EARLY BALTIMORE

Even in this white-controlled political and economic environment, Baltimore's African Americans riveted together a cohesive urban community, both free and slave, exuding a solidarity that affected the formation of social capital. By 1860 blacks had developed a mature community and formed extensive social networks and civic associations. Foremost among these institutions was the church.

The Black Church

Perhaps the earliest and most important black institutions of nineteenth-century Baltimore were its churches. The Sharp Street Methodist Church was established in 1792, Bethel African Methodist Episcopal (A.M.E.) Church in 1817, St. James

Protestant Episcopal Church in 1824, and Union Baptist Church in 1852. All are still active today.

Clearly apparent in the development of the city's black churches was the parishioners' desire to worship without restrictions. In the final decade of the eighteenth century, white Baltimore Methodists began withdrawing their commitment to racial equality.[17] Black Methodists had no decision-making authority in the various white churches, were forced to wait for white members to receive communion before being allowed to do so themselves, and were not considered for ordination as ministers before 1800. Repudiating racial inequality in religion, African Americans formed their own Methodist congregations, the first independent denominations to be organized by blacks.[18] The African Methodist Episcopal Church was founded in Philadelphia in 1787. This independent church movement of black Christians formed the backbone of the struggle toward freedom by African Americans. Baltimore's Bethel A.M.E. was one of the first such organizations in the country, becoming the city's largest and most influential black congregation as early as 1826.

By 1860 sixteen black churches had been established in Baltimore. "Once established, black churches quickly became the social, political, economic, educational, and even cultural centers of the Baltimore black community. Black Baltimoreans' earliest organized efforts at economic self-help, education, and political organization revolved around black churches."[19] The activities of many of these churches served to foster a sense of racial unity, becoming the "cradles of black consciousness and organizations" and "affording a vehicle for collective action for the congregations and the population at large."[20]

Because the churches were such important centers of black culture, their leaders ranked as pillars of the community. Throughout the antebellum period, black ministers played a major role in the life of Baltimore's black community. Some of the prominent ministers of the era included Daniel Coker, a founder of the A.M.E. church (he was elected the first A.M.E. bishop but declined the office) and the individual most responsible for the formation of Bethel; Noah Davis, a former slave and Baptist preacher; Daniel Payne, a Bethel minister and later bishop of the A.M.E. church; Nathaniel Peck, a Bethel lay minister and active promoter of back-to-Africa colonization; Hiram Revels, minister at the Madison Street Presbyterian Church and later the first black member of the U.S. Senate (from Mississippi); and Henry McNeil Turner, a minister in the A.M.E. church who later achieved national recognition as a bishop, politician, and civil rights activist in Reconstruction Georgia.

Black Schools

Although the Baltimore Public School system was established by the mayor and city council in 1829, city officials felt no obligation to provide free public education to black children. Free blacks were taxed for schools their children could not attend.[21] Thus, before 1867, the education of black children was confined to private schools organized and supported by black churches. Most of the churches of the early 1800s had Sabbath schools, which in addition to reading the Scriptures taught basic reading and writing skills.[22] The Asbury Society, associated with Sharp Street Methodist Church, began providing separate schools for whites and blacks around 1802. The school at Bethel A.M.E. reported having approximately eighty students. St. James, the black Episcopal church, conducted both a successful day school and a Sabbath school of about 100 students. The fact that the black schools took in slaves as well as free blacks attests to the cohesiveness of the black community and the value it placed on education.

African Americans also operated private schools with loose ties to black churches. In 1809 Daniel Coker conducted one of the earliest day schools. Called the African Academy, it soon became the most celebrated black school in the city. "Coker offered his students more than just classical literature and history. Coker's school provided an intellectual foundation for the development of racial consciousness."[23] As he would from his pulpit at Bethel, Coker used his school as a platform to oppose slavery, advocate emancipation, and foster pride in the history of African people. The school was so popular that Coker soon offered night classes to adults in the community. When the school closed in 1820, after Coker emigrated to Liberia, as many as 150 students were enrolled, some from as far away as Washington, DC. William Watkins, a Coker student and only nineteen years old, took many of the school's students and founded the Watkins Academy, which continued for nearly twenty-five years. Watkins was also an outspoken antislavery advocate.[24]

By 1859 there were fifteen schools for blacks. Yet despite efforts of black church leaders to fill the void in black education, the schools faced financial hardships and suffered from insufficient materials so that many of these privately run institutions were inadequate for educating the whole person. Significantly, the costs meant the vast majority of blacks could not afford to attend. Nonetheless, these schools continued to grow with their churches and provided the bulk of educational opportunities for the city's black residents.

Black Fraternal, Social, and Civic Associations

Free blacks in Baltimore organized and joined a wide array of black benevolent associations, mutual aid and relief societies, literary and debating societies, and fraternal organizations. Like the black schools, these organizations were often linked to the church. Benevolent societies provided assistance to those less fortunate by soliciting contributions from the more affluent black residents; the Baltimore Bethel Benevolent Society of the Young Men of Color, formed in 1821, was one of the first of these. The African Friendship Benevolent Society for Social Relief was incorporated in 1833. An 1835 report identified at least thirty-five black benevolent societies.[25]

Black workers in the various trades formed beneficial societies, paying dues to provide for the mutual support of members and former members and their families in cases of illness, unemployment, or death. The Caulker's Association, organized as early as 1838, performed a dual service as beneficial society and trade union. Black coachmen, porters, mechanics, barbers, and bricklayers also organized benevolent associations.

During the second quarter of the nineteenth century, free blacks established a number of literary societies, debating societies, and lyceums. "These societies strove to provide moral and mental uplift to their members by engaging in such activities as reading and critiquing famous and contemporary works of literature, declamatory speaking, and writing prose and poetry, as well as sponsoring lectures on current issues and instruction in grammar, rhetoric, logic, and composition."[26] Organizations such as the Young Men's Mental Improvement Society, the Phoenix Society, and the Mental and Moral Improvement Society of Bethel were formed in the early 1830s.

Black fraternal organizations supported picnics, camp meetings, parties, ball games, and other social events. The Friendship Lodge, a society of freemasons, was one of the first such organizations, established in 1825. In 1848 local residents formed the Zion Lodge no. 4 and the Prince Hall Lodge of Free and Accepted Masons. In the 1850s black Baltimoreans established a number of lodges, including Royal Arch Masonry, Good Samaritans, and the Order of Odd Fellows.

By the mid- and late antebellum decades, blacks had formed a high level of social capital. "The Black Church," write C. Eric Lincoln and Lawrence Mamiya, "has no challenger as the cultural womb of the black community."[27] In Baltimore, not only did it give birth to new institutions such as schools, benevolent societies, fraternal organizations, and literary societies, but it also fostered among Baltimore's black citizens a common group identification and racial solidarity born of a collective struggle. The attachments and common bonds that blacks, both slave and free, developed were strong and lasting, helping them cling tenaciously to their place in a city where their fate was closely linked to the mood and attitudes of the dominant white society.

The Threat of Reenslavement

As the antebellum period progressed, the ideological climate in Maryland changed, causing the black community to draw on its stocks of social capital. White opinion about slavery and free blacks shifted. First, the rapid growth of the state's free black population concerned whites in slaveholding southern Maryland. The combination of a huge, free black population and the severe economic depression of the 1830s even concerned white Baltimoreans, who had long tolerated the troublesome presence of free African Americans. With many manufacturing firms suffering and closing for lack of capital, free blacks were dispensable. At precisely the same time Baltimore was stricken by economic stagnation and depression,

Maryland experienced a surge of immigrants from Germany, Ireland, and other European nations, who competed with blacks, slave and free, for scarce, unskilled jobs. Racial tensions rose with competition. Blacks were eventually pushed out as white employers capitulated to the demands of white workers. Further, reports of Nat Turner's 1831 slave insurrection in Southhampton County, Virginia, and of John Brown's raid at Harpers Ferry in 1859 heightened white hysteria over Maryland's growing free black population.

Beginning in the 1820s and accelerating thereafter, Maryland officials, abandoning the state's tradition of tolerance, enacted legislation intended not only to regulate slaves but also to restrict the limited liberties of free African Americans. Though generally reluctant, Baltimore's white leaders enforced the restrictions. In 1841, for example, the legislature made it a felony for a free black knowingly to receive abolitionist literature. The following year, the General Assembly forbade all black societies. Three years later, the legislature targeted lengthy outdoor revivals when it banned all meetings of black residents for religious purposes, except those held in a church building.

The major threat to the liberties of Maryland's free population came when the General Assembly convened in early 1860 to amend the state's constitution. Curtis W. Jacobs, a large slaveholder from southern Maryland and a vocal mouthpiece for supporters of further restrictions on slaves and free blacks, pushed through a proposed constitutional amendment prohibiting future manumissions and reenslaving free blacks. Many provisions of the Jacobs bill were directed at suppressing the free black population in Baltimore: prohibiting assembly of blacks, even for religious purposes, and barring free blacks from either acquiring or holding property. The measure proved to be one of the most prohibitive introduced in any of the nation's legislatures.[28]

Black Baltimoreans worked intensely in rallying opposition to the Jacobs bill. Denied the right to vote, blacks petitioned state lawmakers to defeat the proposal. An association of African-American barbers, for example, presented a petition with more than 1,000 black signatures opposing the amendment. African-American ministers organized weekly protest meetings, inviting prominent local ministers as speakers. At Bethel A.M.E., members formed a "protection society" designed to develop measures to oppose the bill. George Hackett, a former sailor who had served aboard the U.S.S. *Constitution,* was named its president. As the Reverend Mr. Coker's brother-in-law, Hackett had the advantage of being well connected in the black community. He arranged to meet with Curtis Jacobs to express black Baltimoreans' opposition to the measure. The meeting proved inconclusive, though it showed the courage of African Americans in attempting to preserve their freedoms.[29]

Fortunately for Maryland's black citizens, Baltimore's community efforts paid off. In November 1860, Marylanders resoundingly defeated the Jacobs bill; more than 70 percent of the voters rejected the measure. At a time of crisis, social capital facilitated collective action and helped shaped black Baltimore's response to an early threat. Of course, African Americans were aided by the hostile reaction of many whites to the Jacobs bill.[30] Nevertheless, only through united struggle did the African American community help block the powerful movement by whites to reenslave free blacks in Maryland.

Freedom and Civil Rights

In November 1864 the people of Maryland ratified their new constitution, abolishing slavery in the state. The evil of human bondage had been vanquished. In Baltimore, with its strong free-black tradition, African-American citizens looked forward to nothing less than full rights as citizens. Boasting the establishment of influential churches and black organizations and associations that facilitated political activity and the development of racial consciousness, African Americans were prepared to protest when their full citizenship rights were denied. Throughout the remainder of the nineteenth and into the twentieth century, the African-American community drew on its long tradition of civic engagement to fight racial discrimination.

High on the list of race restrictions opposed by the city's black leaders was the state law prohibiting African Americans from serving on juries or practicing law. In 1880 the U.S. Supreme Court ruled that states could not exclude blacks from jury service. In 1884 a group of black citizens, led by the Reverend John Handy, organized the Color Equal Rights League to see that blacks were admitted to the bar.[31] The league received the support of the Mutual Brotherhood of Liberty, a group of African-American ministers, organized in 1885 and led by the Reverend Harvey Johnson, the influential pastor of Union Baptist Church from 1872 to 1923.[32] Known throughout the city as an experienced, articulate, and determined community leader, Johnson "was afraid of no one, because he believed his principles were right."[33] The Color Equal Rights League and the Brotherhood of Liberty pooled their resources, successfully fighting the restriction on black lawyers. In October 1885 Everett J. Waring, a Howard University School of Law graduate, became the first African American admitted to practice in the courts of Maryland.[34]

Black leaders also worked tirelessly to gain and expand educational opportunities for African-American children. Despite the existence of private schools, black leaders felt the city had a responsibility to provide public education for blacks, and they continued to exert pressure on the city government to do so. The issue was raised again in January 1865, in response to growing community pressure. After nearly two years of debate, the city council passed an ordinance supporting the education of black students, declaring it "a cheap mode of saving a people from crime, pauperism, and helplessness."[35] The city council was aware that black leaders, led by the vociferous Harvey Johnson, were preparing to take the issue of black public schools to court if the council failed to respond. The Brotherhood of Liberty wasted no time, retaining Attorney Everett J. Waring to bring a lawsuit, should it be necessary.

When the school year began in 1867, thirteen primary schools were established for black children, but this was only a partial victory. A year after they opened, they were under the control of white teachers. No African-American teachers were hired throughout the 1870s and 1880s. Working with other black organizations such as the Colored Advisory Committee, the Maryland Protective League, and the Central Colored Prohibition Club, the Brotherhood of Liberty sponsored meetings to raise funds for a lawsuit against the city. Mass meetings were held to draft and circulate petitions demanding that the mayor and city council allow black teachers to staff black schools. One rally, attended by hundreds of black citizens, featured Frederick Douglass as the main speaker.[36]

By 1887 the Brotherhood of Liberty had gained the support of three white city councillors who successfully lobbied their colleagues to secure passage of an ordinance authorizing the appointment of qualified African-American teachers to African-American schools established after June of that year. The ordinance stopped short of employing black teachers in schools already staffed by white teachers and also stipulated that white teachers were not to be employed in any school where there were black teachers. Two years later the first public school staffed by African-American teachers opened. The election of a progressive mayor, and the subsequent administrative reorganization of the city's school system, hastened the rapid replacement of white teachers by African-American teachers in black schools. By 1907 the black schools were operated by an all-black staff.

THE TWENTIETH CENTURY IN BALTIMORE

Supreme Court Justice Thurgood Marshall often described his native city as "up-South Baltimore."[37] The majority of whites there traced their roots to rural southern Maryland and other southern states, and they kept black residents firmly "in place" through a southern system of legal and social segregation. Whites were often confrontational with African Americans seeking transportation on city buses, streetcars, and taxicabs. As late as 1955, a survey of 191 public establishments revealed that 91 percent had some type of "exclusionary or segregation" practices singling out black patrons.[38] Blacks did not dare venture into white neighborhoods without fearing arrest and detention based on suspicion of some crime. Downtown, the stronghold of white commercial interests, segregation was so bad that the majority of blacks ventured there only when it was absolutely necessary. Whites refused to address blacks by courtesy titles, referring to a black man as "boy" and a black woman as "girl."

African Americans also faced discrimination in the workplace. Blacks had a monopoly on jobs as laborers, porters, waiters, and domestic servants.[39] In the mid-1930s no department of city government (except the school system, which was required by law to maintain separate schools) employed African Americans at a rate close to their proportion of the city's population. Nor were they employed in the police or fire departments. Because African Americans were confined to low-skilled jobs, their wages invariably tended to be lower than those of white workers. Labor unions, which at times could garner greater wages from employers, did not put much effort into recruiting black members.[40] African Americans were barred from most municipal tennis courts and golf courses; public pools and baseball fields were also segregated. Segregationist values, notions that blacks should be separate and subordinate, prevailed.

During the early decades of the twentieth century, black social capital in Baltimore heightened as a geographically and culturally defined black neighborhood developed, an influential African-American newspaper began publication, an expanded black middle class emerged, historically African-American colleges and universities were established, and civil rights organizations and other race-advancement associations were created. Throughout the century blacks turned to their vast networks of associations and organizations to help fight racial injustice.

Segregated Neighborhoods

Black neighborhoods became important sources of African-American group identity, helping form a distinctly urban and African-American consciousness. Before the 1900s, a small concentration of African Americans lived in an area of south Baltimore commonly called Pigtown. Generally, however, African Americans were widely dispersed throughout the city, and no predominantly African-American community existed.[41] In 1880, for example, although blacks constituted 10 percent or more of the total population in three-fourths of the city's twenty wards, no single ward was more than one-third black.[42] Around 1885, African Americans began to move in a northwesterly direction into traditionally white neighborhoods, particularly into a west Baltimore neighborhood, bounded by North Avenue on the north, Franklin Street on the south, and Madison and Fulton Streets on the east and west. This migration was in response to overcrowding in Pigtown where, after the turn of the century, more than 200 black homes were demolished to accommodate the expansion of Camden Yards Railway Station.[43] By 1904 one-half of the African-American population of the city was living in what is now called Old West Baltimore.

During World War I, as a result of migration from rural areas of Maryland and from the South, mainly Virginia and North Carolina, the black population expanded. Between 1900 and 1920 the number of blacks in the city rose from 79,258 to 108,322, a 37 percent increase. As the black population continued to grow, some African Americans who had the means began to flee to outlying areas. By 1910, Madison Avenue, Eutaw Place, Linden Avenue, and McCulloch Street, all parallel to Pennsylvania and Druid Hill Avenues, became focal points for affluent African Americans seeking housing. In response to white protest over the expansion of blacks into white communities, in 1910 and again in 1911 and 1913 the city council passed ordinances prohibiting African Americans from moving into areas primarily occupied by whites, and vice versa.[44] Total housing supply for blacks was thus restricted.[45]

Much of the African-American population was concentrated in three West Baltimore neighborhoods, Upton, Sandtown-Winchester, and Harlem Park. William J. Wilson has observed that in the early decades of the twentieth century many big-city neighborhoods featured a "vertical integration of different income groups as lower-, working and middle-class professional black families all resided more or less in the same ghetto neighborhoods."[46] West Baltimore typified this description. The most prominent black citizens, a substantial group of renters, and the poorest of the city's working class lived within the neighborhood's boundaries. Black professionals lived along upper Druid Hill Avenue, a quiet residential street with stately three-story townhouses. W. E. B. DuBois is said to have described Druid Hill Avenue as "one of the best colored streets in America."[47] According to another African-American observer, "Druid Hill was the place where upper-crust Blacks lived and to which up-and-coming ones aspired."[48] Black working-class families rented more affordable dwellings. The black poor lived in alley houses—small structures built along narrow back alleys and lacking the basic amenities of urban life.

Baltimore's black institutions meanwhile accommodated its members. In 1908 Union Baptist Church, in East Baltimore, moved to Dolphin and Druid Hill Avenues, closer to its members. Sharp Street Methodist Church, located at the center of the city, collected enough donations to a buy a lot and build a church. Now at Dolphin and Etting Street, it is probably the oldest surviving African-American church built and financed by blacks in Baltimore.[49] Its neighbor, Bethel A.M.E., opened the doors of its new location on Druid Hill Avenue in 1910.

African-American neighborhoods were tightly knit and well-networked. Residents counted on each other, indeed watched over each other. Newcomers to West Baltimore relied on relatives and friends from the neighborhood for information concerning job opportunities. As a longtime West Baltimore resident recalled years later, "When you came up here [from Virginia] you had to report to a resident here, someone you knew. And they notified your family right away. And you stayed there, right there, until you got a job."[50] The Colored YWCA on Druid Hill near Dolphin ran an employment service. And because blacks lived close to each other, word of a new baby, a wedding, or a death spread quickly. "If the larger Baltimore community was hostile, neighbors simply could not be anonymous faces to each other. The daily triumphs of life had to be shared."[51] The segregated neighborhoods of West Baltimore helped build bonds and trust among African Americans.

An Influential Black Newspaper

Another element facilitating black social capital was the *Baltimore Afro-American*. The newspaper was founded in August 1892 when John H. Murphy Sr., a former slave, purchased a small printing press at an auction.[52] During the first decades of the twentieth century the *Afro-American*'s readership expanded, and the paper achieved a circulation of 200,000 and annual gross revenues in excess of $1 million, becoming one of the largest black newspapers in the United States.[53] The newspaper is still published by members of the Murphy family, continuing its historical role as the voice of black social capital.

The *Afro-American* gave readers thorough coverage on the activities of blacks, devoting articles and editorials to African Americans in the community. Extensive articles on black clubs, organizations, and churches were printed. From the start, the paper continually battled for black political rights, better economic opportunities, and the reduction of discrimination. When the state legislature enacted two laws imposing segregation of the races on all railroads and steamships in the state (Maryland blacks in 1904 were frankly unfamiliar with segregated transportation), John Murphy carried editorials describing to his readers the "deplorable" conditions resulting from segregation, calling on blacks to boycott the segregated facilities. Throughout summer 1904, scarcely an issue of the weekly appeared without either an editorial or a story on the boycott.[54]

From its inception the *Afro-American*'s headlines and editorials helped to inform the black community not only of the battles being waged against discrimination but also of social and religious activities. In 1935 a Baltimore Urban League study observed:

> As a lever for racial justice, the Baltimore *Afro-American* has constantly and persistently agitated for economic, social and cultural justice for Baltimore's Negro population. The "*Afro's*" approach to this problem has been a double-edged one. Not only has it pointed out to the white community the various miscarriages of justice, but it has carefully and continuously worked to arouse the Negro community to demand full justice in such matters. . . . As the local spokesman for Negro rights, the *Afro-American* is both respected and feared.[55]

African-American Middle Class

Rigid separation and discrimination created job opportunities for a large number of black Baltimoreans who worked in public services and the business establishments that catered to African-American needs. These residents comprised Baltimore's African-American middle class. In 1935 the Baltimore Urban League estimated that "3,000 Negroes are engaged in some phase of professional employment in Baltimore. For some years this group has been one of the most representative middle-class communities in the country."[56] Black probation officers, nurses, dentists, clerks, and recreation workers found work in providing public service to the black community. Black teachers, school administrators, and ministers made up a large component of the middle class. According to one study, "There were more Negro school teachers in Baltimore than in any other American city."[57] Of course, there were African-American lawyers, doctors, and other professionals who sold their services to black clients. And along Pennsylvania Avenue, black entrepreneurs catered to the African-American community.

Black Colleges and Universities

Central to the formation of this African-American middle class was the presence of Morgan State University and Coppin State University, two historically black institutions of higher learning. Barred because of their race from attending the University of Maryland, African Americans who wanted a college education enrolled at Morgan or Coppin. The former was founded in 1867 to train "those men recently released from bondage for the Christian ministry."[58] The college's theological mission was abandoned in 1905 and an expanded liberal arts curriculum was initiated. In November 1939 the state acquired Morgan as a means to fulfill its obligations to provide higher education for black citizens. Morgan obtained university status in 1975, offering master's and doctoral degrees.

Coppin State was established in 1901 in response to black leaders' complaints about the small number of black teachers in the separate "colored" school system. Coppins' specific purpose was to train African-American elementary schoolteachers. For the first thirty-four years, it offered one-year and two-year programs. In 1934 the curriculum was expanded to three years, and in 1938 the school was given the authority to confer four-year degrees in education. In 1950 Coppin became a state-supported college.

Campus life and student activities strengthened bonds among students. Many Morgan and Coppin students joined the same traditionally African-American sororities (Alpha Kappa Alpha, Delta Sigma Theta, Zeta Phi Beta) and fraternities (Alpha Phi Alpha, Omega Psi Phi, Kappa Alpha Psi, and Phi Beta Sigma), important aspects of Baltimore's black social capital. Morgan State and Coppin State are also essential components of it, providing the basis for a growing black middle class. The colleges trained many educators, clergy, entrepreneurs, and other black leaders. During the 1950s and into the 1980s, the vast majority of black teachers and administrators in the Baltimore public schools were Morgan and Coppin graduates.

The Civil Rights Movement

Perhaps the most significant promoters of black social capital during the first half of the twentieth century were the local chapter of the National Association for the Advancement of Colored People and the leaders of African-American church congregations. Founded in 1913, the Baltimore NAACP is the second oldest chapter in the country.[59] After a long period of aggressive leadership, however, the NAACP had fallen dormant. Then the 1933 lynching of George Armwood on the Eastern Shore galvanized Baltimore's African-American community, inspiring decades of intense activism and reinvigorating the NAACP.[60] The association was led by Lillie May Jackson, a fiercely independent black woman of "aristocratic background."[61] Under her leadership, the chapter became one of the largest branches in the country, second only to New York's.

In the 1930s and 1940s, civil rights leaders in Baltimore scored some important victories. In 1934 Thurgood Marshall, chief lawyer for the Baltimore NAACP, argued successfully for the admission of Donald Murray, a young black man, to the University of Maryland Law School. The association also launched successful legal attacks on Maryland's public school system because black school teachers were paid about half the salary of whites.

The protest movement energized the larger African-American community, resulting in the formation of other black protest organizations. The most popular was the City-Wide Young People's Forum.[62] Organized in October 1931 by nineteen-year-old Juanita Jackson, Lillie May Jackson's daughter, the forum was an important vehicle for organizing young African Americans. In November 1933 it launched the "Don't Buy Where You Can't Work" campaign. It targeted the neighborhood A&P food stores, which depended on African Americans for 100 percent of their business, yet hired only whites. Store managers initially rejected demands to hire black clerks. The picket lines quickly spread to other A&P stores. Baltimore had never seen a more unified response to blatant discrimination. Against such an onslaught of community outrage, in 1934 A&P began hiring African Americans. The Young People's Forum led other protest battles in the 1930s to encourage whites to hire more African Americans as social workers, carpenters, bricklayers, painters, plumbers and electricians and in other skilled occupations.

Among the young blacks who became leaders of the forum was Clarence Mitchell Jr., a reporter for the *Afro-American.* Mitchell and Juanita Jackson eventually married, and their union created a civil rights dynasty of sorts. From the 1940s and into the 1980s the most powerful black name in the city was Mitchell. Clarence Mitchell eventually served as the chief Washington lobbyist for the national NAACP. He played a critical role in the passage of every major piece of civil rights legislation adopted by the federal government in the 1960s. Juanita Jackson Mitchell earned a law degree from the University of Maryland and was the first African-American woman to practice law in the state. She served as legal counsel to the Baltimore NAACP and as head of the Maryland NAACP. The Mitchells dominated the local NAACP. It became their base of power, and several members of the family used that platform as their entry into politics. Clarence Mitchell III was elected to the Maryland legislature in 1962 at the age of twenty-two. His brother Michael won a seat on the Baltimore City Council and later served in the state senate. Parren Mitchell, the younger brother of the elder Mitchell, was the most prominent Mitchell in Baltimore politics, serving in the U.S. House of Representatives from 1970 to 1986. In 1994 Clarence Mitchell IV was elected to the House of Delegates, where his father's career in politics had begun.

The NAACP's civil rights' activism spawned a number of organizations in the 1940s, 1950s, and 1960s. The Citizens Committee for Justice, a coalition of black civic and social groups, was formed in 1941. The committee campaigned against police brutality and for jobs and representation, coordinating a march to Annapolis in 1942 that included nearly 2,000 middle-class African Americans from 125 churches and fraternal organizations to protest unequal treatment. The march resulted in the appointment of a gubernatorial study commission and the first appointment of blacks to the Baltimore school board and police department.[63] The Colored Women's Democratic Club was founded in 1946 to train black women on how to vote and to register voters and to make them aware of political issues. The Me-De-So Club, made up of black professional men who helped finance civil rights activities in the city, was organized in the early 1950s. The Monument Bar Association, Federated Clubs of Colored Women, and the Cooperative Women's Civic League formed as associations that sought to advance change in the African-American community.

The NAACP carefully allied itself with the black church. Leading ministers such as Vernon Dobson of Union Baptist; Marion C. Bascom, pastor of Douglas Memorial; Frank Williams, then president of the Interdenominational Ministerial Alliance (IMA); and Robert Newbold, pastor of Grace Presbyterian, were in the forefront of the city's civil rights struggles.[64] Many other ministers, including J. Timothy Boddie, Arthur J. Payne, Harrison J. Bryant, John H. Tilley, and Edward G. Carroll, were staunch supporters and members of the NAACP. The local chapter, the black clergy, and the *Afro-American* newspaper were the "triple generals" in the crusade for civil rights in Baltimore and Maryland.[65] Whenever the NAACP undertook a fight, the *Afro-American* gave it great publicity, black ministers preached sermons, and literature was distributed at church services.

In the 1950s and 1960s, when the national civil rights movement began in earnest, Baltimore had already established a foundation for an independent African-American protest movement. Black Baltimoreans had "leaders who had been toughened rather than demoralized by degradation. They had the *Afro-American*, probably the strongest black newspaper in the United States. . . . They had strong churches under politically minded ministers, and they had some aggressive female leaders like Lillie May Jackson and her daughters."[66] Led largely by prominent black middle-class professionals, they accomplished some impressive victories: concessions from private employers for jobs, equalization of pay for black school teachers, significant increases in black voter registration, and the hiring of black police officers.

Throughout the twentieth century, black social capital in Baltimore was mobilized to free African Americans from oppression. Its first targets were the legal bases of discrimination: segregation in public facilities, schools, and housing. With the passage of the Civil Rights Act of 1964, the civil rights movement reached its first goals. For the first time in American history, the government committed itself to extending the full rights of citizens to all African Americans. The civil rights movement changed the social and political life of the city. The marches of the 1950s and 1960s stopped; the mobilization of black social capital slowed.

Meanwhile, profound changes were under way within the African-American community. Although great strides had been taken, the vestiges of racism lingered, and the problems associated with the growing black underclass were becoming apparent. The reserves of black social capital created before the 1970s would have to be tapped and reconfigured to address the needs of increasing numbers of socio-economically disadvantaged residents.

A Changing Black Community

Baltimore experienced significant economic decline after the 1950s. As the city began losing industrial jobs in the 1960s and 1970s, economic vitality in many of the African-American neighborhoods in West Baltimore dwindled.[67]

The impact of major structural changes on African-American communities was evident by the late 1960s and early 1970s. Segregated high-rise public housing projects, such as Murphy Homes and Lafayette Courts, constructed to house the thousands of black residents moving to Baltimore during and after World War II, became sources of crime and social alienation, endangering not only their residents but also the surrounding communities of Upton, Harlem Park, and Sandtown-Winchester. In the 1950s and 1960s, federal government-sponsored urban renewal destroyed many black-owned homes and businesses. By the late 1970s Upton, Harlem Park, and Sandtown-Winchester, the first West Baltimore neighborhoods occupied by blacks migrating north from the core of the city at the turn of the century, were deteriorating communities. African-American judges, lawyers, schoolteachers, and principals left the old neighborhoods and claimed homes in Forest Park and Windsor Hills, among the city's oldest suburbs. Elegant Druid Hill Avenue homes gave way to elegant ranch-style homes in Ashburton. The exodus of professionals was part of a vast movement north and west by large numbers of African Americans. Old West Baltimore ceased to be a place for prosperous professional black people to live. Unemployment, crime, and the numbers of female-headed households living at or below the poverty line increased exponentially (see chapter 4). Today, Old West Baltimore is plagued with vacant, boarded-up properties and empty lots dating back to the days of urban renewal.[68]

Key black institutions also experienced decline. Although the *Afro-American* continues to be published, by the late 1970s its circulation had declined precipitously. In the late 1980s, beset with low sales and financial problems, the paper launched "Operation Afro," appealing to the public to support its subscription drive. The community slowly responded. Lacking the leadership of Lillie May Jackson, suffering from limited financial support, and crippled by staff cutbacks, the local NAACP also began to slide in importance in the 1970s. The organization is not the force it once was.

Drawing on Reserves

With the decay of black neighborhoods, African-American leaders realized they could not be content with the achievements of the civil rights movement. By the early 1970s, black leaders, especially the clergy, drew again on the endowments of black social capital, remobilizing their churches and communities for change. Harold McDougall has discussed how in the 1970s African-American churches and fraternal organizations

> responded to urban renewal and the costs it imposed on neighborhoods and low-income residents by transforming themselves into aggressive community improvement organizations. . . . Community protests centered on the city's housing and urban renewal programs. They fought planning that was undertaken for business rather than for people; they called for rent control and for community management of government services and government-subsidized housing. Social activists, including clergy, turned to the creation of parallel institutions at the neighborhood level to try to repair some of the damage that had been done to the vernacular community by overcrowding, state repression, and the loss of middle-class residents.[69]

For many years after the civil rights movement, these neighborhood-level organizations, and many others like them, worked to improve their immediate communities. As McDougall has observed, these efforts "started as many church efforts in West Baltimore have started, with a minister or some other spiritual leader challenging a congregation to do something to upgrade the community surrounding it."[70] Community leaders in Park Heights mobilized to form the Park Heights Community Development Corporation to finance commercial revitalization throughout the neighborhood and to repair and maintain hundreds of vacant houses.[71] Similarly, St. Pius V Catholic Church leaders formed a tax-exempted corporation, joining with the Harlem Park Community Association to improve housing and schools and to attract jobs to the community.[72]

In the late 1970s, however, black church leaders and neighborhood activists in West Baltimore "began to get the idea that some citywide strategy was required."[73] Mobilization in separated pockets of the city was not enough. In 1977 a new organization, Baltimoreans United in Leadership Development, successfully tapped the reserves of black social capital, mobilizing the African-American community on a citywide basis.

BUILD

BUILD was formed in 1977 by an ecumenical group of ministers in response to the apathy that prevailed after the civil rights movement.[74] The earlier activism generated by the black ministers, the NAACP, and the *Afro-American* had slowed considerably. The Reverend Vernon Dobson explained that one reason for the formation of BUILD was to tap into the reserves of black social capital. "I was becoming an old disillusioned preacher," he recalled. "The last demonstration we called, we had had a press conference where we announced we'd have three hundred people. Ten came."[75]

Determined to develop a citywide movement, Dobson, the Reverends Wendell Phillips and Sidney Daniels, and Monsignor Clare O'Dwyer, veterans of the civil rights struggles, joined with five other founding members to lead the sponsoring committee that contracted with the Industrial Areas Foundation (IAF), an organization founded by the late Saul Alinsky, a radical community organizer from Chicago.[76] The IAF provides the full-time staff for BUILD and for similar organizations in New York, North Carolina, Texas, and California.

For the first three years BUILD was made up of a small group of churches that worked on local neighborhood issues such as police protection, arson control, and rat eradication.[77] Initially, its efforts were slow to catch fire. As one organizer recalled, "The IAF really didn't have an organizer who could pull it off. The lead organizers were not able to cross racial lines. They were white and most of the ministers were black. The organizers weren't connecting with people—black or white."[78]

In spring 1980, IAF officials dispatched a new organizer to Baltimore. White and Jewish, Arnold "Arnie" Graf brought with him years of experience. He had been active in the civil rights movement of the 1960s; spent two years in Sierra Leone with the Peace Corps; worked as a welfare-rights organizer in Harlan County, Kentucky; and in 1976 followed Ernie Cortes as lead organizer of COPS, an IAF–affiliated organization in San Antonio, Texas. "The IAF skills Graf brought with him included a thorough knowledge of targets, potential victories, and appropriate strategies."[79]

When Graf arrived in Baltimore, BUILD was heavily in debt and had a small base, only twelve or thirteen churches. Its leaders were discouraged. "People were concerned that their church was paying $2,000 to $3,000 in dues and nothing was working," remembered a BUILD activist.[80] Graf nevertheless proved capable of enlisting strong support among African-American church leaders. He met separately with black leaders, probing their interests, seeking to motivate them. Graf concluded that they needed an issue with "lots of visibility, a great deal of action and momentum."[81]

With the support of Dobson and other black leaders, Graf decided to tackle the issues of low-income housing and bank redlining. Making use of the Community Reinvestment Act, BUILD discovered that most local banks lent only a small portion of their mortgage funds in inner-city and mainly black areas. Provident Bank, for instance, lent $660,000 to families in black neighborhoods out of more than $50 million, barely 1 percent.[82] BUILD then printed out tables and charts showing the disparities and passed them out in the churches. The organization called a meeting on the issue, and about 250 people attended. As one leader recalled:

We then asked people in the churches to anonymously write down how much money they had in the banks. We discovered that of the members of the twelve or thirteen churches, they had over $15 million in the banks. We then demanded changes. Harborplace [the centerpiece of Baltimore's Inner Harbor redevelopment] had just opened. People knew that a lot of the money for the Inner Harbor was public dollars. People in the neighborhoods resented giving money to redevelopment projects while the neighborhoods were falling apart.[83]

When bank officers refused to meet with BUILD leaders about the matter, a group of sixty to seventy members formed long lines at the banks' windows and asked for change into pennies. Police came. Officials panicked. The tactic created such a problem for the banks that bank officers agreed to talk to a BUILD delegation. Over 500 low-income families acquired home mortgages after these talks.[84]

As a result of the 1981 victory over bank redlining, another four or five churches joined BUILD. By the mid-1980s its membership had grown to include some forty-five to fifty predominantly African-American churches and three labor groups, the Baltimore Teachers Union (BTU), the union representing school administrators and principals, and the Hospital and Health Workers Union. In 1993 BUILD had an annual budget of about $300,000 and a full-time staff of four. The churches, however, constitute its main strength.

BUILD uses a combination of training, research, and confrontation. Its leaders are trained to "want power," to know when to compromise, and to pay "attention to others' self-interests."[85] Further, "We conduct research to decide what to do battle with," said a former officer of the group. BUILD also believes in a grassroots philosophy, and its meetings and conventions are usually attended by blacks from all socioeconomic sectors. A Morgan State University professor described BUILD as "an instrument for working at the grassroots level."[86] And its successful campaign against bank redlining illustrates its use of confrontation as an element in its strategy of empowerment.

BUILD has mobilized the black community in ways reminiscent of the civil rights era. In October 1984 its convention drew over 1,500 delegates. In November 1987, at its tenth anniversary convention, more than 2,000 people were present. It is considered by many people to be the most powerful group in Baltimore City. According to a founding member, "BUILD is a powerful organization. It is organized in fifty churches. Each church pays annual dues. Within each church there is a core group of people who organize their particular congregation. . . . BUILD is the only organization in Baltimore that can promise you that 1,000 people will show up and they will."[87]

BUILD's influence is far greater than that of the local chapter of the NAACP and has also eclipsed that of the IMA, a group of African-American ministers formed in the 1940s and representing about 166 churches. A black minister agrees:

IMA never had the staff and leadership specifics around a certain issue. BUILD comes from a different thought pattern. It is built around the ideas of Saul Alinsky. It was difficult for the preachers to organize around a certain issue.

With BUILD, churches committed money and bodies. This is what the IMA didn't have. BUILD is much more organized. They do a little bit of threatening, pleading, and they use a lot of common sense. They study an issue with precision. BUILD can bring the community together.[88]

Since its formation, BUILD has accumulated impressive victories involving bank loans, auto insurance, utility rates, living wages, and other issues.[89] "While many community-based organizations form around a particular issue and dissolve once the issue is resolved, BUILD was able to thrust itself into the forefront of all of Baltimore's urban issues."[90] Because it raises broad-based, community-wide issues, BUILD is able to mobilize hundreds of citizens, demonstrating to political and civic elites that the African-American community's voice will be heard.

SUMMARY

Baltimore's black community has a long history of racial exclusion and segregation. In response to these experiences, it developed significant common bonds and important internal institutions to combat racial discrimination. During the antebellum period, the presence of free African Americans gave the black community resources and leadership to form fraternal orders, literary associations, benevolent and mutual-aid societies, and private schools. These organizations represented early investments in social capital.

African-American churches were among the few stable and coherent institutions to emerge from the antebellum era. Black Baltimoreans increasingly relied on Union Baptist, Sharp Street Methodist, Bethel A.M.E., and other churches to bolster their autonomous existence in a racist society. After the Civil War, black church leaders such as Harvey Johnson played a significant role in fostering high levels of civic engagement devoted to protecting African-American interests. In the twentieth century, the black church—joined by the local NAACP and the *Afro-American*—played a crucial role in mobilizing the black community during the civil rights movement.

Historically derived, black social capital does not suddenly disappear. The social trust, norms of reciprocity, and networks of civic engagements built up among African-American leaders over many decades remain. In the 1980s and 1990s, BUILD draws on these reserves of social capital. A number of the city's progressive churches, Union Baptist, Brown's Memorial Baptist, Enon Baptist, Trinity Baptist, Metropolitan United Methodist, Heritage United Church of Christ, St. Peter Claver Church, and Nazareth Lutheran Church, are active members of BUILD. Several are led by clergy who honed their activists' skills during the civil rights struggle. "The ministers form a peer group, sharing experiences as they struggle with banks, corporations, and the city government."[91]

In many ways Baltimore's African Americans achieved their high stocks of social capital as a direct result of the barriers that white people erected to impede their progress. Segregated black neighborhoods and historically black Morgan State and Coppin State Universities—formed partly because of white hostility, irrational fears, and white supremacy—became important sources of group cohesion, intragroup identity, and black social capital. Black social capital was wrought and refined in the crucible of collective black experiences.

The African-American community developed relative high endowments of black social capital, facilitating cooperation among blacks to address racial injustice. But what about the black community's relationship with the city's larger white community? Dense but segregated networks of civic engagement and social capital sustain cooperation within each group, but networks of civic engagement that cut across communities, "weak ties," as Mark Granovetter calls them, promote wider cooperation.[92] Black social capital thus can work against cooperation with whites, especially when complicated by a history of racial discrimination.

3
Patronage Culture and the Politics
of Biracial Cooperation

Changing the structure or function of an institution while leaving the underlying
political (and institutional) culture untouched may amount to nothing more than
moving boxes on an organizational flow chart.
– BARBARA FERMAN

Paying careful attention to the life patterning social structures and cultural values
that give security, predictability, character, and meaning to life in a given
community may therefore yield a more fine-tuned understanding of local policy
responses.
– MEREDITH RAMSAY

The National Urban League in 1923 conducted an intensive study of employment
relations between Baltimore's industrial sector and the city's African-American
community, believing an examination was warranted because it was the area having
the "most likelihood of inter-racial cooperation." The league study found, however, that black leaders had not cultivated an effective mode of cooperation with
the larger white community. "Until very recently," the report observed, "the occasions on which whites and Negroes came together for a discussion of mutual problems have been rare. . . . White persons as a rule do not attend the meetings of
Negroes. . . . Similarly, it is extremely rare that Negroes get an opportunity to attend
the meetings of the whites."[1] Sponsors of the study believed that community-wide
issues such as employment, public education, housing, crime, and public health
might be resolved more easily if African-American and white leaders could work
out a mode of cooperation among themselves.

Baltimore's African-American leaders had developed an ability to work together based on past experiences and attachments. Black social capital facilitated

42

cooperation among them in addressing myriad issues confronting their community. The scope and nature of the relationship between the city's black and white leaders are significant, however, because effectively addressing community-wide concerns, such as improving the quality of public education, requires not only social capital but also important resources that white leaders had heretofore controlled.

Throughout much of the twentieth century, a tradition of patronage dominated the manner of cooperation between white and African-American leaders. This pattern shifted attention away from broad community aims toward particular benefits—jobs—creating a dilemma for black and white leaders as they attempted to reform the city's public school system during the mid-1980s and early 1990s.

HISTORY OF BLACK POLITICS

When blacks first entered Maryland's electoral arena following ratification of the Fifteenth Amendment in 1870, African-American leaders attempted to work with the city's white leadership to address community-wide goals. Unlike the Deep South states, where laws disenfranchising African Americans were enacted, black voting power in Maryland remained secure.[2] Thus in Baltimore, white political leaders were encouraged to deal with the city's sophisticated and civically engaged African-American community.

Ironically, the geographic containment of African Americans resulting from segregated housing patterns, especially in West Baltimore, lumped African-American voters together so that their voting blocs were able to elect blacks to the city council before the turn of the century. As early as 1890, a major breakthrough was made when Harry Sythe Cummings secured the Republican nomination for councilman from the Eleventh Ward, predominantly African-American but with voter registration about equally split between whites and blacks. Elected with a slim 105-vote majority, Cummings became the first black to hold elective office in Maryland.[3] Thereafter, with brief exception, African Americans maintained a representative on the city council, always from a predominantly black ward in West Baltimore. Between 1890 and 1931, six different African Americans were victorious in city council elections, all as Republicans representing West Baltimore. In addition to Cummings (1890–1892, 1897–1915), the black Republican councilmen included Dr. J. Marcus Cargill (1895–1897), Hiram Watty (1899–1905), Warner T. McGuinn (1919–1923, 1927–1931), William Fitzgerald (1919–1923), and Walter Emerson (1927–1931).[4]

Without exception, the pioneering black councilmen pushed matters that concerned African Americans, especially education. Sythe Cummings, for example, successfully supported a city ordinance establishing a black manual training school or an industrial education program similar to the all-white Baltimore Polytechnic Institute so that African Americans could be trained in the skilled trades and take advantage of the job opportunities in the growing industrial economy.

Cummings also authored the legislation establishing a kindergarten course in all public schools, both black and white. Dr. J. Marcus Cargill introduced a proposal that called for replacing white teachers in black schools with black teachers. His proposal was eventually watered down by fellow councilmen, but the final version of the ordinance meant that eventually black schools had black teachers, and black professionals were hired in large numbers.[5] Other African-American council members introduced ordinances appropriating equal funds for black schools. One crucial issue that each one pushed was a new building for the Colored High School. The ordinance was eventually adopted in 1923, and after being renamed the Frederick Douglass High School opened in 1925 at Calhoun and Baker Streets in West Baltimore.

To be sure, one or two black councillors could never control the vote of the entire city council, and much of their proposed legislation was defeated. Though many of the bills the early black councillors supported represented an acquiescence in segregation, there was little choice at the time. What is significant is that these pioneer black politicians consistently and forcefully spoke out on matters of concern to their community. The vast majority of the legislation they introduced forced the city's white leadership to confront and address matters affecting the entire black community. Thus African-American and white leaders related to each other in efforts to address community-wide goals.

By the mid-1920s, however, the scope and nature of cooperation between black leaders and the white community began to change, inaugurating an era in which patronage and attention to the pursuit of particular benefits rather than to broad community aims dominated. Cooperation between African-American and white political leaders centered on the promise of a government job, an appointment on the city commission, help in dealing with the criminal justice system, or a favorable vote concerning the zoning of a parcel of property. The beneficiaries of this relationship were not always the larger African-American community but leaders of the Democratic political machine and a few African-American surrogates.

Democrats and Machine-style Politics

An examination of the patronage culture that dominated black/white cooperation takes us back to the 1870s. With few exceptions, city elections and political offices were the dominion of a citywide Democratic machine that ruled from the late 1860s into the early years of the twentieth century.[6] Isaac Freeman Rasin, the machine's boss, led the Democrats from the mid-1860s until his death in 1907.[7] Rasin exercised an influence "so complete and dominant over party affairs here as to amount almost to dictatorship."[8] His own personality and personal skills helped shape the political environment to ensure that Democrats maintained their control. On election day he preferred to take nothing for granted—dissident and Independent Democrats occasionally challenged the machine—and because voters still made their choices without privacy, muscle and money counted. With

Voter
Reform

"walk-around money" in their pockets and using various powers of persuasion, Rasin's men "got out the white vote, rewarded the faithful, and made trouble for the rest."[9]

Rasin's organization was built along the same lines as many other big-city machines. Control of patronage ensured jobs for a host of loyal precinct workers, and control of government offices ensured financial contributions from interests desiring governmental action, or inaction. Teaming with Arthur Pue Gorman's state Democratic organization, the two men controlled Maryland politics from 1870 to 1895.[10] "The alliance between Gorman and Rasin was . . . the most important factor that any Democratic aspirant had to take into account."[11] Rasin and Gorman forged a powerful combination, seldom failing to agree on candidates or courses of action. Not until the very end of their lives did the stress of events finally end their close working relationship.[12]

During this twenty-five-year period, all state offices and control of both houses of the legislature remained in Democratic hands. Maryland regularly voted Democratic in presidential elections, and the overwhelming majority of the state's congressional representatives elected during this period were Democrats. Baltimore was important not only for the numerical strength it furnished the state party but also for the reliability of its support. The city went Democratic in every gubernatorial, presidential, and congressional election between 1870 and 1895.

In the 1895 state elections, however, harassed by internal strife and increasingly unable to govern effectively, the long-dominant Democratic party lost power. Republicans won the three top state posts—governor, attorney general, and comptroller—and an overwhelming majority in the lower house of the legislature. Much of the Republican strength came from Baltimore, where black Republicanism and black voter turnout were strong. Republican Lloyd Lowndes, the 1895 gubernatorial victor, carried the city by over 11,000 votes, a number larger than in any of Maryland's other twenty-three subdivisions. Baltimore also elected Republican Alcaeus Hooper, a reform candidate, to the mayor's office. The following year Maryland went Republican in the presidential election and sent a solidly Republican delegation to Congress. In 1897 the Republicans completely captured state government by winning control of the Maryland senate.

Political Power

The Republicans' reign was short. In spring 1899, fueled by a racist campaign using the slogan "This Is a White Man's City," the Democrats reclaimed Baltimore and returned to power in Annapolis.[13] The state's Democrats (with Gorman's urging) then pushed through the legislature a series of laws designed to disenfranchise blacks and to remove forever the possibility of another Republican victory. In 1904, 1908, and 1910, three separate disenfranchisement amendments were passed by the legislature, which used the devices of literacy clauses, grandfather clauses, and property requirements to reduce the number of black voters. The 1904 measure, the so-called Poe Amendment (named for University of Maryland law professor John Prentiss Poe, who drafted it) was the most serious threat to African-American suffrage.[14] Its major provisions had been borrowed from the Mississippi and Louisiana constitutions that had recently disenfranchised African Americans.

The three amendments, however, were defeated in the required referendum by an interesting coalition of African Americans, white Republicans, leaders of government reform organizations, and many white immigrants and their leaders, who feared that literacy tests and the grandfather clause would take away their political power as well. Maryland Democrats encountered special problems in framing disenfranchising amendments because of the large body of naturalized citizens, politically active whites, who could not qualify under the grandfather clause and the literacy requirements. The amendments posed a threat to thousands of the state's foreign-born from Eastern Europe. Baltimore City was particularly sensitive to this threat because most of the state's foreign immigrants lived there. Thus, the Poe Amendment was soundly defeated in Baltimore by almost two to one.

Arthur Pue Gorman was convinced that Freeman Rasin's organization had sabotaged the Democrats and accused the city machine of deliberately holding back support; Rasin later denied the charges. He was a much shrewder politician than Gorman. When faced with a strong Republican and reform threat, it was common for Rasin to place on the machine's ticket men of "unassailable integrity and [he] perfumed the whole business by going into the camp of the enemy and . . . [choosing] . . . as his candidates some eminently respectable businessmen with reform tendencies and an anti-Rasin background."[15] Rasin's machine depended on support from the large white ethnic community, and it was arrayed against the Poe amendment. Because it potentially disenfranchised foreign voters, however, Rasin cared nothing for it. "All Rasin was really interested in," observers claimed, "was the success of his city ticket."[16] Concomitantly, Rasin had a cunning plan for Baltimore's black voters: rather than stripping them of their right to vote, he formed relationships with African-American agents whose function it was to steer blacks away from the Republican party, keep black voter turnout down, or solicit what little black Democratic support could be obtained.

Democrats and the Black Voters

Rasin pursued his strategy by forming the Colored Democratic Association shortly after ratification of the Fifteenth Amendment. Jonathan Waters, an African American, became its first president.[17] Yet he had difficulty convincing African Americans that they should cast their vote against the party of Abraham Lincoln. In 1872 Waters was cornered on the streets of Baltimore by a racially mixed group of Republicans and shot by "an unknown assailant." He was not killed, but there were no reports of any further political activity from him. After Waters, the key black Democratic agent was Walter Sorrell of Baltimore, but little is known about his activities.[18]

Thomas "Tom" Smith was probably the greatest single black beneficiary in the patronage relationship with white Democratic leaders.[19] Recruited by Rasin during the 1904 disenfranchisement amendment battle, Smith became the key intermediary between white machine politicians and Baltimore's African-American community until shortly before his death in 1938. Born during the Civil War, Smith became a saloonkeeper, opening the only hotel in Baltimore for African Americans in 1912. His businesses, political activities, and reputed involvement in "policy," or illegal private lottery, brought him substantial—by African-American standards—wealth. Smith functioned much like other machine-style politicians with a working-class clientele. "Each Sunday morning, from half a dozen to thirty or forty of his followers gathered at the hotel for the usual business of job-finding, assistance in court cases, and other matters relating to the citizens' contacts with government."[20] Police could count on Smith to help locate black criminals, and these same criminals could count on Smith to help them beat the charges.

Tom Smith became "notorious" for his political tactics.[21] Because few African Americans voted Democratic, Smith, using persuasion and violence, worked to discourage registered blacks from casting ballots. Frank Kent, a *Baltimore Sun* political reporter and his contemporary, recalled that the day after each election, Smith, "with his list of voters, came downtown, and . . . check[ed] the names off from the registration books, which showed whether or not those negroes had voted."[22] White leaders paid Smith to keep blacks away from the polls, compensating his service on the basis of the number of registered blacks who had not voted.

Meanwhile, in 1923, following a trend recommended by progressive reformers, Baltimore abolished its bicameral city council, replacing it with a unicameral one. The old system of many small wards was replaced with six much larger city council districts, each electing three councillors. Determined permanently to weaken the Republican party's influence in city politics, the most heavily Republican precincts were gerrymandered into the Fourth District so that the Democrats would have a fairly easy time controlling the other five.[23] The oddly shaped Fourth District grouped thousands of blacks in its southern end and a large Jewish population in the northwest end. Riding on the coattails of a popular Republican mayoral candidate, William Broening, two black former councillors, Emerson and McGuinn, won election to the city council in 1927. Four years later, however, they were not reelected, ending the black presence on the council.[24] It was nearly twenty-five years before an African American returned to the council.

After Tom Smith's death, Democratic leaders formally institutionalized the patronage relationship with black leaders, forming the Citizens Democratic Club (CDC) to direct black voters to the party.[25] The leaders in the CDC were African-American businessmen who benefited from the patronage relationship. Black businessman Lloyal Randolph owned the hotel and bar in West Baltimore where the club regularly met.[26] CDC member William Adams made a fortune in the illegal numbers games in East Baltimore, parlaying his operations into legitimate businesses in the black community and eventually becoming a millionaire.[27] Adams owned most of the restaurants and bars in the African-American community, which helped to develop strong ties within the black ghettos. In 1951 Adams and CDC member Henry Parks founded Parks Sausage Company, at one time the largest black-owned corporation in the country. In 1962 Parks won a seat on the city council.

President Franklin D. Roosevelt's New Deal policies made the CDC's task of encouraging black support for the Democrats much easier. At the federal level blacks were increasingly turning away from the party of Lincoln.[28] However, in local elections black Baltimoreans continued to register and run for office as Republicans. Thus, at the behest of white Democratic leaders, CDC often sponsored bus excursions on election day to get registered African Americans out of the city.

The CDC's handy work benefited James "Jack" Pollack, who ruled West Baltimore's Fourth District from the late 1930s through most of the 1960s.[29] Pollack was one of a multitude of district-level Democratic bosses spawned after Freeman Rasin's death in 1907.[30] Pollack held no elected post. In the mid-1950s, at the height of his power, he reputedly controlled twelve state legislators, five city judges, five city council members, and scores of public employees and minor officeholders. White and Jewish, Pollack refused to support African-American candidates for Fourth District offices although blacks constituted a sizable portion of the district's population. The *Sun* opined that "as long as the Pollack machine held undisputed control in the 4th District . . . Negroes had no place in the organization planning when it came to elected office."[31]

Despite a tight organization, Pollack occasionally was challenged by factions, Independent Democrats, Republicans, or lone candidates, who condemned his boss rule. To protect his hegemony, Pollack turned to members of the CDC to "'cap' and 'skew' what Negro turnout happened along."[32] The CDC's task was to organize the black precincts, distribute "walking-around" money throughout them, and turn out black voters to support Pollack's candidates. Lloyal Randolph was Pollack's key black henchman. From around 1939 to the early 1950s, Pollack's candidates depended on Randolph to organize the black precincts and deliver the black vote. A Randolph contemporary recalled years later that Pollack's longevity in the increasingly black Fourth District was significantly aided by Randolph.

> Lloyal was a veteran political hand. . . . He used to escort the white candidates through black neighborhoods, and he served as a middle man between the Pollack crew and the black community. He used to carry out the functions of a ward boss or political fixer, dispensing what little patronage there was that trickled down from the top. Lloyal was the man who knew how to help get a kid a job. He knew who to call to help merchants resolve zoning or liquor license problems.[33]

A smaller but significant number of black residents lived in East Baltimore. The black precincts there were the bailiwick of Clarence "Du" Burns, a classic machine-style politician. His father and uncle were poll runners for Albert Ritchie, four times Democratic governor during the 1920s and 1930s. In the late 1930s,

Burns registered as a Democrat when most African Americans were Republicans, saying that he wanted to follow his father and uncle. Besides, he recalled, "The Democrats paid $5.00 to the runners and the Republicans paid only $2.00."[34]

In the 1930s and 1940s, Burns was one of only two African Americans working for the Bohemian Club, a party organization led by conservative white ethnics. He worked his way up in the Bohemian club "through precinct work. . . . A candidate had to carry the old 7th and 10th wards to carry the city," Burns recalled. "I learned how the game was played." Burns carried the Seventh and Tenth Wards for the white bosses, becoming in his own words, "one of the boys."[35] He acknowledged that he knew he was being used by white bosses, but this did not bother him. He considered it a part of the game of politics.

In 1947 Burns got his big break. After forming his own political club, turning out black voters for mayoral candidate Thomas D'Alesandro Jr.—the popular city councillor whose power base in the largely Italian and ethnic southeast Baltimore ("Little Italy") propelled him to Congress five times and the mayor's office three times (1947 to 1959)—Burns was rewarded with a patronage appointment as a janitor at Dunbar High School, a position he held for over twenty years until he won a seat on the city council in 1971. "Things happened to me that never happened to me before. When Tommy won, he didn't forget me," Burns recalled years later. After being befriended by D'Alesandro, Burns used his new-found power at city hall, helping East Baltimore's black residents. He was elected city council president in 1983 and appointed mayor of Baltimore in 1986.

The cooperation between black machine-style leaders and white political leaders was based on an exchange of political support for patronage, especially jobs. Although these were entry-level jobs or menial labor, for most of the recipients the alternative was to be unemployed. This relationship embodied the classic machine politics strategy of cooptation of black support through the distribution of jobs that held no political power to individuals who could deliver the votes of family and friends. Some immediate job benefits, in the form of municipal and state patronage positions, accrued to the lower-income African-American community. However, broad community-wide issues were not effectively addressed. For example, the inner core of West Baltimore and the black east side contained almost three times as many substandard housing units as the areas of white population. And wide discrepancies existed between the level of industrial employment opportunities available to the average white and black. In 1950 the average African-American worker sustained twice as much unemployment as the average white worker. Further, marked disparities existed between the segregated school systems. The incidence of part-time enrollment fell much more heavily on black than on white students, black students were more likely to attend schools in dilapidated buildings, and large differences existed in the funds allocated per pupil for use by black and white schools.

Although some working-class African Americans could count some tangible rewards from supporting machine politicians, the middle and upper-classes were slighted by Democratic patronage policies. Blacks were not slated for visible public offices from which they could influence the formation of policy. Black leaders' requests for appointments to the governing boards of state and city institutions were generally ignored.

The fringes of West Baltimore, where Boss Pollack ruled, were populated largely by black middle-class residents: schoolteachers, doctors, lawyers, ministers, college professors, and a few government employees. These black leaders contended that the problems such as poor housing, unequal job opportunities, dilapidated schools, and discrimination in admission to and promotion in civil service were linked to two factors: their own lack of political representation in city and state governments, and the predominant patronage political culture through which the white district and city leadership dealt with a small group of African-American intermediaries who were more interested in enriching themselves than in addressing those issues. The frustrations of the African-American middle class over the pattern of exclusion and unequal treatment led to a heightened (though ultimately unsuccessful) effort to alter the nature of cooperation between black and white community leaders.

Challenging Machine Politics

In the 1954 state legislative elections, black leaders in West Baltimore challenged Pollack's Fourth District organization. Leading the movement were prominent members of the black clergy; the NAACP; Carl Murphy, president of the *Afro-American;* members of the faculties of Morgan State and Coppin State Colleges; black schoolteachers and administrators; and an array of black professionals and middle-class residents who lived in West Baltimore.[36] Their strategy was simple. Since Pollack controlled the Democratic party, they decided to field a strong Republican candidate. The Fourth District had considerable black Republican strength; as late as 1957, over 40 percent of the voters in the Fourth District were registered Republicans, and over half of them were African Americans.

Three black candidates challenged Pollack-backed incumbents in the state legislature. Leading the bid for the state senate was a young Republican, Harry A. Cole, a graduate of the University of Maryland Law School, a former special assistant attorney general, and later a justice on Maryland's highest court. The other two candidates were Emory Cole (no relation to Harry), a Republican, and Truly Hatchell, an independent Democrat. Pollack failed to take the challenge seriously, and the three blacks won. From 1955 to 1958, for the first time in Maryland's history, there were African Americans in the state legislature.

In the 1955 election for city council, Pollack put Walter Dixon, a black candidate, on his Fourth District slate. Dixon won, becoming the first African American in nearly twenty-five years to hold a council seat, but he owed his victory to Pollack's machine. Meanwhile, Pollack was maneuvering to recapture the seats he had lost in the 1954 legislative races. Of particular importance was the senate seat held by Harry Cole. Since only one senate seat was allotted to the Fourth District, the senator had considerable power in the affairs of the state, including patronage.

In the 1958 state elections, Pollack recaptured the three legislative seats by fielding a biracial slate including three blacks. J. Alvin Jones, a leader of the CDC, defeated Cole by a 2,000-vote margin.[37] Verda Welcome, wife of a prominent black surgeon, was the only anti-Pollack candidate to win, becoming the leading symbol of new African-American independence. Although his grip on the Fourth District was tenuous, Pollack's influence continued into the mid-1960s, when his white and largely Jewish voters moved to an adjoining district in northwest Baltimore.

Black Reaction to the Patronage Culture

The machine and patronage traditions often overwhelmed well-meaning African-American leaders. Verda Welcome, who in 1966 became the first African-American woman in the nation to be elected a state senator, entered politics as a crusader against machine politics, emerging as the leader of a statewide civil rights struggle. She formed the powerful Fourth District Democratic Organization (FDDO), the first black-controlled political club in Baltimore. However, as an elected official, Welcome became entangled in a protracted struggle with other politicians over patronage. She began to see her role less as an advocate for community-wide policy issues and more as a fighter for particular benefits such as jobs. In her autobiography, Welcome explains the contribution of her political organization.

> The [FDDO] had become a benevolent machine. Our power can be summed up in three words: money, numbers, and patronage. . . . The third element, patronage, rewards contributors and workers. The reward for a candidate is, of course, victory. But for the foot-soldier or the non-political supporters, the rewards were different. I, like other elected officials, had access to a set number of jobs in the city and state. Our organization could open doors because of our connections with business and community leaders. Our political organization became for some, an informal employment agency. Job-seekers ranged from persons seeking menial labor to professionals and civic leaders seeking references. Oftentimes, a letter from a state senator or other elected official proved to be the ticket job-seekers needed to get the position.[38]

The 1960s and early 1970s spawned several black leaders whose basis for a relationship with white leaders centered on the city's patronage culture. Rival black organizations often fought over turf, political offices, and patronage. Black millionaire/businessman William Adams, for example, a holdover from the days of the CDC and an ally of boss Pollack, often supported candidates challenging the slate endorsed by Verda Welcome's organization. Holding no public office, Adams played a behind-the-scenes role in Baltimore's black politics, maintaining close ties with Pollack and other white politicians, especially those who controlled the issuance of liquor and business licenses and who could influence zoning decisions.[39] After House Speaker Marvin Mandel, a Pollack protégé, was appointed governor by the legislature in 1969, the feud between Welcome and Adams was exacerbated. Governor Mandel directed patronage away from Welcome and into Adams's newly formed Metro Democratic Organization; Welcome's state-level patronage dried up. As she recalled years later, "Mandel practically shut the door on the Fourth District Democratic Organization and anointed Willie [Adams] the de facto boss of the Fourth District."[40] Throughout the 1960s and 1970s, political observers watched as Adams and Welcome battled, not over substantive policy matters but over control of patronage.

Machine politics tended to create considerable distrust and jealously between African-American voters and black politicians and among the political leaders themselves. Black machine-style politicians drew criticism from black civil rights leaders and progressive black clergy because of their tendency to support political candidates with questionable civil rights' credentials or for endorsing candidates on the basis of how many dollars such action would generate for their organization's bank account. Critics complained, for example, that Willie Adams's business interests were such that he could not "use up the political debts he is owed to change things like school policies. . . . There is nothing in it for him." Other observers claimed that African-American elected officials sponsored by Adams had "not made serious efforts to bring the problems of the black community into the forum of city government for airing and debate."[41] Similarly, Clarence "Du" Burns "received a great deal of criticism . . . because of his willingness to cut deals with white political operatives."[42] Black club politicians were often viewed as pawns of white political operatives and criticized for forsaking the goals of equality and equal representation for personal and economic gain.

PATRONAGE CULTURE AND SCHOOL POLITICS, 1960s–1990s

The challenge to the dominant political culture by civil rights leaders and other progressive black leaders was periodically successful. The 1954 and 1958 legislative elections serve as perfect examples. The 1963 mayoral election marked another, more lasting victory, the opening of the political process to a wider array of African-American leaders and broadening the scope of black/white cooperation to include community-wide policy issues such as quality public education.

Before 1963, Baltimore's progressive African-American leaders were virtually ignored by white Democratic party bosses.[43] This attitude changed after a dramatic event in the city's political history: the 1963 election of Theodore Roosevelt McKeldin to the office of mayor. McKeldin's victory marked the first time a Republican had been elected to that office since 1943, when McKeldin himself had accomplished the feat. He attributed his election to the "massive support he obtained in the black and to a lesser extent Jewish precincts."[44] McKeldin's victory pulled thousands of new African-American voters into the political system. Moreover, a broader spectrum of black leaders was being consulted and courted on a sustained basis for the first time in the city's modern political history.

Mayor McKeldin took advantage of the considerable powers of the office to fulfill many of his campaign promises. He had pledged to push for city legislation outlawing discrimination in public accommodations, including housing. Because of a divided Democratic-controlled city council, McKeldin was able successfully to negotiate passage of the Equal Accommodations Act.[45] He used his power to appoint more African Americans to positions within many of the departments of city government. He adopted a policy of appointing roughly equal numbers of blacks and whites to municipal jobs.[46] And he ensured that the city was an "early enlistee" in the War on Poverty, establishing Baltimore's Community Action Program (CAP) just six months after Pres. Lyndon B. Johnson signed the enabling legislation in February 1965.[47] In retrospect, McKeldin actually used the Democrats' desire to recapture black support to push for broader social and political programs.

In the 1967 mayoral election, Democratic party leaders regrouped. Thomas D'Alesandro III, who served as city council president during McKeldin's mayoralty and who was partly responsible for delivering Democratic votes in the city council to pass many of his programs, was elected. Mayor D'Alesandro, working closely with business leaders and leaders in the black community, wanted to avoid the racial conflict that afflicted Detroit, Los Angeles, Newark, and other cities. He continued McKeldin's policy of assigning municipal jobs to roughly equal numbers of blacks and whites. Whenever possible, D'Alesandro "would 'clear' and solicit patronage decisions with club leaders and city councilmen."[48] By 1971, 46 percent of the 41,000 municipal jobs in Baltimore were held by African Americans. Further, in response to black demands for changes in CAP, D'Alesandro was able to negotiate with the city council a revision in the program's charter allowing the Community Action Agency (CAA) to conduct voter registration. He appointed Parren Mitchell, at the time considered by many whites (and a few blacks) to be a "militant" leader, director of the CAA.[49] Mitchell later became Maryland's first African-American representative to Congress.

D'Alesandro, Race, and School Politics

Mayor D'Alesandro also expressed concerns about the state of the public schools and in 1968 launched a successful $80-million bond referendum to support school construction. The bonds were earmarked to address the black community's concerns about their children attending "ramshackle schools, many of them built in the nineteenth century." Consistent with the city's tradition of patronage politics, D'Alesandro also directed school officials to use funds from Title I of the Elementary and Secondary Act of 1965 to hire thousands of "neighborhood people" as teachers' aides, providing employment for many more black residents.[50] Further, he appointed more blacks to the board of school commissioners. By 1970 four blacks served on the nine-member board, the policy-making body that oversees the Baltimore City Public Schools.

Although D'Alesandro was considered a liberal and received overwhelming support from African-American voters, black disenchantment grew. Like many major cities, Baltimore erupted in flames after the assassination of Dr. Martin Luther King. The riots of 1968 deeply wounded the city. One local observer noted that "the riots only exacerbated racial divisions and assuaged any guilt that might have been felt by middle-class parents fleeing the city or choosing private schools."[51] The racial tensions spilled over into the schools. "Board meetings were so raucous in those days that Mayor Thomas J. D'Alesandro III called the [school] commissioners to a private meeting and threatened to fire them all if the 'name calling, picayune bickering and discourtesies' didn't stop."[52]

As more whites left for the suburbs, the racial makeup of the schools changed dramatically. The percentage of African-American students grew, and leaders in the black community insisted that the proportion of school administrators, teachers, and other school personnel reflect this shift. Fueled partly by research that showed white middle-class teachers and administrators often had low expectations of minority youth, which in turn contributed to poorer student performance, many blacks in Baltimore and other major cities espoused community control of schools as their rallying cry.[53]

In January 1970 Superintendent Thomas D. Sheldon proposed a decentralization plan that, he emphasized, did not involve "community control" of the schools. The plan angered the four black school board members and a white liberal who sided with them and was rejected. Sheldon eventually resigned after the liberal majority on the board rejected his nominations for school principals and demanded he submit a list that better reflected the racial composition of the student body. Sheldon was the last white to lead the city's schools on a permanent basis.

In late 1970 Mayor D'Alesandro shocked the city when, at age forty-two, he declared that he would "retire" from politics at the end of his term. The racial strife had taken a toll on the young mayor. "One day it all turned sour," he told a reporter when he made his decision not to seek reelection.[54] As a city councillor recalled years later: "The school board was a battleground. I would go to the board meetings; they would put on a show each week. Tommy D'Alesandro really wanted justice for the school system. He wanted to help the system but couldn't because of the conflict."[55]

The First Black Superintendent

In July 1971 (before D'Alesandro's term expired) the school board voted 8 to 1 to appoint Roland N. Patterson, an assistant superintendent from Seattle, as the city's first black school superintendent.[56] And in December 1971, city council president William Donald Schaefer, after defeating two African-American candidates, was sworn in as mayor.[57] He remained in office until his election as governor in 1986.

Critics and supporters portray Mayor Schaefer as "combative and sometimes vindictive."[58] Observers note that he admired Richard J. Daley, the longtime mayor and political boss of Chicago, and adopted Daley's style of leadership.[59] Kweisi Mfume, who spent seven years on the Baltimore City Council before being elected to Congress in 1986 and who later became the national president of the NAACP, described Mayor Schaefer's style as "punitive." According to Mfume, Schaefer was a "powerfully strong and intimidating political force. Things were done his way, or not done at all; those who dared to dissent wound up on his hit list."[60] A teachers' union leader echoed this sentiment in an interview, declaring that "William Donald Schaefer ordered, coerced, and paid off. He was loyal to his friends and wished death to his enemies." "He is definitely a grudgeholder," says a former state legislator who worked closely with Schaefer.[61] Challenging Mayor Schaefer was nothing short of heresy.

Superintendent Patterson and Mayor Schaefer clashed repeatedly. A reporter observed that city hall seemed to "scrutinize" Patterson "much more assiduously than it had his predecessors," and Patterson was aware of it.[62] His willingness to develop close ties with former black mayoral candidates and militant black leaders did not endear him to the new mayor. Further, Patterson's decentralization plan, designed to give community leaders a significant role in educational decision making, antagonized Schaefer. People had hoped that Patterson's appointment would "quell racial tension in the school system."[63] Ironically, his tenure turned out to be the most racially acrimonious in the school system's modern history.[64]

The superintendent's reorganization of central administration further alarmed city hall. The so-called "Patterson massacre" affected about 450 administrators.[65] Several high-ranking white administrators were reassigned; many were replaced by African Americans. New offices and positions were created, and many persons were recruited from outside the city to fill major central office positions. Patterson's insistence that "good people from outside the system" be considered for top administrative positions threatened Schaefer's reliance on patronage to respond to black demands for jobs.[66] Many observers, including Sen. Verda Welcome, a former schoolteacher, concluded that such patronage exacerbated tension between Schaefer and Patterson. According to Welcome,

The political connection between the mayor's office and the school system had long been a well-kept secret. The thousands of jobs available at city schools naturally made them a magnet for patronage, and mayors had traditionally taken full advantage of this. But Patterson, who had few ties to Baltimore, refused to go along. Schaefer, who seemed to have a problem with strong black men, soon began maneuvering to fire Patterson.[67]

Patterson's attempts to insulate the school system from the influence of black and white political elites alienated not only Schaefer but also middle-class African Americans. Indeed, Patterson's greatest strength in the city was among low-income blacks, who viewed him as their champion. Among middle-class blacks and machine-style black politicians, however, he was tolerated but not widely accepted. Old-line black Baltimoreans tended to view him as an outsider and wanted him to consult with them more.[68]

Race continued to be a major issue, and three major crises in 1974 kept it on the local agenda. First, a teachers' strike erupted in February 1974. Many teachers, fed up with low salaries, poor working conditions, and crowded classrooms demanded an 11 percent increase in fringe benefits and salary. The strike lasted for over a month and literally closed the schools. Mayor Schaefer took a strong stance against the teachers. If he gave in to them, he calculated, other municipal unions would seek similar raises, and the result would be a large increase in the tax rate. A higher tax rate, he argued, would only lead to more white flight and even higher tax rates. The strike took on a racial aspect when it appeared that Schaefer feared alienating middle-class whites at the expense of a black school system. As Edward Berkowitz points out,

> Indeed, the entire episode of the school strike could be read as a betrayal of the city's blacks by the white entrenched political leadership. The city hesitated to spend more money on the school system for fear of making the city, already on the verge of a black majority, even more black. Preservation of the property tax in an effort to maintain a good business climate triumphed over a proper concern for the education of the city's school children.[69]

The teachers eventually settled for a 6 percent salary increase. Although they did not receive all they had demanded, the strike established the Baltimore Teachers Union as a powerful player in city politics.

As city leaders dealt with the strike, the next crisis arose when word leaked that approximately $23 million in federal grants would be lost if administrators refused to desegregate the schools. The federal mandate "further exposed the many racial tensions within the school system."[70] The federal desegregation order, and the desegregation plan that the school board eventually adopted, led to massive demonstrations by white students and parents. More white flight followed. A look at enrollment figures indicates that thousands of whites left the system in 1974 and 1975.

If there were any doubts left that a racial crisis existed in the BCPS, they were quelled in August when hundreds of Patterson's supporters packed a school board meeting after it was learned that the white majority on the board clandestinely planned to dismiss the superintendent. When a motion to fire Patterson was put to a vote, chaos erupted. "An angry crowd briefly surged onto the stage, ripping out microphone cords and slamming papers and books about the meeting table." The *Sun* reported that one black board member "leapt from his seat" and "nose-to-nose" screamed at one of his white colleagues: "There ain't gonna be no vote.

You don't get no vote tonight." Congressman Parren Mitchell, an ardent supporter of Patterson, angrily denounced the attempt to oust him, saying: "Never have I seen the racist scum come through as it has tonight."[71] The racial issue was now more than an undercurrent in school politics; it had become a raging river, the driving force behind the school crisis.

The board was unable to remove Patterson quickly. His supporters filed a lawsuit prohibiting the members from dismissing him without a public hearing. A black judge, Joseph C. Howard, ordered the board to grant Patterson a public hearing, which allowed him to remain in office a while longer. By January 1975, however, sentiments had started to change. Mayor Schaefer had appointed new school board members, three of whom were black, to replace the four members whose terms had expired. Blacks gained a majority on the school board for the first time in history, although a white attorney was appointed as its president. Acknowledging the racial tensions prevalent in the BCPS, editors of the *Sun* observed that the appointment of a white school board president "should serve to allay white fears of a black-dominated School Board during the touchy period when a high school desegregation plan is imminent." The *Sun,* an important molder of elite opinion, applauded the makeup of the new board: "It is obvious that . . . Mr. Schaefer has chosen Baltimoreans with solid community credentials who are not given to predetermined positions or readily identified with pressure groups and who are more likely to vote along educational lines than racial lines."[72] With the extension of Schaefer's authority over the school board, it voted in July 1975 to fire Patterson. A federal court judge upheld the board's action.

Mayor Schaefer and the BCPS

Determined to bring calm to the school system, Schaefer and other white elites reached an understanding with black leaders about control of the school system: a tacit agreement was made that consolidated African-American administrative control of it.[73] In July 1975 the school board named John L. Crew as the second black superintendent. Crew was an insider, a twenty-year veteran of the system who had taken pains to remain neutral in the controversy over Superintendent Patterson. In Crew, Mayor Schaefer had a "more cooperative black professional" who "accepted as legitimate strong mayoral leadership."[74] Alice Pinderhughes succeeded Crew in 1982 and retired in 1988, shortly after Schaefer was elected governor of Maryland. Pinderhughes gained the superintendent's position after a forty-five-year career in the BCPS and owed her appointment to Mayor Schaefer. He persuaded the school board to elevate her and then encouraged the state superintendent, David W. Hornbeck, to waive a state requirement that the city's school superintendent have a master's degree, which Pinderhughes had not earned.[75]

Schaefer's authority over the school system was key in prolonging his hold on the mayor's office as Baltimore became a black majority. His black supporters were appointed as school administrators, principals, and other school professionals as rewards for their political support. African Americans were also hired in lower-level positions as janitors, secretaries, and teachers' aides. "Increasingly, the school district resembled a patronage base. Personnel that orchestrated mayoral activities were put on the school system's pay-roll. Central office administrators critical of the administration were either demoted or transferred. Not infrequently school resources were allocated in a politicized manner to serve as warnings to dissenters at the school building level."[76] African Americans gained administrative control over the schools but became more answerable to Schaefer.

Public education, however, was not the chief concern of the Schaefer administration. The famous Inner Harbor redevelopment project, the World Trade Center, the National Aquarium, and luxury hotels were constructed during his fifteen-year tenure in city hall. Schaefer focused his energy, and the city's revenues, on downtown redevelopment.[77] Indeed, during the Schaefer years, spending on the schools and other city agencies decreased.[78]

Despite decreased funding, Superintendents Crew and Pinderhughes respected Schaefer's budget priorities. "School expenditures, which required the approval of city hall, were subjected to careful scrutiny by administrators who reported directly to the mayor's chief aide."[79] In an interview, Pinderhughes candidly admitted that she "never submitted a budget request to the board without first consulting Schaefer."[80]

Inadequate spending on the public schools had a significant effect on the quality of instruction.[81] As a result of low spending levels, the schools operated with a shortage of books and low staffing levels in libraries and counseling offices. Eliminated from the school budget were enrichment programs such as art and music. Further, low salaries hampered the city's efforts to recruit high-quality teachers.[82]

Critics and supporters agree that Mayor Schaefer's handling of school issues reflected his governing style: quick, decisive action aimed at visible problems. He tended to eschew more complex policy issues. Moreover, as a city council member in the 1960s and 1970s, he had witnessed the struggles of previous mayors who grappled with the challenges (and the racial controversies) of the BCPS. In Schaefer's opinion, the school system was a political land mine, and heavy involvement in its affairs offered few rewards. He typically left school policy (other than the budget) to trusted associates on the school board and to African-American administrators who owed their appointments to city hall.

Consequently, the true function of public education, mastery of sufficient knowledge and skills to assume the rights and responsibilities of citizenship, was lost during the Schaefer era. Even in the diplomatic language of the *Baltimore 2000* report, issued shortly before Schaefer resigned to become governor, the recognition that he did little to help the school district is clear. Future mayors, the report suggested, should play a more substantial role. "The mayor appoints the school board and can set its course. No substantial renovation of the school system can be accomplished without his deep interest, steady pressure, and willingness to apply the political weight of his office to insure results."[83]

Bonds of Personalism

By 1986, at the end of Schaefer's long tenure, Baltimore's top school administrators were a group of middle-class African Americans who had worked their way up the system's bureaucracy. Many of them, like then-Superintendent Alice Pinderhughes, had gone through the turmoil of the 1970s when racial and class antagonism ran high. They had survived the 1980s, when the city's contribution to the education department dwindled in real terms. They had listened in the 1970s and early 1980s, as civic and business leaders began to criticize the schools as ineffective and dangerous. And many of them could recall when the *Sun* had carried uplifting stories about the BCPS' accomplishments and how the newspaper's coverage changed in the 1970s with news stories, and occasionally a series of feature articles, about the system's problems and failures. Indeed, the senior administrators had been together for most of their careers.[84]

A similar pattern existed among the entire professional staff: teachers, counselors, librarians, principals, and assistant principals. In 1993, 63 percent of the professional employees were African American.[85] Teachers in the BCPS are a closely knit group who have long years of experience in the public schools. Statewide, Baltimore City has one of the largest proportions of teachers with twenty-one years' or more experience, nearly 35 percent. In comparison, the statewide average is 28 percent. The BCPS also has the smallest percentage of teachers (22.5 percent) with less than ten years' experience.

These figures reveal that a large proportion of the teachers, like their colleagues in central administration, have been around since the tumultuous 1970s. They have not only worked together for decades, but they have also developed a personal affinity, a kind of personal bond. These bonds of personalism did not begin, nor do they end, in the central administration or at the school site.[86] The majority of the teachers and administrators share similar middle-class backgrounds. Many of these black educators attended the same colleges and universities. Many (such as Alice Pinderhughes, for example) graduated from Coppin State College or Morgan State University.[87] Moreover, many of them are members of the same fraternities and sororities. Reportedly, when Pinderhughes was superintendent, her sorority, Alpha Kappa Alpha, was well represented among the professional staff. According to one top administrator in a 1988 interview, "You've got to recognize a little bit of tradition in terms of blacks. Many of us went to black colleges and universities, and the social outlet there was the fraternities and sororities. That was the orientation for us."[88] And many teachers and administrators attend the same middle-class black churches, further strengthening the bonds of personalism. Union Baptist and Bethel A.M.E. are two of the most prominent whose members include principals, teachers, administrators, and other school-system personnel. They are also two of the most influential churches in city politics.[89]

The Election of Kurt Schmoke

In 1986 William Donald Schaefer was elected governor of Maryland. Following Schaefer's resignation as mayor, city council president Clarence "Du" Burns by fiat became the city's first African-American mayor. Burns held the post for a little over a year and was then defeated in the 1987 Democratic mayoral primary by another black, Kurt L. Schmoke.[90]

Schmoke was nearly thirty years younger than Burns. He grew up on Baltimore's West Side, the son of college-educated parents. Schmoke was a high school and college sports star, a graduate of Yale University and Harvard Law School, and a Rhodes scholar. He worked for a brief period with Piper and Marbury, the city's most prestigious law firm, and then in Washington for Pres. Jimmy Carter, returning to Baltimore to get involved in politics. Although Schmoke had no history with the city's political clubs, in his first bid for elected office he was chosen as state's attorney in 1982. He was able to unite the black community behind his candidacy and also received considerable support from liberal whites and many of the city's prominent civic leaders.[91]

In 1987 the city's first all-black Democratic primary gave voters distinct choices. They could tap the younger Ivy Leaguer, representing a new generation of black political leadership; or they could stick with Burns, the folksy, old-style politician who had worked his way up the patronage ladder from high school janitor to mayor. Two issues dominated the campaign: downtown development and public education. Schmoke expressed the view that economic goals had not balanced neighborhood improvement with downtown development. He concluded that the city was "prettier but poorer."[92] He also capitalized on the recently released *Baltimore 2000* report, which called for dramatic improvements in the city's schools. Indeed, he centered his campaign on reforming public education. Schmoke won the election, capturing 51 percent of the vote and elevating school reform on the local agenda. A member of the school board credited him with sustaining education on the agenda: "Education is an issue. There is so much emphasis on education because it's the mayor's major theme. He has been concerned about education. He has tried to make it a household word. He has gone to the schools and into the community. He's been successful. Everybody is talking about education."[93]

Although BUILD initiated the heightened effort to reform the city's schools (see chap. 7), Mayor Schmoke played an important part in consolidating its priority on the local agenda and in involving other civic leaders and organizations in that effort. Two of the organizations, the Greater Baltimore Committee and the Citizens' Planning and Housing Association, are significant in their contributions.

The GBC represents over 1,000 of Baltimore's top corporations. Its board is composed of chief executive officers of the Rouse Corporation, First National Bank of Maryland, and Baltimore Gas and Electric, among others. Formed in 1955, the GBC has been the vehicle for mobilizing the corporate sector in support of downtown renewal efforts.[94] It was a major force behind the Inner Harbor redevelopment project.[95] With a budget of $1.5 million and a staff of twenty, the GBC is a potentially powerful force.

In the mid-1980s, the GBC became more active in school affairs. One strategy was to designate a staff person to work on local school concerns. Another was quietly to prod city and school officials to adopt more efficient management strategies. Business leaders supported site-based management, for example, after experiencing the successful transfer of authority to their own site-level managers. In 1987 the GBC joined with BUILD and formed the Baltimore Commonwealth, a school compact program. In recent years, the committee helped fund the search for new superintendents; it is customarily consulted whenever the school board moves to replace an incumbent superintendent and when appointing a new one. Further, the GBC has testified before committees of the state legislature in support of increased state funding for Baltimore's schools.

For much of its history, the CPHA concentrated on the physical condition of the city, especially its housing stock. However, in the late 1980s and early 1990s, it added education to its portfolio. A nonprofit organization, the CPHA is also one of Baltimore's oldest citywide civic organizations.[96] Formed in 1941, it was one of the first to respond to the problems of slum housing and urban blight. It has been a biracial organization since its inception. The CPHA was instrumental in the city's decision to establish and monitor housing codes. In 1947, in response to the association's reports, city officials established a special housing court to prosecute housing-code violators.[97] One year later, in response to CPHA recommendations, the Department of Planning was established as a regular agency of city government, charged with developing a strategy for stemming neighborhood blight through preparation of a master land-use plan.

Organizing citizens and communities to address local needs is a key component of the CPHA's strategy; it has helped create nearly 150 volunteer neighborhood associations. The concept of citizen participation formed the basis for its involvement in planning and housing. Its members held positions in the public sector and corporate world. Among its alumni are Robert C. Embry Jr., the city's first housing commissioner and president of the local Abell Foundation; former governor William Donald Schaefer; U.S. senator Paul Sarbanes; the late Verda Welcome; Walter Sondheim, a former president of the Baltimore school board and senior adviser to the GBC; and the late James Rouse, developer of Columbia, Maryland, and Harborplace.

The mobilization of groups such as BUILD and Mayor Schmoke's emphasis on improving the public schools encouraged CPHA leaders to add education to its list of priorities. In 1990 it hired its first education director and established a standing Education Committee. The CPHA transferred its expertise and knowledge of the workings of city government to education issues. Its role involves monitoring the school system, collecting and analyzing school data, and providing technical assistance to parents, community leaders, and other school activists. As an advocacy group, the CPHA encouraged community-centered schools. It was a leader in the Stadium School movement, helping parents establish a community-based and -managed public school in the Memorial Stadium area.[98] The CPHA brings the strength of a respected and credible civic group to education.

SUMMARY

Black Baltimore offers a complex political history. Despite the high level of black social capital, relations between African-American and white leaders centered around patronage politics. The white elites could secure black leaders' cooperation for a relatively low price in contracts, jobs, favorable administration of the law, and a host of personal services. The school system is an apt example. Baltimore's patronage tradition and pre-1960s patterns of biracial cooperation led many citizens, particularly the black middle class, to view the public school system primarily as a key source of jobs and other material benefits.

One of the problems with machine and patronage politics, however, is that it undercut discussions of broad issues, such as housing, employment, and public education. In Baltimore, black machine politicians' preoccupation with the control and distribution of material and personal benefits encouraged them to accept the desires of white civic and political leaders, forsaking real inroad on communitywide concerns.

The compromise and accommodation characteristic of Baltimore's African-American political leaders are intertwined with the city's political culture. In the early 1970s, as a broader segment of African Americans began mobilizing politically, white civic and political leaders were forced to make them junior coalitional partners. With the appointment of Roland N. Patterson as the first black school superintendent, the Education Department became one of the first in city government headed by an African American, becoming the "black" agency of government. Yet when Superintendent Patterson openly criticized the heavy political control exercised by city hall, sought to shield the school system from political elites, and moved to assert autonomy in it, Patterson faced opposition from Mayor Schaefer and to a lesser extent from middle-class African Americans. Insofar as Patterson's reforms went against the grain of the predominant political culture, he met resistance from black school leaders and city officials who had long developed a mode of cooperation centered on patronage.

Baltimore's political culture spawned the expectation that the public school system functions principally as a major source of jobs and patronage, and the city's African-American middle class leaders accepted that as their vision. In the 1980s, when the general consensus among leaders was that reform was necessary, these ingrained expectations became barriers to systemwide school reform.

4

The Political Economy and
City Schools, 1950–1990

*Despite the valiant efforts of many in the black community, along with many white
friends, to build bridges of understanding and channels of assistance to eradicate
the effects of decades of discrimination and bias, there is still a great disparity in
the efforts of government and the larger community toward improving the
conditions for blacks. In education, the disparity is much more evident.*
– ALICE PINDERHUGHES

A beginning point in any examination of education is to observe the connection
between schools and the conditions of the society in which they function. Histo-
rians today recognize the importance of placing the study of urban schooling in
its social, economic, and political contexts. How have such forces shaped the course
of public education in Baltimore?

DEINDUSTRIALIZATION AND INNER-CITY DECLINE

Following the Civil War, Baltimore became a city driven economically by manufacturing, and World War I further spurred this economy. Business boomed for
the city's massive clothing industry because of the government's demand for war-
related apparel. The heyday of clothing production occurred between 1914 and
1919, when over 10,000 workers were employed.[1] Activity at the city's port facilities also grew. Baltimore jumped from its ranking as the nation's seventh most
active port in 1920 to third in 1926.[2] During the 1920s the city added to its highly
diversified industrial base by attracting 103 new plants, including American Sugar,
McCormick Spice, Lever Brothers, and Proctor and Gamble soap factories.[3] Other
manufacturers in or near the city included General Motors, Armco Steel Corpo-

63

ration, Western Electric, Black and Decker, and Pittsburgh Plate Glass, among others. By 1920 Baltimore's population expanded to 733,826. Further, the 1918 annexation permitted the city to extend geographically, tripling its size from thirty to ninety-two-square miles. Baltimore was a city on the move.

Its manufacturing economy provided family-supporting employment for residents. Home ownership was possible. In 1930 over 50 percent of the city's white residents owned their homes.[4] Row houses were built to keep construction costs down and ownership affordable, creating the city's persistent image of brick row houses, one room wide and two or three stories tall, with white marble steps.[5]

The Great Depression of the 1930s, however, slowed the city's growth. Initially, the diversified economy withstood the layoffs a little longer than other industrial centers. In time, however, Baltimore's economic slump "arrived at the same point" as Detroit, Cleveland, Milwaukee, and other manufacturing cities.[6] In 1932 the city's unemployment rate reached just over 19 percent. Especially hard hit were workers in the textile, steel, clothing, and construction industries. In the construction industry, for example, only 119 houses were built in the city in 1934, compared to the thousands constructed annually in the 1920s.[7] By 1934, as Sherry Olson has observed, Baltimore was "at the bottom of the depression."[8] The crisis deepened and persisted until a reluctant Mayor Howard Jackson, who resisted the city's permanent involvement in the distribution of relief, was forced to accept municipal responsibility for Pres. Franklin D. Roosevelt's New Deal relief programs.[9]

World War II turned Baltimore's economy around, bringing a new period of economic growth. The war industry provided many jobs in steel plants, shipyards, and other heavy industry. The Glenn L. Martin aircraft plant in nearby Baltimore County was one of the area's manufacturers that benefited from the war. In 1940 the plant employed about 3,500 people; during the period from 1943 to 1945 some 53,000 workers were building aircraft. Work also increased dramatically at Bethlehem Steel and its affiliated shipyards. Before the war, Bethlehem Shipyards employed about 1,300 workers, but during the war years, employment peaked at nearly 47,000.[10]

Thousands of African Americans came to the city from rural areas of Maryland and from the South, mainly Virginia and North Carolina, looking for economic opportunities in the war industry. In 1920, 108,322 blacks called Baltimore home. Between 1940 and 1950, the African-American population rose from 165,843 to 225,099, an increase of 36 percent. During the same period, the rate of white population growth was only 4 percent. Blacks constituted 19 percent of the city's total population in 1940; by 1950 that figure was 24 percent (see Table 4.1). For the people of Baltimore the greatest single impact of the war was prosperity: prosperity for everyone, especially for once-unemployed workers.

After 1950 the confluence of two major social and economic trends radically transformed the city. First, between 1950 and 1980 the racial composition of the population changed dramatically, from only 24 percent African American to

Table 4.1. Baltimore Population by Race, 1920–1990

	Total Population	White (%)	Black (%)
1920	733,826	625,130 (85)	108,322 (15)
1930	804,874	662,124 (82)	142,106 (18)
1940	859,100	692,705 (81)	165,843 (19)
1950	949,748	723,655 (76)	225,099 (24)
1960	939,024	610,608 (65)	325,589 (35)
1970	905,759	479,837 (54)	420,210 (46)
1980	786,775	346,692 (45)	430,934 (55)
1990	736,014	287,933 (41)	435,619 (59)

Source: U.S. Bureau of the Census, U.S. Census on Population, 1920, 1930, 1940, 1950, 1960, 1970, 1980, and 1990.

55 percent. Its black population nearly doubled, from 225,099 to 430,935. By 1990 Baltimore had become nearly 60 percent African American (see Fig. 4.1).

The growth of the black population in Baltimore coincided with the massive exodus and suburbanization of the city's white population. White flight accelerated during the 1970s, with some 135,000 residents leaving the city during the decade. Between 1950 and 1990, the number of whites living in the city declined by over 430,000, a decrease of 60 percent. A survey conducted in 1977 showed that about one-third of those households said that their "main reason for moving was some negative feeling about the city—taxes, schools, and neighborhood conditions."[11]

Meanwhile, the population of the city's suburbs surged. In 1950 Baltimore's five suburban counties—Harford, Baltimore, Anne Arundel, Howard, and Carroll—had a total population of approximately 455,000 residents. In 1990 the same counties had become home to 1.3 million residents, 86 percent of whom are white.

Besides population differences, the age structure of Baltimore's emerging black majority differed markedly from whites in the city (see Fig. 4.2). Before 1950 the percentage of white school-age children outnumbered African Americans significantly. In 1940, for example, 79 percent of the school children were white and only 21 percent black. After 1950, when the racial make-over of Baltimore began, the school-age population began to change dramatically. Between 1950 and 1990 the number of white school-age children dropped from 140,061 to 41,294, a decrease of 70 percent. During the same period, the number of black children rose from 52,337 to 101,399, an increase of 94 percent.

This demographic trend strongly affected public education in Baltimore. Although the black percentage of the city's total population was 60 percent by 1990, enrollments in the Baltimore City Public Schools were over 80 percent African American (see Fig. 4.3). Meanwhile, the decline of white students and residents revealed the racial dimensions of population shifts and student enrollment. For instance, although the city was over 50 percent white in 1970, the school

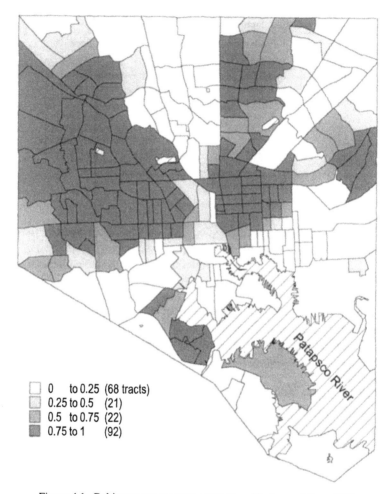

0   to 0.25 (68 tracts)
0.25 to 0.5   (21)
0.5 to 0.75 (22)
0.75 to 1   (92)

Figure 4.1. Baltimore census tract, percentage black population, 1990

system's white student enrollment was just 30 percent, illustrating the percentage gap between white residents and white student enrollment. Many African Americans viewed these differences as evidence that whites had abandoned the public schools. The gap widened during the 1980s and 1990s.

The transition from white to black is also represented in the personnel of the BCPS. As employment opportunities opened in the growing suburbs, many white teachers and administrators left the city system to work in the expanding suburban school districts. As a result, black teachers and administrators found increased employment opportunities in the city's schools. To be sure, Baltimore's dual, segregated school system has long been a source of income and upward mobility

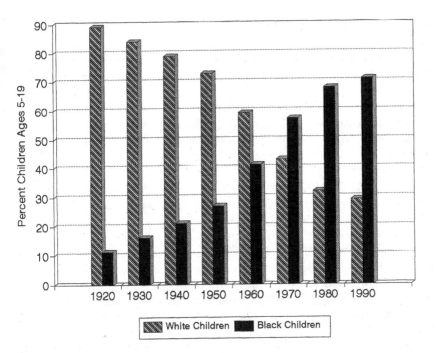

Figure 4.2. School-age children by race, 1920–1990

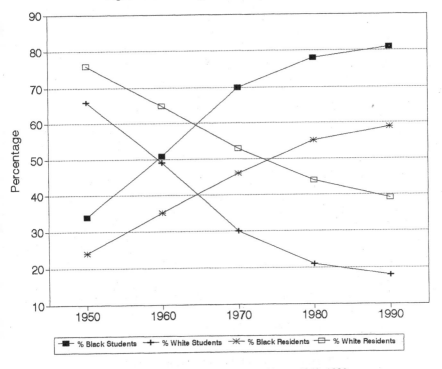

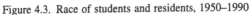

Figure 4.3. Race of students and residents, 1950–1990

for many African Americans, especially the city's black middle class. By the 1990s, however, the public school had become the linchpin of Baltimore's black employment base.[12]

In 1965, 20 percent of the elementary and secondary school assistant principals and principals were African American; by 1993, 70 percent were.[13] In 1965, 53 percent of the city's elementary teachers and 40 percent of secondary teachers were black.[14] A steady climb in the percentage of Baltimore's black faculty occurred, rising to 59 percent in 1972, peaking at 71 percent in 1984, and leveling off to 63 percent in 1993 (see Fig. 4.4). In 1995 African Americans held over 70 percent of the district's 11,414 jobs, including lower-level positions as janitors, secretaries, and teachers' aides.[15]

In part, the demographic shift in the BCPS simply reflected the changes in the overall city population. But it also reflected the reluctance of financially secure families to send their children to the city's public schools, opting instead to send them to private schools. "The white middle class in Baltimore," according to a 1967 NEA study, "is rapidly separating the educational fortunes and destiny of its children from those of the other children—the Negro children, the children of poverty, the majority of the children."[16] The dynamics of demographic change in Baltimore between 1950 and 1990 were such that matters of race, poverty, and unemployment were disproportionately felt in the public school system.

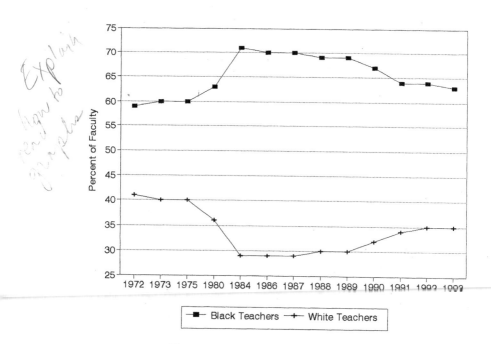

Figure 4.4. Race of Baltimore teachers, 1972–1993

BLACK BALTIMORE AND ECONOMIC CHANGE

At the same time these dramatic demographic trends were occurring, the city was also undergoing a major economic restructuring. Its manufacturing economy began to experience decline during the 1950s. In 1951 Baltimore had 1,811 manufacturing establishments; in 1959 the number had fallen by 12 percent. The decline intensified between 1970 and 1980, and by 1990 the central city had only 844 manufacturing plants. Concomitantly, the number of workers in manufacturing has severely declined. In the early 1950s, 127,000 Baltimoreans were employed in manufacturing. This figure dropped to 102,000 in 1970; to 70,000 in 1980; and to 44,000 in 1990. By 1995, only 33,000 such jobs remained.

Employment fell considerably in primary metal plants, shipbuilding and repair, and transportation equipment production. Bethlehem Steel Shipyard shut down operations during the early 1980s, laying off some 1,500 people.[17] Baltimore's deteriorating port added to the city's industrial woes. Unable to adapt to new containerized cargo techniques that were revolutionizing shipping, the city suffered from competition with other ports nearby such as Newport News and Norfolk, Virginia, threatening another source of well-paying, low-skill jobs.[18] These were the blue-collar jobs that had enabled industrial workers to build middle-class living standards throughout the twentieth century.

Grocery stores and other retail establishments in the city closed, shifting retail trade away from the city to the suburbs, further eroding Baltimore's economy. Data showing the location of retail sales in the region are dramatic. In 1950, 80 percent of the retail sales in the Baltimore region were located in the city. By 1992 the figure had dropped to 18 percent. Suburban malls, supermarkets, theaters, and restaurants accounted for 82 percent of the region's retail trade.

Economic transformation, especially when complicated by racial concentration and a history of racial discrimination, is a painful and socially disruptive process. In Baltimore and other frost-belt cities, manufacturing jobs were replaced by advanced-corporate and service-sector jobs.[19] White-collar jobs have expanded, but jobs typically filled by people without education beyond high school have shrunk considerably. Such changes thus have hurt poorly educated and low-skilled citizens.

John Kasarda has examined the consequences of this economic restructuring on urban black employment. He concludes that most urban blacks "simply lack the education to participate in the new growth sectors of the urban economy."[20] Other scholars have also commented on the disproportionate impact that deindustrialization has had on African Americans.[21] Barry Bluestone and Bennett Harrison note that the systematic decline in the industrial base has had a more severe impact on blacks than on whites.[22] Martin Carnoy observes that "the gradual white-collarization of manufacturing had a significantly different impact on minorities than whites. Whites moved up into the expanded ranks of managers and professionals, but for both blacks and Latinos little movement occurred, and only from unskilled to semiskilled blue-collar jobs to clerical positions."[23]

Despite improvements in their overall educational attainment, a great majority of African Americans still have little schooling and therefore have been unable to gain access to new urban growth industries. Thus, for low-skilled African
Americans, economic restructuring appears detrimental. Only 8 percent of African Americans in Baltimore have received a college degree; comparatively, the
percentage of whites is nearly three times as large. Many white residents have
been poised to take advantage of economic restructuring, with the requisite education and training necessary for employment in the new service and advanced-
corporate economy.

For black Baltimoreans as a whole, labor market exclusion has spawned stag-
gering increases in poverty, welfare dependency, and other symptoms of community distress.[24] Median income in the city is well below the state average and is
less than half the amount of the state's wealthiest counties. Data from the 1990
census are instructive. The median family income for the city is $28,217—more
than $10,000 under the state average of $39,386. In Baltimore County, a jurisdic-
tion containing the city's oldest and most immediate suburban neighborhoods, the
median income of $44,502 is 58 percent higher than Baltimore City's median
income. Howard County, just outside Baltimore, has a median income more than
twice that of the city.

Even more dramatic are the poverty figures. More than one in six families in
Baltimore falls below the poverty level—three times the state average. Poverty is
concentrated in the inner core of the city (see Fig. 4.5). As is the case nationwide,
the poverty rate among children is much greater than among adults; nearly one-
third of the school-age children are living below the poverty line. For the state,
the proportion is about one in ten. The suburban counties fall well below the state's
average and even further below Baltimore's.

Behind the figures on income and education is another story, a story of weak
economic self-sufficiency. The exodus of both affluent residents and jobs left the
city with a large proportion of its residents dependent on government services—
"public dependents," as Sherry Olson has described them.[25] A high level of teen
births also contributes to economic dependency. Nearly one in ten girls in the
fifteen- to seventeen-year age range (96.8 per 1,000) gives birth (see Table 4.2).
This is three times the national average and five or more times greater than the
rates for Baltimore and Howard Counties. Despite various efforts to lower that
figure, it has held constant for several years.[26]

Growing poverty in the community has meant an increasingly impoverished
BCPS student clientele. In 1995, 67 percent of the students enrolled were eligible
for reduced-fee meals, an indication of their poverty status. In contrast, only
25 percent of Baltimore County students were eligible. The statewide figure was
31 percent. In fact, according to the Governor's Commission on School Funding,
the BCPS serves the largest concentration of students in Maryland living in poverty and with special needs. In 1992 there were 255 schools across Maryland with
45 percent or more poor children; 148 of these schools (or 58 percent) were in

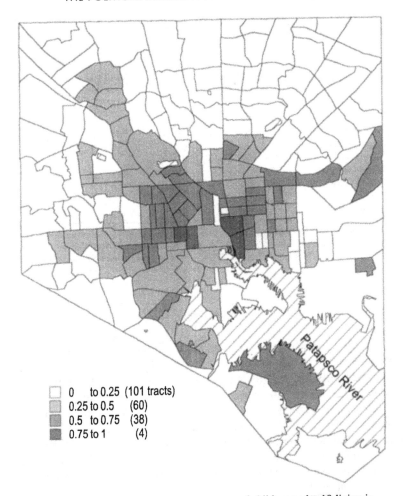

0   to 0.25 (101 tracts)
0.25 to 0.5   (60)
0.5 to 0.75   (38)
0.75 to 1   (4)

Figure 4.5. Baltimore census tract, percentage of children under 18 living in poverty, 1990

Baltimore City. Only Baltimore had schools with 90 to 100 percent of their students living in or near poverty.[27]

Although much of the BCPS' clientele earlier in the century came from poor households, the sheer size and concentration of the misery in the city of the 1980s and 1990s presented the school system with an unprecedented challenge. Never before, in so many schools in the system, had so large a portion of the student population come from such conditions of economic and social havoc. The result was a full-fledged crisis in the BCPS.

Table 4.2. Adolescent Births, 1989

| | JURISDICTION OF RESIDENCE | | | |
	Baltimore	Baltimore County	Howard County	Montgomery County
Births to mothers under 15 yrs. old	19	14	3	17
Rate/1,000 females under 15 yrs. old	5.3	0.1	0.6	0.8
Births to mothers 15–17 yrs. old	1,253	219	39	182
Rate/1,000 females 15–17 yrs. old	96.8	19.8	11.8	14.8
Total births to mothers under 18 yrs. old	1,272	233	42	199

Source: David Imbroscio, Marion Orr, Timothy Ross, and Clarence Stone, "Baltimore and the Human Investment Challenge," in *Urban Revitalization: Policies and Programs,* ed. Fritz Wagner, Timothy E. Joder, and Anthony Mumphrey Jr. (Thousand Oaks, CA: Sage Publications, 1995), p. 48. Reprinted by permission of Sage Publications.

CHANGING EMPLOYMENT ENVIRONMENT AND POOR SCHOOLS

Before the 1960s students who dropped out of school or, despite holding a high school diploma, were illiterate or lacked basic arithmetic skills could still often find employment in the region's numerous factories. The decline in factory employment, however, has eliminated many of these job possibilities for unskilled youth. John Kasarda reports that between 1970 and 1984 Baltimore experienced consistent job losses in industries where employees' education averaged less than a high school diploma and consistent employment growth in industries where workers on the average acquired some higher education. As early as 1980, nearly 40 percent of those employed in Baltimore had at least some higher education, up from 22 percent in 1970.

Moreover, as manufacturers have invested in new technologies to remain competitive in the increasingly global economy, employment, both in factories and in large segments of the fast-growing service industry, has required increased literacy and mathematical skills. In a recent study, William J. Wilson found that today's employers are looking for workers with a broad range of "hard" and "soft" skills. The former are testable attributes such as literacy, numeracy, and basic mechanical ability, the product of education and training. The latter are "strongly tied to culture" and are "shaped by the harsh environment of the inner-city ghetto."[28] "Soft" skills include personalities suitable to the work environment, good grooming, and group-oriented work behaviors. Mayor Kurt Schmoke has consistently acknowledged the mismatch between the training and education of the city's workforce and the increasing demands of employers:

A highly trained, literate workforce is now in great demand in Baltimore, and that demand will escalate in the coming decade. One indicator of the economic changes that have already taken place can be summed up in one simple statement: the Johns Hopkins University has replaced Bethlehem Steel as the city's single largest private employer. Today, computer systems, biochemical manufacturing, banking and financial services, and telecommunications are the fastest-growing industries in the Baltimore/Washington corridor. Unfortunately, there is a growing mismatch between the needs of these highly technical industries moving into the region and the skill levels of our local citizens. If Baltimore is to continue to expand economically, we must be able to get more of our students to graduate from high school and continue on to college and more of our adults to enroll in literacy and other training programs to sharpen and improve their skills.[29]

These employment and education trends were evident across a number of large northeastern cities.[30]

In the early 1980s civic and political leaders reached two basic conclusions concerning the BCPS. First, the schools are extraordinarily important to a hopeful future for Baltimore and its residents. The school system is the one instrument society has for ensuring that young people acquire the "soft" and "hard" skills that employers require, including skills not being fostered through family or neighborhood life. In 1986 the local Goldseker Foundation commissioned urban consultant Peter Szanton to conduct a study to forecast the city's economic future; *Baltimore 2000* took a decidedly pessimistic view.[31] Yet it pointed to an improved public school system as the "best hope" for the city: "The schools are society's last best hope for providing the neediest young people with sufficient confidence, self-discipline and respect for themselves and others to give them a chance for productive and satisfying lives. It is clear, moreover, that personal qualities, not the mastery of academic subjects, matter most to entry-level employers."[32] The second conclusion was simply that the schools were failing the city's youth and that systemic reform of the BCPS was necessary. According to an adviser involved in the report, "The system is simply a disaster."[33]

Not much had changed ten years after the publication of *Baltimore 2000*. In 1995 the dropout rate among BCPS students was more than three times greater than the statewide average. Table 4.3 shows the percentage of elementary and middle schools in the Baltimore region reaching the "satisfactory" standard established by the Maryland School Performance Assessment Program (MSPAP), tests that measure performance in reading, mathematics, writing, language, social studies, science, and attendance. The state instituted MSPAP in 1989 as a way to hold individual schools accountable for what students should know and be able to do as a result of their educational experiences (see chap. 9). The data show that a smaller percentage of BCPS schools reached the satisfactory standard than other

Table 4.3. Maryland School Performance Program Report: Elementary and Middle Schools in the Baltimore Region, 1993-1995

	1993-1994 Elementary/Middle	1994-1995 Elementary/Middle	1995-1996 Elementary/Middle
Baltimore City Public Schools	24.0/31.8	26.1/34.4	25.3/35.0
Anne Arundel County	64.2/67.3	70.3/67.4	73.9/70.6
Baltimore County	57.9/71.7	65.4/74.9	64.8/76.8
Howard County	73.5/85.0	80.4/88.7	82.6/87.7
Harford County	61.9/74.3	74.4/81.4	76.7/81.6
Statewide	53.2/64.8	59.2/68.9	60.7/69.6

Source: Christopher S. Lambert and Jennean Everett Reynolds, The State of Baltimore's Schools: Data and Information on the Current Status of Baltimore City Public Schools (Baltimore: Advocates for Children and Youth, June 1997), p. CS-2.

Note: The figures reported are "school performance" indices that reflect the average performance representing the school's distance from the state's "satisfactory" standard. Indices above 100 indicate that average performance exceeds the satisfactory standard; an index of 100 indicates that average performance equals the satisfactory standard; and an index below 100 means that average performance is below the satisfactory standard. Elementary schools' performance is based on student attendance and performance on third and fifth grade MSPAP tests. Middle schools' performance is based on student attendance, eighth grade MSPAP tests, and performance on the Maryland Functional Test in reading, writing, and math.

school systems in the region. In 1995, for example, only 25.3 percent of BCPS elementary schools, compared to 64.8 percent of Baltimore County's and 82.6 percent of Howard County's, reached the state's satisfactory standard. The percentage of Baltimore middle schools reaching the satisfactory standard was also well below the other surrounding counties and the statewide percentage for all three years.

Other relevant data point to a school system in need of reform. In 1995 BCPS students averaged a score of 723 on the Scholastic Aptitude Test (SAT). The state average was 909, the national average 910. In some BCPS schools students scored much lower: Lake Clifton High School students averaged 616; students at Frederick Douglass High School, once Baltimore's premier black high school, averaged a dismal 597. Furthermore, the percentage of BCPS graduates who continued their education at a four-year college is smaller than the statewide average. In 1995 only 33 percent of the BCPS graduates completed the University of Maryland System requirements for entrance into its four-year colleges. The statewide figure was 51 percent.

The BCPS faces still other challenges. A recent management report outlined the less visible ones, such as incompetent school and central office administrators, a "culture" that does not support "effective management," and "entrenched" attitudes among teachers and administrators that the BCPS cannot be improved.[34]

CHANGING POLITICS: THE SCHOOLS AND STATE GOVERNMENT

Because public education is a state responsibility, there is no escaping the influence of state governments in local school affairs. For a considerable part of the twentieth century, Baltimore has been the political powerhouse in the state. Its ward-level political bosses tightly controlled the city's Democratic vote, delivering it to a specific candidate in state primary elections. In a predominantly Democratic state, this support guaranteed final victory.[35] Political bosses such as Isaac Freeman Rasin, Sonny Mahon, Frank Kelly, William Curran, and more recently James "Jack" Pollack and Irving Kovens were able to use their clout to reach out across the state and unify competing interests behind a single candidate for governor.[36] From 1920 to 1960, except for four years, a Baltimore resident controlled the governor's mansion. Only three governors have been elected from outside the city since the 1950s. Two of them, however, Spiro Agnew (elected in 1966) and Harry Hughes (elected in 1978 and 1982), had strong city connections. Parris Glendening, a former executive from Prince George's County, was elected in 1994, becoming the first Maryland governor elected from the Washington, DC area since Gov. Oden Bowie (also of Prince George's County) was elected in 1868.

Baltimore's demographic transformation after World War II altered the state's political topography, weakening the city's influence in state affairs. In 1930 Baltimore contained nearly half (49.3 percent) of Maryland's population. A half century later, in 1980, only 18 percent of Marylanders resided in the city. Baltimore's population decline had an impact on state politics; a dramatic drop occurred in the proportion of the city's votes cast in gubernatorial elections from 1954 and 1994 (see Fig. 4.6). In 1954, 36 percent of the statewide vote for governor was cast in Baltimore; four decades later city voters contributed only 11 percent. Growth in the state's population after World War II occurred largely in predominantly white suburban counties, giving those voters the power to deliver more votes in a statewide election than those in Baltimore.[37] In Prince George's and Montgomery Counties, Washington, DC–area suburbs, the combined proportion of votes cast in the 1994 gubernatorial election was slightly over 20 percent.

It is important, however, not to exaggerate the city's declining influence in state politics. In the early 1990s two Baltimore legislators, Delegate Howard "Pete" Rawlings and Sen. Barbara Hoffman, chaired the legislature's two budget-writing committees. The city remains a major force in deciding Maryland's Democratic primaries, largely because 90 percent of its registered voters are Democrats, and the state remains decidedly Democratic, although the Republican party has gained ground in recent decades. In the 1994 general election, Parris Glendening squeaked out a victory over Republican Ellen Sauerbrey by only 5,993 votes. Glendening carried only three of Maryland's twenty-four political jurisdictions—Prince George's County, Montgomery County, and Baltimore. Without the strong showing in the city, he would have been defeated.[38] Still, the city's influence in state

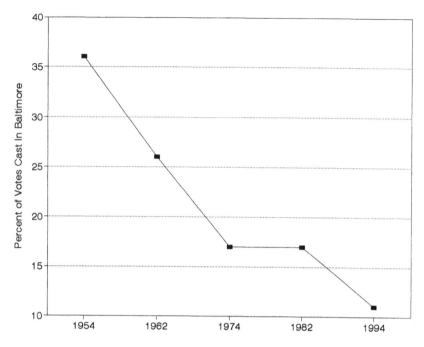

Figure 4.6. Baltimore's influence in gubernatorial elections, 1954–1994

government is not as significant as it was twenty or thirty years ago (see Table 4.4, which shows a corresponding decline in its representation in the General Assembly). The number and percentage of state legislators from Baltimore City have dropped during the past three decades.

There is also a racial dimension to Maryland's postwar demographic trends, which influences state politics. In 1960, 63 percent of the state's black population lived in Baltimore. Today, they are more dispersed, many living in the suburbs, especially in Prince George's County, a black-majority suburb. Baltimore, how-

Table 4.4. Baltimore's Political Representation in the Maryland General Assembly, 1966–1996

Year	House of Delegates	Percentage of Total	State Senate	Percentage of Total
1966	43	30	12	25
1974	33	23	11	23
1990	27	19	9	19
1996	29	20	10	21

Source: General Assembly of Maryland, List of Commitees and Roster, 1966, 1974, 1990, 1996.

ever, remains the center of the state's African-American population. In 1990 blacks constituted 24 percent of the state's population, and Baltimore was home to nearly 40 percent of all black residents.

Thomas Edsall, who covered Baltimore and Maryland politics for the *Sun* in the 1960s and 1970s, predicted that the transformation of Maryland's population would corrode state-level politics. Race and class, Edsall contended, would be the foundation of the conflict, and Baltimore would be at its epicenter:

> The demographic changes taking place in the state point toward the prospect of increasing internal dissension within the Democratic party. . . . Not only do the suburban communities that now dominate the state provide fertile territory for the GOP . . . , but growing suburban strength in the legislature is likely to produce the kind of political conflict pitting affluent, and largely white, suburban jurisdictions against less affluent, and largely black, Baltimore city.[39]

As Baltimore's influence in state politics waned, city officials found themselves looking to Annapolis for support, especially for public education. The vast majority of states fund their educational systems through local property taxes. Under this system of financing, the extent of educational services depends heavily on the adequacy of each community's tax base. Maryland adopted a school equalization program in 1922.[40] The General Assembly prescribed a minimum educational program and a reasonable local property tax rate to finance it. Any subdivision that could not raise enough money at that tax rate received state aid to fill the gap. Decades ago, Maryland, as did other states, designed educational aid to assist then poorer suburban school districts.[41] In the first four decades of Maryland's aid to public education, Baltimore actually helped its less wealthy suburban neighbors fund their school systems.[42] In 1950, for example, Maryland contributed $90 per pupil to its suburban schools and only $71 per pupil to Baltimore; in 1964 the circumstance was the same—suburban schools received $199 per pupil from Annapolis and Baltimore only $171.[43]

Today the situation has changed. There has been a colossal rise in the percentage of Baltimore's school budget supported by state funds (see Fig. 4.7). In 1993 Maryland provided 63 percent of the city's education budget, up from 25 percent in the 1950s.[44] With a restricted property tax base, the BCPS finds it increasingly difficult to maintain quality services, which results in hard decisions about resource allocation and more dependency on state assistance.

Through a state school funding equalization program, Baltimore receives more state education aid than any of Maryland's school districts. Yet despite this assistance, the city spends considerably less per pupil than the state average (see Table 4.5). Significantly, the disparities are not based on Baltimore's unwillingness to tax. Its property tax rate is double that of most jurisdictions in the state. Maryland's formula gives more aid to poor school systems than to rich ones, but the wealthier districts, with a greater tax base, spend more per student. In 1995, for example,

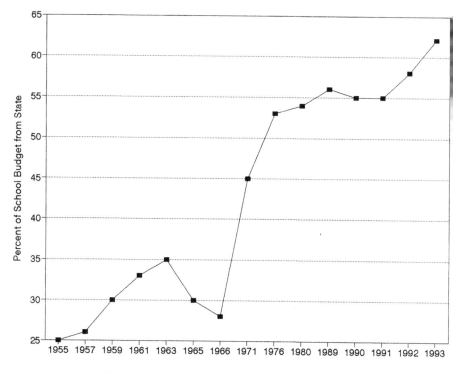

Figure 4.7. State aid to Baltimore schools, 1955–1993

Montgomery County, one of Maryland's wealthiest jurisdictions, spent nearly $8,000 per student, but only 19 percent of that amount came from the state.

Baltimore's leaders and school officials have maintained for years that this gap in spending translates into less of almost every kind of school resources for the BCPS and an inability to compete effectively with more affluent subdivisions. In 1979 Baltimore joined with three rural school districts (Somerset, Caroline, and St. Mary's Counties) in a lawsuit challenging the constitutionality of Maryland's education financing scheme on the ground that it failed to ensure complete equality of funding among affluent and poor school districts.[45]

The city lost its suit, but the effort influenced Gov. Harry Hughes to appoint a task force to study state education funding.[46] It recommended a new funding formula weighted heavily toward Baltimore and other poorer subdivisions. The legislature adopted this formula, which never "equalized" Baltimore's spending with most of the rest of Maryland.[47] For many years, such funding schemes caused little debate across the state. Montgomery County, a relatively liberal, affluent, white enclave, was generally content to help poorer neighbors. But the recession of the early 1990s gave Montgomery its own funding problems.[48] Consequently, Montgomery County officials and other suburban leaders began accusing state

Table 4.5. Spending per Pupil in Maryland's Largest School
Districts, 1995

School District	Spending Per Pupil
Baltimore City	$5,873
Anne Arundel County	6,452
Baltimore County	6,337
Carroll County	5,795
Harford County	5,697
Howard County	6,793
Montgomery County	7,697
Prince George's County	6,272
Statewide Average	6,338

Source: Maryland State Department of Education

leaders of inattention to their needs while Baltimore mismanaged millions of state education aid. As the amount of state assistance to the city climbed, state education officials and legislators (especially suburban legislators) began closely scrutinizing the management and performance of the BCPS.

SUMMARY

The demographic and economic changes that have occurred in Baltimore since the 1950s profoundly affected the city, its residents, and schools. In 1997 the black population was 65 percent; whites made up only 33 percent. Today, Baltimore is racially isolated within its metropolitan area and among Maryland's other twenty-three political subdivisions.

The number of manufacturing jobs located in the city declined significantly, with new growth taking place primarily in the service sector. "Of net [job] growth in the region, half reflects high-wage, knowledge-intensive jobs, while the other half reflects low-wage jobs that pay half as much: from child care to cleaning carpets in hotel rooms or picking up styrofoam cups on the waterfront. Nothing in between. Nothing to match the 90,000 well-paid, unionized factory jobs that have disappeared."[49] Unlike the European immigrants whose entry into the labor market coincided with the rapid growth of entry-level industrial jobs, the influx of blacks after 1950 occurred when the city's economy was no longer providing plentiful blue-collar jobs that could support families with a decent standard of living. As one local writer declared: "The city no longer wears a blue collar. As the blue-collar worker becomes an endangered species, the American dream in overalls goes with him."[50] Youth can no longer expect to find unskilled or semiskilled employment in factories, and as employers continue to raise the educational ante and emphasize both "soft" and "hard" skills, struggling BCPS students are likely to be relegated to low-wage, dead-end employment. While the nation's economy grows and many Americans are doing well, large segments of inner-city residents are in danger of being left behind.

Poverty has been spreading throughout Baltimore. A number of studies have documented the growth of poverty neighborhoods. David Rusk has calculated that between 1970 and 1990, "the total number of poverty neighborhoods increased from seventy to ninety." "For most Baltimore neighborhoods," writes Marc Levine, "the 1970s were years of increasing poverty, deteriorating housing, and shrinking economic opportunities."[51] Although the regional poverty rate dropped from 11 percent in 1970 to 10 percent in 1990, the poverty rate in Baltimore increased from 18 percent to 22 percent. The city is, as Rusk bluntly puts it, the "region's poorhouse." "The heart of Baltimore City's slow decline," he adds, "is that it is cast in a highly specialized role within the metropolitan community: Baltimore City must house, educate, and serve the social needs of far too many poor black residents."[52]

What does all this mean for social capital, especially intergroup social capital? As Baltimore became predominantly African American and poor, whites tended to criticize the city, its leaders, and its schools. Edward Berkowitz has observed that the schools "began to attract unwelcome notice from critics who charged they were unsafe and ineffective." The increased criticism, Berkowitz adds, was "not unrelated to the fact that Baltimore was becoming a black city."[53] The effect was to heighten whites' fears that the city and its schools were in serious decline, a reaction not only among whites in the Baltimore region but also in Montgomery and Charles Counties and in other parts of Maryland, where disdain for Baltimore is matched only by contempt for the other nearby majority black city, Washington, DC.

Many black leaders thus hold the view that the city is finally under their political control, allowing them to shape its future. For many of them, the main concern is to incorporate black political and economic power there. In grasping and consolidating this power, African-American leaders have had to depend increasingly on reserves of black social capital.[54] Their concerns about the tenuousness of black political power in turn heighten their tendency to promote black social capital. The pattern has been for suburban whites and Baltimore's African-American leaders to see the world in terms of "we" and "they," which hampers formation of intergroup social capital.

5
School Reform Through Site-based Management

You've got a lot of school folks out there who are so immune to this. They make no changes whatsoever. I had several principals who said to me, "Why should I listen to you? You'll be gone soon" or "Why should we work with this reform of Dr. Amprey's because he's going to be gone and somebody else is going to come in here with other reforms." Bottom line—Baltimore City can never reform itself. It's impossible. The only hope is to bring in outside forces.
– ASSISTANT SUPERINTENDENT, BALTIMORE CITY PUBLIC SCHOOLS

The 1987 election of Mayor Kurt Schmoke boosted school reform to the top of Baltimore's agenda. Just as former mayor William Donald Schaefer used his formal and informal powers to redevelop downtown Baltimore, Mayor Schmoke vowed to use the visibility of the mayor's office to promote education. In an effort to publicize the opening of the Baltimore National Aquarium, a major addition to the Inner Harbor redevelopment project, Schaefer appeared in an 1890s' swimsuit and, accompanied by a rubber duck, jumped into the seal pool. Similarly, Mayor Schmoke donned a crossing-guard's vest while escorting a group of kindergartners to school. A visit with Schmoke earned his guest a bookmark with "Baltimore: the city that reads" printed on it. If Schaefer, as one observer put it, "was a master entrepreneur for economic development," Kurt Schmoke became a master entrepreneur for improved educational opportunity.[1]

Mayor Schmoke, however, was not the initiator of the heightened effort to improve the Baltimore City Public Schools. Baltimoreans United in Leadership Development deserves the credit for creating the political environment that facilitated Schmoke's and other leaders' efforts in reforming the city's school system.

In 1983, four years prior to Schmoke's election, BUILD began to investigate the shortages and disparities in supplies in the BCPS. Its findings reinforced the certainty among many African-American leaders and school activists that action was needed to reform the city's schools. In collaboration with community leaders, politicians, teachers, principals, and the business community, BUILD eventually developed a systemwide school reform plan. Site-based management and the creation of neighborhood school autonomy were its key components.[2]

SBM moves decision-making authority from the school district's central administration to local schools.[3] The basic idea is simply to give principals, teachers, parents, and other community members more authority to make management decisions concerning the operation of their individual schools. One school may decide to replace its wiring to ensure Internet access to students. Another school may vote to hire additional English as Second Language (ESL) teachers to support a growing immigrant population. In a centralized school district, each school must consult district administrators for approval; with SBM, school constituents gain autonomy over decisions.

SBM has become a popular reform method in public school districts across the country. In the late 1980s, Chicago received national attention for its effort to establish SBM throughout its troubled school district. Under measures adopted by the Illinois legislature, the influence of the central bureaucracy was substantially curtailed; and significant authority in the operation of the schools shifted from professional educators to parents and community members. Chicago's 1988 reforms "encouraged expanded participation among parents and community members, teachers, and the principal by devolving to these local actors significant formal authority and new resources to solve their local problems."[4] The reforms empowered parents and community members through creation of local school councils. By 1993 more than 95 percent of the fifty largest urban school districts in the United States had similar SBM programs in at least some of their schools.[5]

Mayor Kurt Schmoke, with his formal authority over the city's schools, played a critical role in elevating SBM to the top of Baltimore's agenda. Further, a broad coalition of parents, religious leaders, community members, business and civic leaders, and professional educators formed to give school constituents more control over their own schools. Altering the governance of local school districts is a political process, however. Changing the relationship between district administrators, principals, teachers, parents, and the school community is also a political decision. Making SBM a top policy priority, and implementing such a program, requires broad support from all levels, from the superintendent to the parents. A high level of intergroup social capital can facilitate the institution of SBM.

INITIAL SIGNS OF STRUGGLE

The emergence of SBM as a reform idea in Baltimore began under the superintendency of Alice Pinderhughes, who had worked her way up through the school system, rising in 1982, after over forty years in the BCPS, to the top position. She was known for welcoming input from outside the school system, smoothing the way for scholars at Johns Hopkins University, the University of Maryland, and other universities conducting urban education research. As an education researcher at Johns Hopkins recalled, she was "a very strong supporter of what we were doing. She was involved from the very beginning, showing up at our training sessions to show support." Pinderhughes worked closely with BUILD, embracing its school reform plan, including the adoption of SBM. Further, she had better relations with the business community than her predecessors, having reached out early in her tenure to the Greater Baltimore Committee, and its education committee became more active during her tenure. "We began to have meetings," Pinderhughes remembered. "It was really like another school board meeting. We went over everything in these meetings, the budget, curriculum, you name it."[6]

In 1982, with Pinderhughes's support, the GBC held a series of informal meetings with BUILD, other African-American community leaders, and BCPS officials. In April 1983 the GBC released a report that urged the BCPS to consider decentralizing some of North Avenue's (BCPS headquarters) functions. To improve the budgetary process, the GBC recommended "school-based budgeting."[7] Two years later, Pinderhughes launched the idea as a pilot program. It would "permit principals, in consultation with teachers and community representatives, to allocate funds across a variety of budget categories according to priorities established at the school level."[8]

Seven schools were selected to experiment with school-based budgeting; however, the program was established "only on paper."[9] It met "strong resistance" from administrators at central headquarters who refused to relinquish their budgetary authority or the necessary information to principals and staffers at the participating schools. As a result, school-based budgeting never got off the ground.

Curiously, neither BUILD nor the GBC used their political muscle to prod the school bureaucracy to support the pilot SBM program. It is unclear why BUILD did not push the matter. One possibility is that it simply was skeptical because of the GBC's endorsement of SBM. BUILD leaders might have grown suspicious, assuming that if SBM failed to improve student performance, then the fears of some African-American leaders would be realized: that the real aim of some people within the business community was the adoption of school vouchers and other market-based school reforms. Some BUILD leaders, however, believed that parents wanted good schools for their children but that they did not wish to run them, thinking they lacked the expertise to do so. The predominantly white GBC leaders feared that using their political influence to push for school-based budgeting would bring them into conflict with the black-led school bureaucracy. They were reluctant to undertake this battle.

A LEADERSHIP CHANGE IN THE BCPS

Four years into Pinderhughes's tenure, Mayor William Donald Schaefer, who personally had named her to the school system's top post, resigned to become governor. City council president Clarence "Du" Burns completed Schaefer's term but faced Kurt L. Schmoke in the 1987 mayoral election, and education took center stage.

Superintendent Pinderhughes continued to support SBM. In April 1987, six months before the Democratic mayoral primary, she released her vision for the BCPS, "Focus on Individual Success," a document with SBM as the central reform.[10] After the release of her report, she appointed a task force to examine SBM and devise a plan to incorporate it throughout the school system.

Jo Ann Robinson, a school activist and former chair of the League of Women Voters' Education Committee, and Charlene Griffin, a staff member in the superintendent's office, were asked to cochair the task force. It included a broad spectrum of educational stakeholders, including the City-Wide PTA Council; students; Jeff Valentine, the education staffer for the GBC; Robert Clark of the CPHA; Jerry Baum, executive director of the Fund for Educational Excellence; Susan Leviton, president of Advocates for Children and Youth; Sarah Daignault of the League of Women Voters; Carol Reckling of BUILD; and representatives from the Baltimore NAACP, the Baltimore Urban League, and other community and civic organizations. Members of the two most powerful school employee unions, Public School Administrators and Supervisors Association (PSASA) and the Baltimore Teachers' Union, were also members.

Although many members of the task force actively supported SBM, PSASA and the BTU were less engaged in its work and deliberations. The president of PSASA, Arnett Brown, publicly criticized SBM, arguing that "like all the initiatives of the past . . . [SBM] would give principals more to do without making substantial change." The BTU also "attached little importance" to the task force's deliberations.[11] The reluctance of teachers and principals was an ominous sign for supporters of SBM.

The task force deliberated throughout the 1987 Democratic mayoral primary campaign, during which Schmoke held a commanding lead in the polls over Burns. As veteran observers of Baltimore politics, the leadership of the teachers' and principals' unions correctly read the political tea leaves, anticipating that a victory by Schmoke would most likely mean a change at North Avenue. Union leaders suspected that Pinderhughes's recommendation on SBM would not be seriously considered if a new mayor were elected and she were replaced. Traditionally, new superintendents arrived with their own policy ideas, regardless of their predecessor's plans. In September, just as the task force neared completion of its work, Kurt Schmoke won the primary.

Despite the changing political terrain, the task force continued to meet. The BTU withdrew as an active participant although Arnett Brown continued to work with it. A few days after the primary election, the task force submitted its final report to Pinderhughes. The Schmoke administration, however, politely ignored the task force's recommendations. "Nothing happened. City Hall looked the other way. It didn't think much of the plan," recalled a member. The report never received full consideration from the Schmoke administration. One month after his election, Mayor Schmoke asked Pinderhughes to retire.[12]

Few people were surprised. Political observers maintained that Schmoke's decision was influenced by Pinderhughes's critics, who argued that during her six years as superintendent she had not pushed hard enough for change, being too much a product of the city system to lead a large-scale shake-up. Some educational stakeholders asserted that although Pinderhughes welcomed SBM and other reforms, she did not have the political skills to accomplish them. Jeff Valentine, the GBC's education liaison, noted in an interview that "Pinderhughes did not know how to dismantle the road blocks that would prevent [SBM] from moving forward. In her case, it was far less an issue of a commitment than how do you control this bureaucracy."[13] The school system needed strong leadership to overcome bureaucratic resistance and to provide direction for the entire system. As the education mayor, Kurt Schmoke wished to put his stamp on the BCPS in a fresh start.

After ushering in the retirement of Alice Pinderhughes, Schmoke played an active role in the national search to find a replacement. In summer 1988, he rejected his school board's initial majority choice and asked that Richard C. Hunter, an education professor at the University of North Carolina, be named as the new superintendent. Schmoke told board members that Hunter promised to build on the support of the civic and business communities cultivated by Pinderhughes. And Hunter told Schmoke that he strongly supported SBM. After considerable prodding by the mayor, the board reversed its initial choice to make way for Hunter.[14] Hunter was given a three-year contract, becoming the first outsider to lead the BCPS since Roland Patterson in the early 1970s. It did not take long, however, for Schmoke to acknowledge that Hunter's appointment was his first major mistake as mayor.

INTEREST GROUP POLITICS

With over 6,000 members, the vast majority of whom are African Americans who have worked together in the BCPS for decades, the BTU constitutes a significant proportion of Baltimore's black social capital. During the 1970s the union worked to improve the overall quality of public education, encouraged parents to work with students, and expanded teacher training. By the 1980s, however, the BTU had shifted its political engagement to traditional union issues: salary, fringe benefits, and working conditions.[15] According to a former member, the union's leadership became principally concerned with central collective-bargaining issues:

> When I joined BTU, I was very content with the organization. But once we began to do things that were more along the lines of union striking, picketing, and that type of thing, my philosophy of education didn't allow me to participate. So I was very glad that I was able to move on. I would like for

them to be spending their time concentrating on trying to encourage and help these parents work with these students and be more up on a professional level where you're training and helping our teachers and your principals and that type of thing.

In the early 1980s, when BUILD, the GBC, and other civic organizations launched the school reform movement, public school teachers remained on the periphery. By the mid-1980s, however, many civic organizations were advocating improvements in public education, an education mayor was determined to push school reform, and a new superintendent had been appointed. The teachers' union then became involved in reforming the BCPS.

The union began to look for ways to develop opportunities for their members to have a voice in educational policy making.[16] In November 1985 the BTU and PSASA became constituent members of BUILD. Irene Dandridge, an African American and BTU's president for over fifteen years, decided that joining the powerful coalition of black churches would raise BTU's presence in the fledgling reform movement. "We wanted to align ourselves with a group that had some power. It was that simple," she explained.[17]

Initially, the BTU thrust itself into the debate over SBM by opposing the plan recommended by the Pinderhughes task force, arguing that it gave too much authority to principals. It "was not true SBM. The task force's plan only allowed the principal and his top aides to decide what books and materials would be used," explained a BTU officer. Nevertheless, the BTU saw SBM as a way to gain more leverage in the distribution of scarce resources by shifting jobs and funds away from the central bureaucracy to the schools themselves. Dandridge believed SBM would "further teachers' collective interests."[18]

In early 1988, calling themselves the Coalition for School Reform, BUILD, the BTU, and PSASA launched a series of meetings to formulate a different SBM proposal. Led by Dandridge, Carol Reckling, and Arnett Brown, the coalition produced a plan to incorporate SBM in three schools: one high school, one middle school, and one elementary school.

Mayor Schmoke quickly endorsed what was essentially the teachers' union's SBM proposal, setting aside the plan developed and supported by the broad coalition brought together under the Pinderhughes task force. Schmoke's endorsement of the new SBM proposal clearly illustrated the political clout of BUILD and the school unions. "BUILD and BTU can turn out the vote," recalled an annoyed member of the Pinderhughes task force.[19]

NEW SUPERINTENDENT, NEW MAYOR

As the experience with the pilot school-based budgeting showed, an effective SBM plan required the support of the superintendent and other central office administrators. When Richard Hunter arrived in August 1988, he met with Irene Dandridge, Carol Reckling, and Arnett Brown. Initially, Hunter agreed to implement their plan but later learned that many community and civic leaders opposed it because they had been left out of the process. Hunter became concerned about the lack of community input for the proposal the coalition had put forth. When after nearly a year he had not yet decided which three schools would participate in the pilot SBM project, Dandridge accused him of dragging his feet, even though he supported it publicly.

In early 1989 Hunter rejected the coalition's SBM proposal in its entirety. Although deeply concerned, Mayor Schmoke was reluctant to overrule his hand-picked school chief. Still determined to have a voice in shaping the SBM plan, the BTU maneuvered around Hunter's opposition by institutionalizing the proposal into the union's 1989 collective bargaining agreement with the city government. In other school districts, Dade County, Florida, and Los Angeles, for example, SBM was achieved through the collective bargaining process as an agreement between the teachers' union and the school district.[20] Following these models, the BTU brought in a contract facilitator from the American Federation of Teachers (AFT) to assist in negotiations with the city.

During closed-door sessions with the mayor, union officials, and the school board, Hunter continued to reject the restructuring proposal.[21] Officially, the superintendent is not part of the collective bargaining process; however, the city charter requires the superintendent's approval before the city can accept a contract with the teachers' union. Hunter continued to oppose the coalition's proposal, arguing that it was a plan devised solely by the teachers' union.

Eventually, the contract negotiations ended in an agreement in which a joint committee of central office administrators, teachers, and representatives from BUILD would revise the coalition's SBM plan. And, as a result of Schmoke's and Hunter's insistence, the new plan involved more than the three schools proposed under the teachers' union plan. Hunter also demanded that the school board approve the final SBM plan. He hoped this move would allow more interest groups, especially parents, to have input into the process.

The joint committee eventually approved a new plan for twenty schools to pilot SBM. Each school would establish committees, "restructuring teams," composed of one PTA member, one union teacher, the principal, and one union paraprofessional (more members, up to twelve, could be added at the team's discretion). The restructuring team would decide such issues as budgeting, academic programs, and procurement. Meetings would be held monthly, during school hours. Unlike the school committees formed under similar plans in other cities, Baltimore's restructuring teams would not have power to hire or fire staff. A systemwide Committee to Support Restructuring, composed of representatives from the mayor's office, the BTU, PSASA, BUILD, the president of the school board, and the superintendent, would "oversee" school-based management and "decide on requests of additional schools to participate in the program."[22]

OPPOSITION FROM CIVIC GROUPS

When the school board held public hearings on the proposal in late summer and early fall 1990, many school activists opposed it. Officials of the GBC declared the plan too vague and timid, complaining that it lacked provisions authorizing those at the school site to terminate underperforming teachers and other staff. For many years, the GBC had criticized school officials for failing to hold teachers accountable and to terminate incompetent instructors. The coalition's proposal, business leaders maintained, did little to remedy this situation.

Activist parents and leaders of civic organizations protested that they had not been fully consulted about the proposal. Sarah Daignault of the League of Women Voters complained, "There is only limited parent involvement."[23] The Citizens Planning and Housing Association officially denounced the process. In an interview, a CPHA official explained that "the problem [we] have with it is that things were done behind closed doors. BTU, BUILD, school administrators, and city hall were involved. There was little input from parents and students." Chickie Grayson, CPHA's president, said she received complaints from other organizations that had tried unsuccessfully to obtain copies of the plan from the school system. When asked if parents and community groups should have been given a wider role, Superintendent Hunter stated that he and the board were bound by the newly approved union contract to work with administrators, teachers, and representatives from BUILD. Jo Ann Robinson, who had headed the Pinderhughes SBM task force, voiced great frustration: "We as parents find ourselves dealing with the same old problems that we very much resent having to face once again—lousy communication, a yawning gap between school system rhetoric about the importance of parent involvement and school system practices which provoke parent protest, and the token nature of the involvement opportunities which are presented to us."[24]

Robinson and other parents criticized the proposal for not creating parent and community boards, like those in the Chicago schools, giving unprecedented power to teachers and parents. Under the coalition's proposal, they argued, central office administrators maintained their strong role. According to the editors of the *Sun,* the plan "fail[ed] to allow individual schools to govern themselves."[25] Moreover, several opponents of the coalition's plan observed that the school-level restructuring teams were stacked mostly with teachers, making the program essentially the teachers' union's proposal.

In response to complaints that the larger community had not been involved in the plan's development, its proponents asserted that BUILD represented the community. To those who criticized the plan for not giving the restructuring teams the authority to fire underperforming teachers, Carol Reckling responded that plotting a moderate course would be more likely to win the support of school system administrators. The coalition decided against proposing changes "just for the dramatics," she added.[26] And to criticism that parents would not have a strong voice in school governance, Irene Dandridge told reporters that "educators still need to run schools, but the parents are going to be . . . invited into the educational process." Sheila Kolman, vice-president of PSASA, responded to critics that "restructuring is not a new way to make decisions or manage the schools. The principal is still ultimately responsible."[27]

As a way of quieting community opposition, Joseph Smith, school board president, told the BTU, BUILD, and PSASA to make changes in the proposal. First, Smith sought to diminish the BTU's influence in the operation of the schools by removing the requirement that all teachers on the restructuring teams be union members. Smith insisted that parents or community representatives constitute at least 40 percent of the membership of each team. Further, the school board also directed that the proposed central office committee designed to oversee SBM systemwide be made an advisory board. This move would alleviate some board members' fears about the panel becoming a potential rival, infringing on their authority in the educational policy-making process. The BTU, BUILD, and PSASA were forced to accept the school board's changes.

IMPLEMENTING SITE-BASED MANAGEMENT

As approved by the school board in October 1990, the SBM plan allowed twenty pilot schools to begin operating in September 1991. The 177 schools in the system were asked to submit applications. A school's principal and 90 percent of its faculty were required to agree in order to participate in the new program. After the application deadline, however, only twenty-seven (15 percent) of the schools had presented proposals. Ultimately, only fourteen applications were approved.

Tight deadlines and a climate of uncertainty contributed to the low level of participation. As Superintendent Hunter explained in an interview a few years later, "No one understood exactly what school-based management would mean as far as additional working hours, additional responsibilities, because the plan was so vague."[28] At Margaret Brent Elementary School, teachers voted against entering the pilot program because they believed it would be too demanding. "After we found out how much was involved, they decided against it," the school's principal observed. Ann Brooks, principal at Moravia Park Primary School, said her school's teachers liked the idea but decided against it. "They decided they would try some things on an informal basis. They wanted to study it a little further," she said.[29]

Supporters of SBM assumed that principals wanted more control over their school's facilities. But because they were not trained as facility managers, most principals preferred such functions to remain in the hands of the central administration. Thus, PSASA had put obstacles in the way of efforts to implement the pilot program. The head of the principals's union, for example, refused to use union funds to help train principals for the expanded duties expected of them under SBM. Training, PSASA officials asserted, was the responsibility of the school system.[30]

Top central office administrators displayed little enthusiasm for SBM. Although making public pronouncements in support of decentralization, Superintendent Hunter was reluctant to relinquish control to the principals, teachers, parents, and other school constituents. He was especially reticent when it came to increasing the participation of noneducators in school affairs.

Indeed, Hunter made a concerted effort to diminish the involvement of the GBC in SBM.[31] To avoid working with Jeff Valentine, Hunter selected Osborne Payne, an African-American owner of a chain of McDonald's restaurants, as the business community's representative on the systemwide Advisory Committee on Restructuring. As a newcomer to Baltimore, Hunter did not know Payne was an active member of GBC's Education Committee, worked closely with Jeff Valentine, and respected his position on school matters. Payne accepted Hunter's invitation to serve on the committee but asked Valentine to replace him. To Hunter's chagrin, Valentine then attended the meetings.

Further, the role of the advisory committee was not clearly defined. Was the committee to assess programs proposed by individual schools? Provide benchmarks for achievement? Reward and punish schools for reaching or not reaching these benchmarks? Jerry Baum, the committee chair, complained: "The Committee is there to support restructuring. What that exactly means has been a problem during deliberations."[32] In March 1991, after reviewing the applications and listening to presentations, the advisory committee's work came to a standstill.

The implementation of SBM reform highlights certain difficulties discussed by Jeffrey Pressman and Aaron Wildavsky.[33] The compromises incorporated into the final plan became more difficult to sustain as policy was turned to action. In particular, the concessions forced on the educators during the school board deliberations and public hearings weakened their sense of ownership of the entire proposal.

THE OUSTER OF SUPERINTENDENT HUNTER

As early as spring 1989, Mayor Schmoke became frustrated with the slow implementation of SBM, a central component of his plans to revitalize the city's schools. Near the end of his first term, he acknowledged that the governance of the schools had not changed. "The restructuring proposal we were going through was really not moving. The bureaucracy was finding a way to slow it down to choke it. It looked good on paper, but in fact the schools weren't operating any differently than they had before."[34] Schmoke also began to question whether his hand-picked superintendent could bring about the "renaissance in education" that candidate Schmoke had promised voters in 1987. The mayor began playing an active and aggressive role in the operation of the Education Department, raising questions about Hunter's leadership. The most publicized incident occurred in 1989 when Schmoke directed Hunter to reverse his decision rejecting a proposal to allow the

Barclay School (an inner-city public school) to adopt the curriculum of an elite private school (see chap. 6). The Barclay controversy was the first public disagreement between the two men.

Other well-publicized controversies occurred. In November 1989, when reports reached city hall that some schools lacked an adequate supply of textbooks, Mayor Schmoke visited a warehouse (with news cameras and reporters following) where he found stacks of books. In December Schmoke summoned Hunter to city hall to complain about the lack of cultural field trips for school children. Later, complaints focused on safety in the schools; Schmoke berated the superintendent for lack of concern when a reporter walked into five high schools unchallenged for a television report on school security. Schmoke's next move was to become more directly involved in school operations. After several principals complained that Hunter refused to meet with them, Schmoke held what one observer described as "an extraordinary" series of meetings with the principals to encourage them to consult directly with city hall on educational matters. Further, after Hunter presented the 1990 school budget to the school board, Schmoke publicly vowed that his own staff would "carefully review" the proposal to ascertain whether it reflected his belief that programs and ideas emanate from the schools, not from central administration.[35]

Schmoke's sudden crusade for schools and the strife between him and Hunter became the talk of North Avenue, left many teachers and principals scratching their heads, raised the eyebrows of many state officials (especially those who controlled the state's purse strings), and made headlines in the local newspapers. The controversy became the leading story on the evening news. Corporate leaders, school activists, central office administrators, teachers' union officials, and principals openly questioned Hunter's capacity to lead the school district effectively. The editors of the *Sun* declared Hunter's appointment "Schmoke's worst grade."[36] It was only a matter of time before some educational stakeholders quietly encouraged the mayor to ask the school board to fire Hunter before his contract expired in July 1991.

Other observers were more sympathetic toward the beleaguered superintendent. George N. Buntin, president of Baltimore's NAACP, sent a letter to city hall urging the mayor to keep Hunter, in the interest of African-American unity. Buntin argued that three years were not long enough to show improvement in a large and deeply troubled school system.[37] Another African-American leader, a member of the Maryland legislature, contended that Schmoke "undermined the superintendent by his actions." The legislator also questioned Schmoke's motives:

When Hunter was here, Hunter was *his* choice. He overruled the board and selected Hunter because Hunter was a professor in North Carolina. He fits the mayor's image of a very cool, intellectual person. But when he wasn't working out, the mayor proceeded to embarrass him publicly on several occasions. He just undermined his credibility. I assumed the mayor was doing that for his political benefit because if he wanted to get rid of him, all he needed to do is tell the people who appointed him that this man is not working out and this is why, and ask him to leave. Plus, he had a contract that was going to expire that just wouldn't have to be renewed.

A group of prominent black ministers also stood behind Hunter. Privately, they told Schmoke they did not like the idea of the city's black mayor publicly berating a fellow black leader. And Schmoke faced pressure from other prominent black leaders who complained that the "white establishment" was out to get Hunter.[38]

The school board was split on whether to force Hunter to resign. Some board members believed that he needed more time to learn the system and to have an impact on student achievement. Hunter, for his part, made it clear he would not depart easily and that he intended to serve out his contract. As an education reporter perceptively observed, "The affair grew into a hotly contested behind-the-scenes debate in which some groups lobbied heartily for the superintendent and others worked as intensely against him."[39]

In April 1990 Schmoke temporarily cooled the growing tensions between Hunter's supporters and critics who were pushing for his immediate exit. Mindful of the potential racial division the controversy could create, Schmoke wanted to avoid the extreme polarization and protracted legal struggle that had arisen when the school system's first African-American superintendent, Roland N. Patterson, had been dismissed nearly fifteen years earlier. Such an explosion would surely stain Schmoke's tenure and potentially threaten his reelection.

Employing what Peter Bachrach and Morton Baratz would have described as a classic "nondecision," Schmoke asked the school board to hire as deputy superintendent Edward Andrews, a popular former Montgomery County superintendent and an education professor at the University of Maryland.[40] Andrews would run the day-to-day operation of the school system. Schmoke hoped he would appeal to educational stakeholders in a way that Hunter had not. The school board agreed, and Hunter was told he could remain as superintendent. By hiring Andrews, Schmoke was able to avoid, for the time being, a decision on whether to let Hunter go. "I hope we can avoid in the future the mayor publicly debating with the superintendent, but when I see problems I won't be shy about raising them with him," Schmoke announced.[41]

Despite the strategic moves, criticism of Hunter continued from school personnel, civic leaders, and school activists. Editors of the *Sun* called the decision to keep Hunter "a bad and timid compromise from a mayor who elevated education to his No. 1 priority during the election campaign and then overrode the school board to hire Dr. Hunter."[42] Schmoke's own leadership was called into question: he appeared indecisive.

With Hunter's three-year contract due to expire in summer 1991 and a reelection campaign looming, a decision concerning his fate was imminent. In December, citing Hunter's lukewarm support of SBM, Schmoke asked the school board not to renew the superintendent's contract. In a candid and unusually forceful statement, the mayor said he doubted Hunter's ability to run the schools:

> I urged him several times to build the school system from the bottom up, not from the top down. . . . I asked Dr. Hunter to meet with the principals individually. He has not done that. I asked for a vocational education action plan. I didn't get one. The members of the school board had to push for it. That shouldn't be their role. The board should set broad policy. . . . I believe in school-based management. I am profoundly skeptical of Dr. Hunter's commitment to that direction. Even today he will say he agrees with school-based management, but I look at his actions.[43]

A few days after Schmoke's announcement, the school board voted unanimously to replace Richard Hunter after his contract expired.

RACIAL POLITICS AND THE SEARCH FOR A NEW SUPERINTENDENT

As an outsider with no ties or political connections in the city, Hunter was isolated from its power centers. Although he came to Baltimore with a national reputation as an expert in urban school administration, he had difficulty maneuvering the treacherous political waters of the Baltimore school system. General agreement therefore arose that a replacement superintendent should have some ties with the region or some familiarity with the city's politics, or both. The other important qualification was a strong commitment to restructure the school system through SBM.

Despite his frustrating experience with Hunter, Mayor Schmoke showed no sign of backing away from the school issue. Determined to find someone to help him lead the reform effort, Schmoke privately lobbied Deputy Superintendent Edward Andrews to take over as new superintendent. Andrews, however, politely turned down the mayor's overtures.

Although many observers applauded Andrews's performance with the BCPS, he admitted that being deputy superintendent was much more difficult than his experience as an associate superintendent in Montgomery County.[44] The daily commute from the Washington suburbs to Baltimore was taking a personal toll on him and his family life. Moreover, as a knowledgeable observer of state educational politics, Andrews also was keenly aware of the racial dynamics in the BCPS. For nearly two decades it had had a succession of African-American superintendents. The appointment of a white superintendent (even by a school board appointed by an African-American mayor) would be viewed by black leaders as a major political setback. For a white educator, like Andrews, from a wealthy, suburban school district to lead the BCPS was politically untenable. He concluded that his appointment as superintendent would heighten racial tensions and create controversy.

Schmoke was not the only Baltimore leader hoping to convince Andrews to stay on as superintendent. Several prominent corporate executives affiliated with the GBC were impressed with his effort to hold principals more accountable for their school's performance. As deputy superintendent Andrews forced nearly a dozen principals to resign, retire, or accept reassignment.[45] Business leaders also tried to persuade him to take the top job. To address his concern about the daily commute to Baltimore, they offered to pay the monthly mortgage for a fully furnished condominium overlooking the Inner Harbor development. Andrews declined.

Undeterred, Mayor Schmoke and GBC leaders continued their behind-the-scenes effort to find a permanent replacement for Hunter. They turned to David Hornbeck, former Maryland state school superintendent (who later became superintendent of Philadelphia schools). But Hornbeck's candidacy created problems. According to one close observer, some school board members were concerned about his insistence on implementing a detailed reform plan that included a clean sweep of top administrators. Further, Hornbeck's appointment would also break the BCPS tradition of being led by a black superintendent. Schmoke appeared willing to change this, despite warnings. "Schmoke, in the midst of a tough re-election campaign, was advised by a group of [black] ministers that the next superintendent had to be black."[46]

WALTER AMPREY: AN OUTSIDER AND AN INSIDER

Meanwhile, the school board conducted the official search, with plans to have a new superintendent in time for the 1991 school year. By April the board produced a list of five finalists, which reflected the members' and the mayor's interest in finding a candidate with ties to the Baltimore region. It included two white superintendents from out of state—Leonard Britton, former head of Los Angeles schools, and Alfred Tutela, former superintendent of Cleveland schools. The other three candidates had close ties to the Baltimore region: Jerome Clark, a Prince George's County associate superintendent; Lillian Gonzalez, an assistant superintendent in the District of Columbia schools; and Walter G. Amprey, a Baltimore County associate superintendent asked personally by Mayor Schmoke to become an active candidate. In July the school board appointed Walter Amprey; he took over the BCPS in August 1991.[47]

A native Baltimorean, Amprey was a graduate of the city's schools and worked in the BCPS as a teacher and a principal. He moved to the neighboring Baltimore County system in 1973 and became a well-regarded associate superintendent. During his years there, Amprey maintained contact with school administrators, teachers, and black leaders in Baltimore City. "It was a mark of his continuing connection with the city, where he has friendships and professional and fraternal associations, that his name was mentioned to Mayor Schmoke. Those connections could give him a foundation on which to build if he becomes superintendent— a factor that is important to the mayor and school board." In a sense, Amprey arrived in his new job already an insider. As he explained, "It helps to know Baltimoreans. It just does. I'm a Baltimore kid. I know the players and the players know me and the players that don't know me know about me, because I've been here all my life."[48]

As an experienced and sophisticated observer of Baltimore politics, Amprey understood the relationship between North Avenue and city hall. He seemed quite comfortable with Mayor Schmoke's leadership in school affairs. The issue for educational stakeholders was whether Amprey and the central administration could effectively implement a strong SBM plan. The political pressure to do so was mounting, not only from city officials but also from the state capital.

ENTERPRISE SCHOOLS

During the 1991–1992 school year, just as Amprey was settling into his new job, the pressure to implement SBM escalated with the release of a management study of the BCPS. In early 1991 Baltimore delegate Howard "Pete" Rawlings, then the cochair of the Maryland House of Delegate's Appropriations Committee, asked Associated Black Charities' (ABC) president Donna Stanley if her organization would lead an effort to study the management of the BCPS (see chap. 9). ABC hired an international consulting firm, Towers/Perrin/Cresap, to conduct the study. Although ABC's priorities focused on economic and community development in the black community, the organization had never been involved in the school system. "We were concerned about education," says an ABC officer; "we just had not been involved in the administrative issues before."

Released in June 1992, the Cresap Study's major recommendation was the establishment of SBM, or what it called "enterprise schools":

> Under this concept each school should be granted the authority and autonomy to mobilize resources and develop instructional strategies to improve student achievement. . . . Principals of enterprise schools should be given the authority and autonomy to manage all of their school's resources; to make key decisions about selecting, evaluating, training and terminating staff assigned to their school; to determine what support services are needed; and to design and implement an effective instructional program. In exchange for this authority and autonomy, principals should be held accountable for their school's performance.[49]

Enterprise schools would be given wide latitude to control their own budgets and to buy some services from vendors other than the central administration. The central office would increase or shrink, based on whether it could offer services to schools of a quality and price that schools, in a free market, would choose to buy.

The Cresap Study, as it became known, also recommended the establishment of a task force to develop and implement the enterprise schools concept. And it recommended that school officials phase in SBM, starting with twenty to twenty-five schools and adding twenty to twenty-five more each school year until the city's 177 schools all became enterprise schools. The study urged BCPS officials to conduct detailed assessments and evaluations during each phase of the implementation.

Many of the city's key educational stakeholders, including Mayor Schmoke, enthusiastically endorsed the Cresap Study. Superintendent Amprey wholeheartedly supported all but six of the 101 recommendations and quickly appointed a twenty-one-member "enterprise schools task force" to formulate and implement a site-based management plan for the BCPS. Completed in May 1993, the final report of the task force recommended that the BCPS identify twenty schools to be given the authority to function as enterprise schools during the 1993–1994 school year.[50] Principals interested in SBM would be invited, on a voluntary basis, to submit school plans. The task force would evaluate the plans and then make recommendations.

In keeping with the recommendations of the Cresap study, the task force agreed to encourage twenty-five additional schools annually to become enterprise schools until all schools were operating under SBM.[51] The initial twenty-four enterprise schools included the fourteen pilot schools that were just beginning to operate under the SBM proposal adopted by the school board during Hunter's tenure. Ten additional schools were identified and selected by the task force.

THE FAILURE OF SCHOOL-BASED MANAGEMENT

In spring 1994 Superintendent Amprey made an unexpected announcement. He declared that beginning in the 1994–1995 school year, all of the system's schools would become enterprise schools. The bureaucracy at school headquarters had become "a virtual gridlock of policies and procedures," Amprey asserted. "We're blowing the system wide open so the order of the day will be that [principals] will have creativity and autonomy."[52] According to Amprey, with the new approach, all BCPS principals would have more independence to decide how to spend money for libraries, janitorial services, teacher training, gifted and talented programs, and other school functions. Principals, working with teams of teachers and parents, would have more autonomy to tailor education funds according to each school's needs.

Despite Amprey's announcements, however, little changed in the schools. An external evaluation (mandated by the Maryland legislature) completed in January 1995 found that principals had no more authority than they had had previously. "Too much control of funding remains in the central office," the report found.[53] Principals reported that they had little control over school personnel, a major tenet of SBM. On the other hand, some parents maintained that decision making was dominated by the principal. An officer in the Baltimore City-Wide

PTA maintained that parents were not invited to attend meetings of the school councils:

> I don't attend the meetings because I don't agree or feel like going along with everything the principal wants. She comes to present the program as: "This is what I want to do." She has all these teachers around and none of them say no because they know if they say no, they're out of a job. Whatever she wants, this is how we're going to run it. Well, that's not what we were told that site-based management would be. I continually complained about it and I even laughed [about it]. For two years my name appeared in the hallway as a member of the [school improvement] team and I was never called to a meeting.

Many of the problems associated with the enterprise school program could be attributed to the poorly planned and fragmented way in which it was implemented. Amprey, for example, did not follow the Cresap Study's recommendation that the concept be phased in—adding a number of schools each year. Evaluators also chastised school officials for moving toward full implementation of the program without an assessment of the twenty-four pilot schools: "BCPS chose to implement the concept in all schools . . . without an adequate support system or an assessment of the pilot phase."[54] Further, teachers and principals lacked sufficient training in SBM.[55] "There is just confusion in all areas . . . as to how to move from a traditional school system to an enterprise school system," commented a member of the evaluation team.[56]

It is not clear why Amprey moved so abruptly. Some observers speculated that he felt pressured by the increased oversight of state officials. Others believed he had become frustrated with his own inability to get the huge bureaucracy under him to relinquish authority to principals, teachers, parents, and school communities. What is clear is that nearly fifteen years after former superintendent Alice Pinderhughes sought to experiment with SBM, the school system had changed very little.

SUMMARY

An examination of Baltimore's efforts to institute SBM throughout the BCPS sheds light on the possibilities and limitations of social capital. As in several other urban school districts, SBM became the method preferred by the city's mayor, school activists, parents, and business leaders to achieve school reform. Although cleavages existed within the African-American community, there was a consensus about the need for better schools. No one was opposed to improved education. Despite the vast reservoir of black social capital, the school leadership was unable to reform the school system.

Countervailing forces offset the consensus for systemwide SBM: entrenched political interest groups. Their blatant espousal of partial interests came at the expense of broader community interests. In this instance, a coalition of professional school administrators and union leaders, what Wilbur Rich called the public school cartel, prevented SBM from being fully implemented.[57]

The Baltimore case illustrates that race and racial tensions are powerful forces that can hamper the development of intergroup social capital, circumstances revealed most clearly during Superintendent Richard C. Hunter's tumultuous tenure. Hunter was less than enthusiastic about SBM. To paraphrase Mayor Schmoke, Hunter said he supported SBM, but his actions suggested otherwise. Nevertheless, when Schmoke sought to remove Hunter, the city's civic leadership divided. African-American ministers and leaders of the NAACP rallied behind Hunter, arguing that white civic and business elites were "out to get" him. They also chastised Schmoke for jeopardizing racial unity by publicly criticizing the city's highest-ranking black school official. Given this racial backdrop, Schmoke was forced to keep Hunter, perhaps longer than he should have. Racial politics also constrained the search for qualified candidates to replace Hunter.

Mayoral leadership is an important component in the formation of intergroup social capital at the local level. Mayor Schmoke played a key role in mobilizing a broad range of local actors to restructure the school system. The number of groups and organizations—the GBC, CPHA, BUILD, League of Women Voters, ABC, PTAs—participating in efforts to develop SBM were partly the result of Schmoke's leadership and the visibility he gave to school issues. Without his consistent prodding and persistence, school officials would not have made an effort to change.

Schmoke's leadership was simultaneously shaped and constrained by the scope and nature of black social capital in Baltimore. Politically, Schmoke had to be attuned to the concerns of black educators and their allies in the church community, even when their stance seemed at variance with generally accepted notions of good school policies. Nevertheless, neighborhood activists interested in reforming their schools turned to Mayor Schmoke to push administrators to act in the communities' interest.

6
Neighborhood Mobilization:
The Barclay and Stadium School
Movements

It has to be grassroots. I figured it has to be. What happens is if it starts where I advocate it, then that's mine to sell. But if the people at the grassroots buy it, and they want it . . . they wouldn't give up. And a lot of teachers did the fighting. And so, it has to be a grassroots effort, not only the administrator, but the parents, and the students, and the staff, and everyone, and even the community leaders.
– Gertrude Williams

Formal authority, leadership by a mayor or others in positions of official power, can ratchet up preexisting levels of social capital and facilitate cooperation, especially when schools are involved. The political environment created by Mayor Kurt Schmoke's leadership, and his emphasis on school reform, did exactly that by encouraging parents, teachers, and community leaders to improve local schools in innovative ways. The analysis of efforts to apply social capital toward school reform therefore shifts to the individual school site, first, the Barclay School area and second, the Stadium School.

THE BARCLAY-CALVERT COLLABORATION

Barclay is a kindergarten-through-eighth grade public school. A neighborhood school, it is located in the center of the Charles Village, Greenmount, Remington, and Abell neighborhoods, not far from the campus of Johns Hopkins University (see Fig. 6.1). The area is one of closed factories and old row houses built in the 1940s. One of Baltimore's many open-air drug markets thrives less than four blocks away, with dealers just as likely to sell drugs at noon as they are at midnight. Although other neighborhoods contend with an even greater

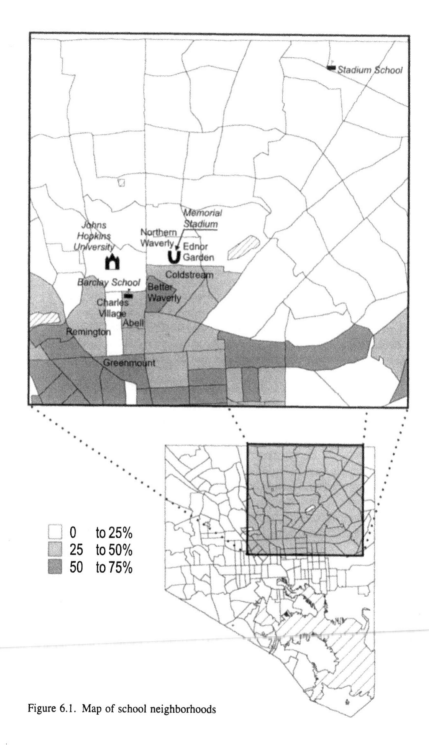

Stadium School

Memorial
Stadium

Johns
Hopkins
University

Northern
Waverly

Ednor
Garden

Coldstream

Barclay School

Better
Waverly

Charles
Village

Abell

Remington

Greenmount

0   to 25%
25   to 50%
50   to 75%

Figure 6.1. Map of school neighborhoods

array of problems, the Barclay location is not considered the most desirable in the city.

The great majority of Barclay's students are children of working class or unemployed African-American, often female-headed, single-parent families. The student population is 94 percent black, and a large number (82 percent) receive free or reduced-price lunch, a larger percentage than the citywide average of 67 percent (see Table 6.1). Barclay also serves small numbers of students from the Charles Village community, whose parents are graduate students at Johns Hopkins University.

An active group of parents of current and former students constitutes the Barclay School community. They are proactive. As a Barclay administrator explained, "Even the children who don't have much economically come from homes where the parents pushed. . . . They're pro-education and have been for years." In the late 1970s, parents honed their bureaucracy-fighting skills during a successful ten-year battle to expand from an elementary to a combined elementary–middle school.

Recognizing the Problem

During the mid-to-late 1980s, Barclay's principal and parents had grown concerned because the students were not achieving at the city or national averages on a variety of measures. "Achievement test scores and attendance rates had fallen to disconcertingly low levels, and student discipline in the classrooms and halls was no longer at a level deemed satisfactory by faculty or administration. In short, by the mid-1980s Barclay was having the typical problems of an inner-city American school."[1] Its steering committee of parents, community leaders, faculty, and staff, who usually met monthly to discuss school matters, took an unusual position about why their children were not performing. The problem was not the students, they concluded: it was the curriculum adopted by the BCPS. It did not challenge students' young minds. The "watered-down" public school curriculum,

Table 6.1. Basic Population Characteristics of Barclay Neighborhoods

	Remington	Abell	Greenmount	Charles Village	Baltimore City
White	81%	29%	6.5%	59%	39%
Black	13	29	90	35	59
Median income	$22,981	$21,330	$11,439	$12,292	$24,045
Families below poverty	30.2%	33.6%	50.4%	28.9%	17.8%
Children under 18 in poverty	34.6	44.3	71.9	13.3	32.5
College degree or more	12.7	25.2	6.3	31.5	17.8

Source: Baltimore City Department of Planning, *1990 Census Data by Neighborhoods* (April 1993); Baltimore City Department of Planning, *1990 Census Data by Census Tracts* (April 1993).

they contended, prevented students from achieving their best. According to a Barclay staff member, it demanded little and expected even less from students, and the students obliged. "There's a tendency in public schools to think that because of a child's economic background that economics has something to do with brain power. And that because a child is extremely poor or comes from a certain community that they should need to lower expectations. We were concerned because we know the quality of children that usually come into this school."

Gertrude Williams, the African-American principal at Barclay, was especially concerned about her students' academic performance. As principal there for over two decades, she reached out to parents and citizens in the Greenmount, Charles Village, Remington, and Abell communities. She cultivated a strong rapport with churches, small businesses, and community leaders. College students from nearby Johns Hopkins tutored and read to Barclay students as a result of Williams's effort to involve the university. She attended community meetings and was active in involving parents. "Some of these parents know," Williams has declared, "that if they don't come to parent meetings, I'll be at their door the next morning."[2] As an astute observer of Baltimore politics and school affairs, she also encouraged the young parents of her students to register and vote. "Only when you are a voting citizen can you have a voice in your city government," she said. Gertrude Williams's leadership is an important component of the social capital that permeates the Barclay School community.

The Calvert Way

With the support of Barclay's parents and faculty, Williams began to search for what she considered a more challenging curriculum. Determined, as she put it, not "to reinvent the wheel," she mentioned her search to a fellow member of the Fund for Educational Excellence's governing board, who directed her to the Calvert School.

Founded in 1897, the Calvert School is exclusive and private (prekindergarten through sixth grade) and has an overwhelmingly upper-middle-class student body and an outstanding academic reputation. Located about a mile across town on the other side of Johns Hopkins, Calvert seems a world away from Barclay. It serves Baltimore's most highly affluent residents. Tuition starts at $5,300 per student annually for half-day prekindergarten and rises to $10,500. Beginning with kindergarten, the annual tuition rises from just over $7,000 to $8,500.[3] Many of Calvert's students go on to attend some of the region's most exclusive private prep schools, such as Gilman and Roland Park Country School.

Gertrude Williams found Calvert's curriculum attractive. Far from revolutionary, it relies on basic academic principles. The reading program is a combination of children's classics and phonics, and many of the books have not changed in a half century. The school's history curriculum is based on a children's history text published during the first half of this century, and much of the content has not changed. Calvert students are taught geography and history every year, beginning in the second grade. The required quantity of class work and homework, however, surpasses standard American norms, as students spend an average of three or more hours on work at home.[4]

The Calvert School offers its highly structured, certified curriculum for kindergarten through eighth grade for home study.[5] It is designed so that it can be taught by parents around the world. Historically, the majority of parents paying for the home study have been members of the U.S. foreign service or military who are often stationed in areas that do not offer English language schools. Perhaps because the curriculum is monitored from a distance, the entire program places an unusually high emphasis on student-generated products. Both in the home-study program and at the day school, students create folders of work that are regularly reviewed by teachers, parents, and school administrators.

The most unique features of the Calvert curriculum are the intensive writing program (students write every day on a variety of topics and are taught how to write in cursive in the first grade) and the requirement that all work be revised until the student's product contain no errors. As early as the second grade Calvert's students are able to write coherent compositions or essays in elegant penmanship and without spelling or grammatical errors.

The Abell Foundation and the Barclay-Calvert Program

"I was really excited to have the structure and the high expectations" that the Calvert curriculum offered, explained Williams. "And I knew the background. A lot of prominent people have come through there," she added. "We sought a curriculum that would work, that would enable our children to go anywhere and be knowledgeable, to speak intelligently, and to read, write, and compute."[6] Williams alerted Barclay's teachers and steering committee and invited them to visit the Calvert School; most came away delighted. With their support, Williams began the process of replacing the BCPS' curriculum with Calvert's. As she recalled years later, "We thought, wow! It's going to go right through the [school] board." In retrospect, Williams underestimated the challenges.

One of the first challenges was financing the collaboration. Implementing the Calvert curriculum required additional resources. Barclay would have to purchase Calvert's home-study course materials at a cost of approximately $670 per student, pay for staff development, upgrade its computer laboratory, and hire a teacher with experience at the Calvert School to help coordinate implementation and to lead Barclay's faculty through Calvert's philosophy, curriculum, and instructional materials. The idea was to begin implementing the Calvert curriculum with kindergarten and first grade and then expand it to second, third, and fourth graders each year over a four-year period.

To fund the collaboration, Barclay's supporters turned to the Abell Foundation, one of the most active in Baltimore. The legacy of the A. S. Abell Company, which for 150 years owned the *Baltimore Sun* and *Evening Sun,* the foundation makes grants in education, health and human services, arts and culture, conservation, and economic development. Abell is also one of Maryland's largest foundations. One recent study showed that in 1992, it had assets of $153.4 million.[7] It is one of the few foundations that has delved into the venture-capital arena. "No other organization," writes one local observer, "has nearly the same impact or influence as the Abell Foundation."[8]

Abell distributes the bulk of its vast resources in Baltimore and has become an enormous force in the city, particularly in education reform. Between 1989 and 1993, over 40 percent of Abell grant dollars went to education-related projects, with 80 percent of that going to education programs and projects in Baltimore.[9] In such a cash-strapped city, the Abell Foundation has enormous influence in school affairs. Among these programs is the Center for Educating African-American Males at Morgan State University, supported by nearly $500,000. Foundation officials also played an influential role in jump-starting the process that eventually led the city to contract out the operation of nine of its public schools to a private firm (see chap. 8). As a business leader explained, the "Abell Foundation sees itself as a change agent and a catalyst. It's essentially rolling out ideas, and whatever sticks they will go with and what doesn't they'll pass on and come up with a couple of new ones."

Abell's involvement in education and Baltimore school issues reflects the preoccupation of its president, Robert C. Embry Jr. Embry is a Baltimore native and a graduate of Harvard Law School. He also has children who attend BCPS schools. He served a brief stint on the city council in the 1950s, was the city's first housing commissioner, and worked at HUD during the Carter administration. Embry was also one of the chief architects of the city's downtown redevelopment strategy.

A trusted and close aide to Mayor William Donald Schaefer, Embry was appointed president of the Baltimore School Board in 1985 but resigned a year later to explore the possibility of running for mayor after Schaefer became governor. Initially, local observers speculated that with two African-American candidates in the Democratic primary, Embry, who is white, could win the party's nomination by capturing the white vote while the other two candidates split the majority black vote. Early polls, however, showed Embry behind both candidates, even among white voters. Ultimately, he decided not to enter the mayoral campaign, believing that his entrance would heighten racial polarization. "I felt it was not healthy for the city and not likely that I could win," he said.[10]

Governor Schaefer later named Embry to the Maryland State Board of Education, and he served as its president from 1990 to 1994. Embry's political connections and his position as president of Abell make him especially influential in Baltimore's school affairs. A Johns Hopkins researcher, who has worked closely with the school system, explained Embry's role in school affairs:

Because the president of the Abell Foundation, Bob Embry, is also the president of the state [school] board and one of the presidents of the Baltimore

City School Board in the past, a good friend of the governor, a lot of things that happened in the city ultimately you can track back to his involvement. He had the money and really total control over the biggest foundation in the city. So he can back up his interest with serious money as well as a lot of sources of power and influence. . . . When he says something, people listen. I'm sure that there are many people who resent his involvement, but they would not deny that he's influential.

Indeed, a number of black school administrators and community leaders complained that Embry was determined to run the schools from his position as president of Abell. Alice Pinderhughes, who served as superintendent during Embry's brief stint as school board president, "was often forced to take a back seat to Embry, who envisioned grand and controversial plans to combat the schools' problems."[11] Pinderhughes commented, "Embry would have loved to be superintendent or mayor of Baltimore. Now he realizes that neither are possible, he is trying to do what he can."[12] A veteran BCPS administrator, fearful of Embry's influence in school affairs, derisively described him as "would-be mayor, would-be governor, the director of the school district and all of that. He's a powerful voice here." Another central office administrator explained that Embry's "tentacles run through this entire [school] system." He continued: "Bob Embry is on the phone an average of once a week either to tell me something I'm supposed to do, or to offer me money to put in one of his favorite entities. . . . He has money and he uses it. He uses the influence of the Abell Foundation to bring about whatever he wants. The worse thing you do is say no to Bob Embry. You only say no once and you'll be gone."

Despite the criticism of Embry's role, many Abell-supported reforms have been successful. Foundations can provide important start-up funds, encourage innovation, and generate analyses and reports on schools. Peter Marris and Martin Rein's observation about the Ford Foundation can be applied to the Abell Foundation: its vocation is reform.[13]

In spring 1988 Williams and Jo Ann Robinson, head of Barclay's steering committee and former chair of Alice Pinderhughes's task force on school-based decision making, wrote a grant proposal requesting $500,000 over four years and presented it to Embry. A few months later Abell's board approved the proposal. Williams then submitted the proposal to Superintendent Alice Pinderhughes, who never acted on it and retired a few months later. Williams and the Barclay parents had to wait for Baltimore's new superintendent, Richard Hunter, to approve the collaboration.

BTU Opposes Barclay-Calvert

The Baltimore Teachers Union officially opposed the adoption of the Calvert curriculum. Irene Dandridge, its president, thought that the rigorous curriculum and the requirement that students rewrite essays until they were error-free would increase teachers' workload. According to one observer, the BTU opposed "the move to the new curriculum because it would increase their management responsibilities at the schools." Although some teachers (many of whom were later allowed to transfer to other schools) objected to the collaboration, the majority of Barclay's teachers (who were BTU members) endorsed the program.[14]

The battle to incorporate the Calvert curriculum into Barclay's took on racial overtones when Jo Ann Robinson assumed the role of chief spokesperson for the project so that Barclay's principal would not have to defy her supervisors at North Avenue. Robinson's daughter had been a Barclay student but had since moved on to high school. Although Robinson, who is white, had no children enrolled at Barclay, she continued to volunteer at and support the school. Some members of the black community "grew suspicious" of her, however, believing that she was pushing the proposal in order to provide an elite school for white students. Dandridge publicly questioned her motives: "Mrs. Robinson has one vision of the Baltimore City Public Schools, [and] I think her vision and my vision are totally different. My vision includes the worst child in the school system."[15] Eventually, Robinson turned the role of spokesperson over to other Barclay parents but continued working beyond the media spotlight.

A "Rich Man's" Curriculum?

In August 1988 Superintendent Richard Hunter arrived in Baltimore, promising to support site-based management and community involvement in school affairs. The Barclay-Calvert proposal was marking time in the school system's bureaucracy just as Hunter was settling into his new job. One of the first decisions facing him was whether to allow the Barclay School to adopt the Calvert curriculum.

Hunter was unenthusiastic about the collaboration, describing the Calvert curriculum as outdated and arguing that it did not incorporate enough multicultural material. He noted that the history curriculum lacked an adequate treatment of minorities and women, which he thought was especially critical for Barclay's largely African-American student population. Hunter reportedly told backers of the proposal that Calvert's program was inappropriate for Baltimore public school children, that it was "a rich man's" curriculum designed for "high-achieving students."[16]

Like most new superintendents, Hunter had his own ideas about school curriculum and reform. Though expressing support for site-based management, Hunter firmly believed that the central administration should maintain authority over the district's curriculum. Approving the Barclay-Calvert proposal, he surmised, would lead to a hodgepodge of different curricula. Hunter argued that the collaboration ran counter to his aim of establishing a "single agenda" for the school system.[17]

One school observer believed that Hunter not only rejected the proposal but also seemed to be "going out of his way to do so in a manner that would demonstrate his unwillingness to relinquish any control over the schools."[18] Hunter advocated altering the practice, for example, that allowed individual schools to seek and obtain grants without going through central administration. This approach, Hunter asserted, undermined his authority. A central clearing process, he argued, would ensure that all externally proposed projects satisfy the school system's priorities and overall needs.

Many observers perceived Hunter's opposition to the Barclay-Calvert collaboration as his way of making a point about outsider influence in school affairs. A Johns Hopkins education researcher, who had worked closely with the school system since the early years of Superintendent Alice Pinderhughes's tenure, complained that Hunter resisted outside involvement in school affairs. "During Hunter's time, this was an extremely centralized district in which dictates from North Avenue told everybody what they had to do to the very fine detail. Hunter was also very resistant to innovation, to outside involvement in the schools, and I think very paranoid in a lot of ways about people fiddling with his schools."

Hunter was especially suspicious of the involvement of Robert Embry. During his brief tenure as school board president, Embry had earned a reputation for contesting the leadership of Alice Pinderhughes. When Hunter arrived in Baltimore, many of the central office administrators informed him of Embry's continued influence as president of the city's largest foundation. As one central office administrator put it, "[Embry] is a very powerful man. . . . The Abell Foundation has millions of dollars and money talks. When you have a financially strapped school district and you put money some place then that money is power in terms of influencing the process of education." As the new superintendent, Hunter reportedly wanted to make it clear "that he would not take orders from Embry."[19] In March 1989, after the proposal had lingered in the school bureaucracy for nearly a year, Hunter officially rejected it.

Mayor Schmoke Steps In

The superintendent's rejection of the collaboration triggered a response from Barclay parents and supporters. The level of social capital among the parents facilitated collective action, helping shape the response. Parents from the Greenmount, Remington, Abell, and Charles Village communities mobilized to reverse Hunter's decision and joined with the staff publicly to challenge his assertion that Calvert's philosophy was based on a "rich man's" curriculum. "We don't want a poor man's curriculum at our school," Williams retorted.[20] The parents held press conferences, marched on school headquarters, and jammed school board meetings. As a Barclay administrator described it, "The parents said 'no, we will have this program. This is what we want for our children.' We would take up a whole side of a [school] board meeting and we would wear these yellow and blue shirts. . . . We didn't have to talk [at the meetings], you just appeared."

Hunter infuriated not only Barclay's staff and parents but also raised concerns among school activists and many educational stakeholders. The denial of the Barclay program troubled them and sparked doubts about his receptiveness to new ideas. Hunter did not appear committed to giving more power over curriculum and finances to teachers, principals, and parents. About this time, the *Sun* began aggressively reporting on the Barclay story, devoting a number of lead editorials to the issue. Editors even went so far as to call Hunter "Dr. No" and "Hunter in Wonderland."[21] According to the *Sun,* "Dr. Hunter's game in the Barclay matter is not education but his belief in centralized administration, centralized initiative and centralized power. That bodes ill for everyone in the city's education system from pupils and parents to teachers." Barclay parents also won the support of many elected city officials. Carl Stokes, whose city council district included the Barclay School, and city council president Mary Pat Clarke, a resident of the Charles Village community, lobbied the school board and later Mayor Schmoke to reverse Hunter's decision.

In June 1989 an annual public forum was held in the Wyman Park Community Center. Usually only a handful of residents showed up, but this day, knowing that Mayor Schmoke regularly attended these forums, a restless crowd of about 300 Barclay parents and supporters filled the rows of folding chairs. When it was her time to speak to the audience, Gertrude Williams explained how the Calvert program could benefit Barclay. When she finished, the crowd erupted in cheers. After the forum, Schmoke invited Williams to city hall for a private meeting.[22] At first, Mayor Schmoke deferred to Hunter on the Barclay proposal, believing Hunter had made "a professional judgment" and that as mayor he was "not about to second-guess the superintendent."[23] However, a number of factors converged, leading Schmoke to intervene and to overrule his new, hand-picked superintendent.

First, the Barclay parents had gained the notice of local journalists. The news coverage of angry parents picketing city hall and North Avenue stirred the sympathies of many people who were fed up with the decline of the BCPS. The school that refused to bow to the powerful superintendent began to grab media attention. "Barclay School Affair Tests Hunter's Leadership," one newspaper headline read.

Second, Embry's involvement in the Barclay proposal encouraged Schmoke to intervene. By the late 1980s the Abell Foundation had become the chief private-sector contributor for education-related projects in Baltimore.[24] According to a local business and trade journal, "An Abell grant confers not only the heady empowerment of money, but instant legitimacy and status."[25] In cash-strapped school districts, local foundations have enormous influence, wielding what Clarence Stone calls "systemic power."[26] City and school officials tend to favor Embry-backed educational proposals because the Abell Foundation controls an enormous number of resources. One observer of Baltimore schools, who is fearful of Embry's influence in the BCPS, recalled his involvement in the Barclay School issue and portrayed his role in school affairs: "He is one of the ones who try to rule the city with his money. He has thrown some money around. He has thrown some at the Department of Education. He saw to it that the superintendent was overruled because he wanted the Calvert plan at the Barclay School. He saw to it. And that superintendent got out of this city."

In June Schmoke instructed the superintendent to work out a solution with the Barclay parents and staff. The mayor's action marked the beginning of his personal involvement in the schools and the first of a number of public clashes with Hunter. By August Schmoke learned that Hunter had taken no action on the Barclay proposal and ordered the superintendent to meet with Gertrude Williams. But repeatedly, according to news accounts, the mayor discovered that nothing was being done. "This went on for weeks and months, and it kept escalating to increasing frustration for the mayor, increasing anger," recalled one mayoral aide. "The meetings weren't held, the calls weren't returned, until the mayor intervened," said one of the people involved in the proposal.[27] In March 1990 Schmoke and Hunter held a two-hour private meeting during which, according to Schmoke, they discussed "personal and policy issues."[28] The mayor had become increasingly irritated, directing Hunter to expedite the approval of Barclay's proposal. The next day, Hunter officially approved the Barclay-Calvert collaboration, ending a bitter two-year struggle.

Implementation began in fall 1990 in kindergarten and first grade, with one grade added each year thereafter. The only independent evaluation of the Barclay-Calvert collaboration was completed in 1994, and it showed that the program raised standardized test scores.[29] Students consistently scored at or above the national average in reading for both public and private schools. Data from the Maryland State Performance Assessment Program also indicated progress in the six areas it measured; Barclay students scored above the district averages in each area. Discipline and attendance also improved.

Highlighted on network television and in national magazines and newspapers and visited by educators from around the country, Barclay by 1997 had a waiting list of hundreds of students seeking admission. Reportedly, "well-to-do white parents have even begun to move into the area to make sure their children can enroll in the school."[30] In fall 1994, school officials began implementing the Calvert curriculum at Carter G. Woodson Elementary School, another high-poverty public school.

The Barclay story captures the experience of real people under difficult circumstances attempting to reform their neighborhood school. The key supporters of the collaboration—the steering committee of parents, parents of former students, teachers, administrators, and community leaders—developed trust, confidence, and a sense of efficacy based on the decade-long and successful struggle to convert Barclay from an elementary to a combined elementary/middle school. The Barclay story illustrates the capacity of Barclay parents to draw on these stocks of social capital to implement an innovative school reform program.

Barclay also reveals the challenge Baltimore leaders face in developing the intergroup social capital necessary to reform the BCPS. This was most apparent in Superintendent Hunter's resistance to Robert Embry's role in the process. As a newcomer to Baltimore, Hunter opposed the Abell Foundation's influence in the

BCPS no doubt because he was swayed by the many black school administrators who complained about, resented, and were threatened by Embry's influence. Black political autonomy over the BCPS is jealously guarded. Although much of the public criticism was directed at Hunter, interview data confirm that he did not lose any friends among African-American school administrators for resisting a prominent school program backed by Embry.

Further, Barclay sheds light on the important role of government and governmental institutions in facilitating social capital. My extension of Robert Putnam's social capital model suggests that government and government officials also influence civic behavior by engaging different sectors of the community. In the Barclay case, Mayor Schmoke played an essential role in promoting social capital, using the authority of his office to encourage the school bureaucracy, the Barclay community, and Abell Foundation officials to work toward a solution. The Barclay experience shows that institutions matter in the development and mobilization of social capital.

A few years after Barclay parents drew on their stocks of social capital, parents and teachers in the neighborhoods near Memorial Stadium began mobilizing to start their own public school. The Stadium School movement provides evidence of the benefits of intergroup social capital in reforming inner-city schools and confirms that a big-city mayor can affect social capital, especially intergroup social capital.

THE STADIUM SCHOOL MOVEMENT

The Stadium School is the first public school in Baltimore operated by parents and teachers who have increased authority. During the 1995–1996 school year, its faculty comprised seven teachers and six noninstructional staffers. It is a small school, with about eighty students enrolled in grades four through eight. Approximately 95 percent of its students are black, and more than 70 percent of all students are eligible for free or reduced-price meals. It draws its student body from the Northern Waverly, Ednor Garden, Coldstream, and Better Waverly neighborhoods located northeast of the city center, around Memorial Stadium's vast ballpark (see Fig. 6.1, p. 100).

Situated approximately three miles northeast of downtown, the four neighborhoods are racially and socioeconomically diverse (see Table 6.2). In many ways, they are microcosms of Baltimore City. Over 70 percent of the residents are African American and nearly 30 percent are white. The median household income is almost identical to the income of households across the city although two of the neighborhoods, Coldstream and Better Waverly, have a higher percentage of families living in poverty. The percentage of impoverished families in Better Waverly is more than double, and in Coldstream, four times the citywide poverty rate.

Table 6.2. Basic Population Characteristics of Stadium School Neighborhoods

	Northern Waverly	Ednor Garden	Coldstream	Better Waverly	Baltimore City
White	21%	29%	19%	26%	39%
Black	77	58	78	72	59
Median income	$26,741	$35,946	$14,611	$28,148	$24,045
Families below poverty	7.9%	6.4%	36.5%	21.1%	17.8%
Children under 18 in poverty	11.9	13.2	52.9	37.5	32.5
College degree or more	15.6	30.1	9.5	19.3	17.8

Source: Baltimore City Department of Planning, 1990 Census Data by Neighborhoods (April 1993); Baltimore City Department of Planning, 1990 Census Data by Census Tracts (April 1993).

Civic Engagement

The movement to launch the Stadium School began in fall 1992 as a grassroots effort undertaken by a biracial group of five teachers and about thirty parents. The teachers were an energetic group, frustrated by their lack of autonomy in the classroom. Jay Gillen, a veteran teacher in the BCPS, was one of the leaders. He had experienced considerable inflexibility while teaching at the Harbor Learning Center, an alternative high school in Baltimore. Of particular concern to the teachers was the new enterprise schools concept. "The enterprise schools gave principals more autonomy, not teachers," asserted one teacher organizer. "There was no flexibility for the teachers. Everything requires the principals' approval. If she didn't like it, it didn't happen." The teachers were influenced by Joe Nathan, a former teacher and director of the Center for School Change at the Hubert Humphrey Institute of Public Affairs at the University of Minnesota, and a nationally known leader in the movement for public school choice and charter public school programs.[31]

The parents involved in organizing the Stadium School were deeply concerned with the quality of their children's education. Many were especially worried about their children's transition from elementary to middle school, with fears about overcrowding. Over 1,200 students were enrolled at Hamilton Middle School, for example, one of four middle schools zoned for the neighborhoods, and it was typical. Such large student bodies, the parents maintained, threatened the educational experience and nurturing that adolescent students need to maneuver the difficult transition to high school.

Other parents argued that the middle schools were underperforming academically and did little to prepare students for high school. Moreover, the location of the middle schools—several miles away from the four neighborhoods—required students to use public transportation. For many parents, the thought of their children (many as young as eleven) negotiating the intricacies of mass transit was daunting.

These concerns led teachers and parents to open Baltimore's first autonomous public school. Deciding to call it the Stadium School, they initially hoped to open it inside the offices of the centrally located stadium, once the home of the former Colts and the Orioles. The organizers believed that having the school inside Baltimore's old granddaddy of a ballpark "would encourage students, parents and teachers to think differently about their relation to learning and to each other."[32]

The Concept

The group was encouraged by Mayor Schmoke's leadership in school reform and his support of site-based management. Indeed, Schmoke's highly publicized interest in improving the quality of public education helped create the political environment that gave rise to the Stadium School movement. Moreover, the idea of creating an autonomous public school governed by parents and teachers was consistent with the 1992 Towers/Perrin/Cresap Study, which recommended that the BCPS recast itself as a network of enterprise schools, each having the authority and autonomy to make a difference in student learning. Although the teachers believed that the enterprise school concept gave too much authority and autonomy to principals, they argued that in spirit it sanctioned a more diverse management structure, allowing parents and teams of teachers to manage public schools under the authority of the school board.

In fall 1992 Gillen convened and led a steering committee to develop a proposal to present to the BCPS. Within a couple of months the organizers had written a detailed fifty-one-page proposal that included a rationale for the Stadium School, the demographics of the population to be served, a curriculum, a plan for the governance of the school, goals for students, daily schedules, school finances, and more. The proposal called for the creation of a public school, operated with public money, with considerable independence from the system's headquarters. It envisioned a small school directed by teachers and with significant authority vested in parents and members of the community. A "school governing council" of parent, student, and community representatives, as well as all members of the school faculty, would operate the school. The faculty, however, would constitute a majority of the council. All major policy decisions, the establishment of a school budget, staff hiring, staff evaluation, school safety, procurement, and other management issues would be the responsibility of the governing council.

The school would involve the entire community. An assessment team, consisting of a student's parent or guardian, an adult from the larger community (minister, neighbor, business owner, police officer, physician), and the student's school adviser, would measure and report on the student's academic progress. While acknowledging the central role of the larger community, the proposal emphasized the involvement of parents in their own children's education. Conceptually, the founders of the Stadium School envisioned active parent involvement at both the school governance level and in the home learning environment.

Unlike the Barclay School, which adopted a traditional curriculum, the Stadium School's founders proposed a unique curriculum with "environmental education" as a thematic focus:

> The school's purpose is to provide a demanding academic program, focusing on the humanistic, environmental and ecological needs of the community, and on the relation of those needs to the regional and global ecologies. Students will learn through active, collective participation in solving real problems faced by their own communities. Credits will be earned and students promoted not through completion of course "hours," but through the students' demonstration that they have applied skills or knowledge to change the world about them or themselves in tangible ways. They will see the results of their learning as their neighborhood environment becomes healthier, more beautiful and ecologically more stable.[33]

The students would take courses in math, history, literature, and social studies, which would engage them in projects "thematically organized around environmental education." They would gain interdisciplinary knowledge (in math, writing, reading, language skills) by interviewing experts, record keeping, data collecting and analysis, use of survey instruments, and use of the library.

Organizers wished to open the school with 80 to 120 fourth through ninth graders, although they proposed eventually to serve students from prekindergarten through the twelfth grade. The student body and faculty would match the ethnic diversity of the four neighborhoods. No student would be denied admission because of prior academic or behavioral records. The school's promoters promised to meet state requirements, based on the Maryland School Performance Assessment Program, within five years or shut down. The proposal included estimated start-up costs of $500,000. The organizers planned to present the proposal to the school board and to obtain its approval in time to open during the 1993–1994 school year.

School Bureaucracy

In February 1993 the Stadium School proposal was formally submitted to the BCPS for approval. As in the Barclay-Calvert case, the parents and teachers supporting the school hit a brick wall, with immediate resistance from Superintendent Walter Amprey. Amprey, who had replaced Richard Hunter in August 1991, argued that the Stadium School proposal did not fit with his "overall vision" of the school system, despite agreeing that it appeared educationally sound. "The main issue is governance," he told reporters. "We like the concept of a teacher-driven school, but we want to have it within a current school to make sure it fits in with the overall vision of the school system."[34] Instead of creating a new school, he supported the operation of the Stadium School within an existing school—a "school within a school."

The Board of School Commissioners supported the superintendent. The school system, board president Phillip Farfel asserted, had no intention of creating new schools. "If we're going to establish new programs, they'll be schools within schools," he said.[35] Farfel argued that the Stadium School, as proposed, would detract from efforts to improve the existing 177 schools and would remove necessary oversight to ensure that it complied with the system's goals. A number of local observers contend that Amprey and the school board were simply reluctant to give the parents and teachers authority over budgeting, personnel, and curriculum. "The Stadium School [is an effort by] a group of teachers who want to start their own school but who also want pretty much total autonomy. The school system is not prepared to provide this," says an educational researcher. Amprey and school officials were also concerned that granting such authority to the organizers would open the floodgates for other groups and communities to propose starting their own schools. The school system's principals also opposed it. Representatives from the Public School Administrators and Supervisors Association viewed the proposal as a direct assault on principals' authority to lead their schools.

Organizing Political Support

As school officials questioned and delayed the proposal, parents and teachers organized support. The professional and volunteer staff of the Citizens Planning and Housing Association played a central role in orchestrating and directing the parents' grassroots mobilization. Throughout the campaign Hathaway Ferebee, CPHA's executive director, members of its Education Committee, and other staffers assisted parents and teachers, provided short seminars on leadership development, gave technical assistance, organized meetings with top school administrators, maintained a written record of all negotiated agreements, and explained the bureaucratic stages of proposal approval to make the school a reality. Lawyers on CPHA's board volunteered legal services to the group working with BCPS attorneys on such matters as insurance coverage, acquisition of a site for the school, and drafting the "memorandum of agreement" that would govern the relationship between the school and the BCPS. With its many years of experience in community issues and in dealing with city government, CPHA became a powerful resource for the organizers of the Stadium School. "CPHA was the most vital piece," explained a parent activist.

From the start parents interested in organizing the school were a biracial group, nearly an even mix of whites and blacks. Gillen, white, and Alexine Campbell, an African-American parent, emerged as the leaders of the movement. The biracial composition of the group prevented the spread of damaging accusations that they were a fly-by-night group of white parents seeking to start a school for their children with public funds. The experience of Jo Ann Robinson, the white parent who originally had taken the lead in the Barclay-Calvert collaboration, suggests that such a charge potentially could have derailed the project.

With support from the CPHA, the parents launched a typical community organizing effort. Meetings were held at the homes of parents and teachers, in neighborhood libraries, and at the headquarters of the various neighborhood associations. "We distributed flyers throughout the community—door-to-door, on utility poles; we talked to parents at school bus stops," recalled a teacher organizer. Proponents often used Superintendent Amprey's own words, the school board's public positions, and excerpts from the Enterprise School Task Force Report to illustrate that their proposal was consistent with site-based management.

Supporters were astute in terms of touching the right bases, recruiting influential allies, and neutralizing potential opposition. As one observer explained, running the idea by the school system administrators was the first step, "then finding the superintendent was not particularly sympathetic to the concept as they wanted to do it; then going to the mayor; going to the city council, and others. Trying to develop as many allies as possible, they would force the superintendent to back down."

Mayor Schmoke told supporters that he "likes the concept and supports the project and would like to see it happen."[36] "Mayor Schmoke was always very supportive," recalls a teacher. Schmoke promised to budget about $500,000 of city funds to help start the school. Although he repeatedly endorsed the project, the mayor said he would leave the final decision to Amprey and the school board.

Stadium School organizers conferred with Robert Embry of the Abell Foundation, Timothy Armbruster of the Goldseker Foundation, and Jerry Baum of the Fund for Educational Excellence, influential nonprofits with education portfolios. They hoped to leverage financial commitments to fund the school's start-up costs. However, none of the nonprofits believed that the organizers' proposal would win approval from the school system, and they did not wish to expend the capital and institutional goodwill on a proposal that was dead on arrival. Although none committed to funding the project, each vouched for the educational soundness of it. Indeed, the Abell Foundation provided $500 in postage to help organizers fund a massive mail-out of flyers to residents and promised to provide funding if the proposal were eventually approved.

Other important educational stakeholders, including experts at Johns Hopkins University, also supported the proposal. Irene Dandridge, an early supporter, liked the idea of having a teacher-directed school. The BTU, however, insisted that the teachers have an equal voice on the school's proposed governing council; indeed, the proposal gave teachers a majority on the council. Councilman Carl Stokes, chair of the city council's Education and Human Resources Committee, and city council president Mary Pat Clarke backed the proposal. Several members of the Maryland legislature, including state senator Julian Lapides, urged city officials to approve the proposal. Lapides personally lobbied Superintendent Amprey on behalf of the school's supporters.

The campaign to win approval of the project continued for nearly a year. In March 1994 proponents held two huge rallies attended by more than 100 parents chanting "give us our school" and carrying placards reading "listen to the community." At the rally, organizers distributed school board members' telephone numbers and told supporters to flood the members' home with phone calls, urging them to approve the Stadium School project.

In early March supporters packed a school board meeting and formally asked members to approve the proposal so they could open the school in time for the 1994–1995 school year. "We can no longer wait for decent schools. Our children need a decent education," declared Jay Gillen. The parents and teachers complained that Superintendent Amprey had refused to consider the school seriously. "We cannot understand the hostility we have met, or why we have to do battle so hard to get your support for a school that responds to our needs and aspirations," Alexine Campbell told the school board. City councilman Carl Stokes spoke in favor of the school and urged the board to stop the delaying tactics and to approve the proposal. "I'm very disturbed, frustrated and angry at times at how much we fight with [parents], and how many obstacles and hoops we put them through. These folks know what needs to be done, and they're ready to go. Let's do it now," Stokes urged.[37] Although the board did not vote on the proposal, the president announced that it would consider it carefully and respond by the next meeting, scheduled for mid-March.

Approval

The political pressure and community mobilization surrounding the Stadium School resembled the battle mounted by Barclay School parents. Indeed, a number of observers began to say that Superintendent Amprey's behavior was similar to that of his predecessor, Richard Hunter. In a lead editorial, the *Evening Sun* criticized Amprey's insistence that the Stadium School did not fit in with the "overall vision" of the school system as "the same kind of reasoning the city heard from Richard C. Hunter."[38] Amprey's "opposition to the Stadium School Project is mystifying," the editorial declared. To supporters of the school, Amprey appeared to be wavering on his commitment to site-based management.

Ultimately, school officials had little choice but to approve the Stadium School proposal. Mayor Schmoke reportedly asked Amprey and the school board to work out a solution. At its March 17 meeting, school board president Farfel announced that the board and Superintendent Amprey would work with the school's supporters to make the proposal a reality.

Between spring and summer 1994, Stadium School organizers met with school officials to develop and approve an agreement for the school's operation. A number of difficult issues had to be negotiated before it could open in September. To handle these thorny details, Amprey instructed his two top deputies, Patsy Blackshear and Lillian Gonzales, to work with Hathaway Ferebee and other Stadium School leaders.

Funding was the first critical issue. In 1992 school officials had hired a private firm, Educational Alternatives Incorporated (EAI) to operate nine BCPS

schools. Ferebee and other Stadium School proponents insisted that school officials fund their school at $6,000 per pupil, a figure equal to the amount provided
the nine EAI schools. Over $2,000 more than was spent on students in the other
schools, the amount was deemed "unaffordable" to school administrators.[39] Instead, they recommended that the school operate at the funding level proposed
for all enterprise schools. Ferebee and the Stadium School representatives persisted on the funding issues, arguing that the "BCPS must give community based
new schools the same level of financial support [given the] for-profit company."[40]

A second issue concerned the grades the school would serve. Supporters of
the new school contended that it should not be constrained by existing grade-level
configurations; they envisioned a school with grades 4 through 9. In their view, a
ninth grader who was not ready for the large, departmentalized setting of a comprehensive high school or a sixth grader who still required the nurturing environment
of an elementary school should not be forced into a different setting prematurely. A
brochure distributed by school organizers explained that

> early and late adolescence are times of intense change in students' lives. As
> teens loosen ties to parents, they intensify their relationships with peers, move
> from concrete to abstract thinking, test new values and try new roles. These
> changes do not take place all at once, or at the same age for all children.
> Adolescence is enormously variable and unpredictable in its details, and
> schools should recognize this by holding open as many roles as possible for
> adolescents to practice with: they can advance when they are feeling adven-
> turous, or slow down when they need more time.[41]

Consistent with the idea of site-based management, Stadium School negotiators
restated their need to be able to group children in the manner they believed best
for students' educational needs. School administrators, however, maintained that
the school should be a middle school comprising grades 6, 7, and 8, consistent
with other middle schools, and that it should comply with state regulations.

The other critical issue was the facility. Where would the school be housed?
The Memorial Stadium's owners had agreed to let the school be located in the
business offices there. For Ferebee and other supporters, the stadium site was crucial because of its centrality to the Coldstream, Waverly, Better Waverly, and Ednor
Garden neighborhoods. Students could walk to school. Moreover, as the proposal
indicated, "The stadium's current vacancy and plans for redevelopment of the site
are crucial environmental issues in our community, ripe for study and active involvement of both students and families."[42]

School administrators agreed to help secure Memorial Stadium and to allow
the school to operate in a neighborhood church until the physical alterations of
the stadium were complete. However, central administration officials and the Stadium School negotiators reached an impasse on the issues of funding and grade
structure. On May 27, 1994, the school administrators wrote the school board
president asking him to "please assist the members of the Stadium School Proj-

ect . . . in resolving these issues so that we can progress with the opening of school in September."[43] Farfel, school administrators, Ferebee, and other Stadium School leaders then met to discuss funding, grade structures, and facilities. Farfel agreed to examine the issues closely and to make a decision at the board's meeting two days later.

On the day of the meeting, about 100 parents rallied in front of the school headquarters to demand that the community-based school receive the same funding per student as the EAI-operated schools. After Farfel announced that it was delaying its decision for "further review," a bitter exchange ensued. When parents interrupted the school board's deliberations, Farfel ruled them "out of order" and abruptly ended the meeting.[44] The school's supporters immediately took the issue to Mayor Schmoke. Schmoke and Superintendent Amprey then met with Ferebee, Alexine Campbell, Jay Gillen, and lawyers from CPHA at city hall. Schmoke reiterated his support for the school and said he hoped to budget $500,000 for it; he also promised to help organizers secure space at Memorial Stadium to house the eighty students enrolled. However, he indicated that the per pupil spending and grade configuration was a decision Amprey and the school board would have to make.

In mid-June Farfel wrote Ferebee indicating that the board had agreed to modify its position on grade configuration and supported opening the school with grades 4 through 9. However, on the funding issue, Farfel continued to maintain that the project "would operate within the existing cost parameters" for all enterprise schools. He indicated that in that program the system's schools would receive funding above the current systemwide average. Moreover, school board president Farfel insisted that the Stadium School "operate in a BCPS facility."[45] Citing legal and economic concerns, he offered space in one of two sites, near the neighborhoods. He asked that the school supporters agree to these modifications to avoid further delay in the implementation of the project. In the end, Ferebee and the other organizers agreed to the stipulations.

In September the Stadium School opened with eighty students. However, for some parents and teachers the opening came with a bitter pill. It turned out that to make repairs necessary to meet building and safety codes, school officials would have to spend about $400,000 to upgrade Memorial Stadium, three times the original estimate. As an alternative, Amprey and the school board decided to bus the students to a former junior high in northeast Baltimore, four miles away (see Fig. 6.1). School organizers had fought more than two years to get their neighborhood school; then they found out it would not be in the neighborhood at all. As one parent put it, "What they offered us is like a slap in the face. All the organizing we did to get a school, then they're just going to throw us out of the community anyway? Everything they presented to us was a crock."[46]

It is still too early in the process to evaluate the prospects for the Stadium School supporters' most ambitious goal of meeting MSPAP standards by its fifth year in operation. As of 1998, MSPAP test results showed that eighth graders scored better than those at several other middle schools drawing from the Northern Waverly, Ednor Garden, Coldstream, and Better Waverly neighborhoods. But comparisons are difficult because the Stadium School is so small that one student's scores can dramatically affect the test results.

Perhaps the most lasting result of the Stadium School movement was Mayor Schmoke's endorsement and support of a reform program called the New Schools Initiative (NSI). NSI allows nonprofit organizations—such as groups of parents and teachers, community organizations, universities, labor, or service organizations—to design and operate new public schools. NSI schools are public in that per pupil classroom funding plus maintenance, transportation, and food service costs are paid by the BCPS. However, NSI permits schools to operate relatively autonomously from the central school administration, as the Stadium School does. In 1997 ten schools operated under NSI.

SUMMARY

Social capital is a resource used to engage communities in working toward shared goals. Putnam and other social capital theorists have argued that successful outcomes are more likely in "civically engaged communities." If a community wants better schools and improved educational opportunities, the possibility of achieving such a goal is made easier if it has high stocks of social capital. This was evident in the Barclay School case.

For nearly two decades, the Barclay School has had an active steering committee of parents and teachers who interacted throughout the school year. Moreover, it is blessed to have the support of small business owners, church leaders, and citizens throughout the Greenmount, Charles Village, Remington, and Abell communities. Every year, Barclay School holds an Annual Appreciation Luncheon; over 100 people participate. Many are parents, and some are parents of former students. Others are from the school district or are people from the community who have become involved in the school. A school serving an affluent suburban community would count itself lucky to have such support. The luncheons and the steering committee provide two examples from a series of remarkable demonstrations of social capital.

The Barclay-Calvert collaboration would not have happened had it not been for the leadership of Barclay's principal, Gertrude Williams, who spearheaded the drive to adopt the demanding Calvert curriculum. She risked her career by fighting Superintendent Richard Hunter over allowing the experiment. And as principal, Williams reached out to parents and teachers, empowering them to work for the good of the students. Many principals are reluctant to do so, fearing that they will try to take over. Williams's official power as principal, and her abilities and leadership skills, helped mobilize the Barclay community's social capital.

The organization of the Stadium School is another empirical referent of social capital at the school-site level. Here was a group of parents, teachers, and other community leaders who organized to start their own public school, a task perhaps more challenging than an existing public school adopting a private school's curriculum. The Stadium School idea developed from the concern of parents preparing to enroll their adolescent children in middle schools. By drawing on their shared concerns about the efficacy of the city's middle schools to provide students with an adequate educational environment, parents in the Northern Waverly, Ednor Garden, Coldstream, and Better Waverly neighborhoods were able to respond collectively.

Stadium School proponents, such as Jay Gillen and Alexine Campbell, benefited from the knowledge of CPHA officials and volunteers. The association had many years of experience training and organizing community groups and, since its inception in 1941, has worked closely with local government and city officials on a wide range of issues. For many parents and neighorhood residents, the Stadium School movement represented their baptism into the workings of city government and the school system's bureaucracy. CPHA's professional staff, led by the capable Hathaway Ferebee, and its many volunteers provided direction to this group of novice school reformers.

The CPHA was also significant because of its history of working across communities. The association has been a biracial organization since its formation. "The organization was founded on a biracial basis and was the first citywide civic organization to have dinner meetings with blacks and whites in attendance. Black and white had the opportunity to work together on common interests and the satisfaction of achieving mutual objectives."[47] Most of the work of the CPHA is done through a series of committees formed to address single policy issues, providing "opportunities for individuals to work together on problems on which they basically agree without requiring them to subscribe to a whole range of policies advocated by an organization." In the late 1990s the CPHA continues to serve as the training ground for Baltimore's civic and community leaders. Its volunteers include African-American and white citizens who work together on a wide range of community issues. During the effort to start the Stadium School, CPHA's Education Committee was chaired by an African-American lawyer, continuing the association's "early commitment to biracial cooperation."[48]

Additional resources played a vital part in helping the Barclay and Stadium School communities achieve their goals. The financial support of the Abell Foundation is critical in the Barclay-Calvert collaboration. The foundation has funded a full-time coordinator for the program, the purchase of over $50,000 in books during the first four years, time for staff development (approximately $30,000 the first four years), a computer laboratory and other equipment and materials. Between 1990 and 1994, Abell's total funding was nearly $500,000. As one observer noted, "When the principal needed to negotiate with central administration of the district, she has had the unusual leverage which accrued through her individual tenacity and the Abell grant. It would be difficult to overestimate the importance of this funding stability."[49] In the Stadium School case, the additional resources came in the form of valuable assistance by the CPHA. The many lawyers who make up a significant number of its body of volunteers provided a variety of free legal work for the project. In short, social capital counts, but resources are also integral.

A common thread running through these two cases is the role of the city's most important government official, Mayor Kurt Schmoke. His emphasis on educational reform and his support of site-based management undoubtedly helped foster the kind of political environment that encouraged the proponents of the Barclay-Calvert collaboration to seek out a curriculum they thought best for their school. Schmoke's decision to reverse Superintendent Hunter's decision on the collaboration was critical. Similarly, Schmoke's insistence that the central school administration devolve more authority and autonomy to parents and teachers inspired the organizers of the Stadium School to launch Baltimore's first public school operated by parents and teachers with public money but independent from the BCPS' headquarters. In early 1997, in his last months as superintendent, Walter Amprey publicly acknowledged that he remained opposed to allowing teachers, parents, and other private groups to operate schools independently of the school system.[50] Schmoke's formal authority over the school district was crucial and forced a reluctant superintendent to approve the Stadium School. In short, the Barclay and Stadium School experiences show that in Baltimore, the formal authority of the mayor's office enabled Schmoke to facilitate cooperation among school officials, parents, and community leaders.

7
Civic Elites and the Baltimore Commonwealth

One day it will be said that in the city of Baltimore in the last quarter of the twentieth century, strange and unusual things began to happen. Well-known somebodies with something from someplace began to meet with little-known nobodies from no place. The upper crust began to meet with the middle crust and with those who have no crust at all. It was a peculiar people. A strange and unusual coalition that negotiated and fought and worked together.
— THE REVEREND GRADY YEARGIN

Robert Putnam's measures of social capital are based on membership records of organizations such as PTAs, labor unions, bowling leagues, garden clubs, bird-watching groups, choral groups, soccer clubs, and other voluntary associations.[1] Social capital, however, is more than a function of the civic engagement of a mass populace, especially in American urban politics. It is also a measure of the engagement, relationships, and levels of trust among civic elites—corporate executives, government officials, the heads of nonprofit foundations, church leaders, and officers of major civic organizations. These are the men and women who do the heavy lifting—who help develop new programs and initiatives and provide the resources to implement and sustain them. Without peak-level coordination among these civic elites, initiatives such as school reform, improvement in job opportunities, and related issues are not likely to succeed.

The 1980s witnessed a tremendous growth of interest among educators, business leaders, foundation heads, and others in public education and the need to enhance the life chances of minority students, especially those in the inner city. As a result, a number of communities formed partnerships with businesses, community organizations, key leaders in government, and leaders of private institutions. For the most part, these partnerships are local in origin and impact, such as

122

the Boston Compact, initiated by local business leaders.[2] Yet as Baltimore's effort to institute site-based management throughout its public schools reveals, popular policy ideas alone do not ensure that local actors are equipped to construct and sustain the necessary coalition or to form the level of intergroup social capital needed to effect those ideas.

Conceptually, an urban regime represents the cross-sector elite component of intergroup social capital. An analysis of black and intergroup social capital in the context of influential white and black partners in Baltimore's urban regime should therefore illustrate the challenges African-American civic leaders faced as they attempted to tackle the issue of school reform through the formation of linkages with white corporate and civic leaders. Moreover, the importance of financial resources, especially private-sector investment, to successful school reform must be kept in the picture.

To analyze the engagement and social capital among Baltimore's civic elites, I present an in-depth study of the formation of the Baltimore Commonwealth and the CollegeBound Foundation. Modeled after the Boston Compact, these programs are efforts to provide a "certainty of opportunity" for graduates of the BCPS. Signed in 1985, the Baltimore Commonwealth is an agreement between the BCPS and the business community to hire high school graduates who agree to specified improvements, such as better school attendance and higher academic performance. The essence of the Baltimore Commonwealth is a pledge by the school system to improve education and learning outcomes in return for jobs.

The CollegeBound Foundation grew out of the planning process that sparked creation of the Commonwealth. It is a program designed to increase the number of college-bound BCPS graduates by assisting students with fee waivers for college entrance applications and standardized tests, help in filling out paper work and financial aid forms, and counseling on college choice and career planning. CollegeBound also provides small grants (between $500 and $1,000) to fill in the gap for students whose loans, grants, or other financial assistance falls short.

CATALYSTS FOR ELITE INVOLVEMENT

In his unsuccessful 1983 campaign to unseat Mayor William Donald Schaefer, William H. Murphy Jr. challenged the city's corporate, civic, and political leadership to reexamine the impact of downtown development from a broader perspective. Murphy's campaign captured the attention of civic elites by spotlighting problems long ignored by city government. A successful judicial candidate in 1980 and a member of the prominent black family who owns the *Afro-American*, Murphy attacked Schaefer, citing the deteriorating conditions of the black neighborhoods, rising black youth unemployment, and the city's failing school system. He criticized the mayor for building a glittering downtown area while ignoring these persistent problems. Murphy expressed his belief that downtown redevelopment did not do enough to ameliorate the plight of the city's disadvantaged residents:

> In the last twelve years, this great city has built marvelous buildings in the center of town which have created a spirit of hope for the rejuvenation of Baltimore. But all around these beautiful buildings in the shadows of affluence are large numbers of children with dashed hopes of a decent education; broken families with unemployable parents; hundreds of thousands of functionally illiterate people of all ages, races, and creeds, and thousands of people without decent low-cost housing.[3]

Murphy was unable to sway the majority of the city's voters to abandon Schaefer. However, his candidacy provided the spark that ignited a dialogue between the city's African-American and white civic leaders about concrete steps to address quality public education and limited job opportunities, especially among African-American youth.

Murphy's relentless attack on the Schaefer regime also caught the attention of BUILD. Its foray into education reform came during the 1983 campaign when it began investigating the shortages and disparities in school supplies in the BCPS. BUILD discovered that the schools were short not only of paper products but also of textbooks, film projectors, and an array of other basic resources.[4] Its investigation forced Mayor Schaefer to promise that if reelected he would be "a cheerleader for the school system" and work to make the city "believe in our school system."[5] Although Schaefer never lived up to his promise, BUILD's efforts encouraged Superintendent Alice Pinderhughes to consider ways to reform the BCPS.

The school system, however, was only part of the problem with black youth unemployment, and thus, school reform was only part of the solution. BUILD leaders argued that discrimination against African-American youth by local employers was another critical element. The same conclusion was also reached by the U.S. Commission on Civil Rights after it held hearings in Baltimore in November 1981 to examine the level of minority participation in the economic development and revitalization of the city.[6]

The commission heard from witnesses who testified that "employer perceptions" contributed to the inability of many Baltimore youth to secure jobs. Dorothy Mead, district director of the Baltimore Office of the Equal Employment Opportunity Commission, testified that employers in the growing hotel industry "are hesitant to hire blacks in positions that are highly visible to their customers."[7] BCPS officials testified that of the 6,000 local high school graduates in 1981, by November of that year only 278 had been hired for permanent positions in the city. Although approximately 1,500 BCPS graduates went to college after graduation, roughly 4,000 were looking for work.[8] Local businesses failed to hire minority youth in significant numbers.

In May 1983 the commission issued its final report. Derisively entitled the *Greater Baltimore Commitment,* it lambasted the corporate community in general and the Greater Baltimore Committee in particular for its "dismal" record in the area of African-American youth employment. "There is no question that employers in Baltimore are not hiring local high school graduates, who are predominantly minority, in significant numbers although many such students have entry level job skills and adequate academic skills," the report stated. Moreover, "Too few blacks hold positions in white businesses that offer the potential to acquire managerial and financial experience."[9]

For BUILD leaders, the educational situation had become a two-edged sword. If young people believe there are no jobs available after graduation and that little or nothing will come of their training and education in school, why should they demonstrate their best in the classroom? Arnie Graf, BUILD's lead organizer, maintained that Baltimore's youth needed to know that hard work in school has it rewards, including the possibility of a satisfying job. The Baltimore Commonwealth was a program that could address both challenges, serving the common good as a wide array of citizens assumed responsibility. It would encourage superior performance from the city's students and leverage a commitment from area businesses to hire them into permanent jobs.

In the 1980s a number of school districts formed school compacts to provide priority hiring for graduates in return for improvements in grades, attendance, and overall performance.[10] In most cities, business representatives, school officials, and community leaders adopted a number of standard measures—grade point average, average daily attendance, punctuality, and performance on standardized college entrance exams—to assess student achievement in fulfilling compact promises. BUILD's initial compact proposal was considerably less stringent. Mindful of research that showed wide disparities in the performance between white and black students on college entrance examinations, BUILD's compact proposal did not include standardized test scores as an achievement measure. BUILD leaders, however, believed in motivating students through realistic achievements. Hence, they developed a compact that would guarantee an entry-level job to every high school graduate with good attendance.

As one of Baltimore's most powerful black-led organizations, BUILD represents a key component in black social capital. Union Baptist minister Vernon Dobson, the Reverend Douglas Miles, Carol Reckling (a former BUILD president), and Marian Dixon, its president, understood that any program purporting to provide jobs for local high school graduates required black social capital and the cooperation of the white business community.[11] Urban regime theory holds that a policy effort must be commensurate with the resources a coalition is able to assemble. Given the amount of resources controlled by the business community, it had to be part of a program like the Commonwealth. A prominent black minister who was active in BUILD emphasized how important the corporate sector was in attaining success in such a program: "You need a coalition. The coalition would consist of groups like BUILD and the Association of Black Charities. Then you would have to get 'Uncle Bubba' in the coalition. 'Uncle Bubba' are whites—

white businessmen. They control the money. It is an economic necessity that they be a part of the coalition."[12]

The business community is organized under the Greater Baltimore Committee. Because of the GBC's historic involvement in local affairs, corporate-sector support for the Commonwealth appeared to be a given. The GBC's involvement went beyond revitalizing downtown. In the mid-1950s school desegregation reportedly "went off without incident" because of the positive role played by prominent business and civic leaders associated with the GBC.[13] The Voluntary Council, one of the GBC's offshoots, worked to eliminate racial discrimination in employment and housing in the 1960s.[14] A member of the GBC described the organization's concern for social issues, asserting that "the [business] leadership of this community has welcomed every opportunity to make this an open society and right the wrongs [of racial injustice]. Every issue that has come up—we have come up on the right side on race, integration, and everything blacks supported."[15]

By the 1960s, however, Marilyn Gittell and T. Edward Hollander reported that the "business community ha[d] not displayed an interest in education and remains aloof from issues when they are raised."[16] In the mid-1970s, although some adopt-a-school programs were launched, the GBC's involvement in school affairs continued to decline.[17] An official conceded that by the mid-1970s the business community "abandoned the school system and gave it to a segment of the black community."[18] Moreover, as the hearings from the U.S. Commission on Civil Rights revealed, private-sector employers compiled a sorry record in terms of hiring minority youth.

CORPORATE ELITES AND THE COMMONWEALTH PROPOSAL

Clarence Stone warned that the mechanics of regime cooperation are complex and problem-laden, noting that "there is no one formula for bringing institutional sectors into an arrangement for cooperation, and the whole process is imbued with uncertainty."[19] Baltimore's experience with the Commonwealth and the College-Bound Foundation illustrates how race pervades efforts at cross-sector elite cooperation in support of school reform. Garnering support from the business sector for the two programs proved to be a complex problem.

Many of BUILD's early campaigns were aimed at the corporate community. During BUILD's infancy, business leaders tried to ignore its demands and often refused to meet with its leaders. As Alan Hoblitzell, chief executive officer of Maryland National Bank, recalled: "I was initially skeptical [about meeting with BUILD leaders]. I had read about their adversarial nature, their confrontations, things like that. The question was whether you could sit down in a cooperative vein to deal with problems that are common."[20] A black minister active in BUILD described how the organization has worked with the GBC: "The Greater Baltimore Committee has only come into partnership with the community kicking and screaming. It has to be through pressure. What the business community always responds to is the threat of disruption of business. That's always been the way of getting the corporate community involved."

BUILD strategized its pressure in order to gain vital corporate support for its Commonwealth proposal. Before approaching the GBC with its concerns about African-American youth employment and presenting its proposal, BUILD completed two strategically important tasks. First, taking advantage of the emotion and mobilization in the African-American community generated by Murphy's 1983 mayoral campaign, BUILD leaders launched a massive voter registration effort that added some 10,000 new voters to the books, creating reserves of voters to bolster support for future initiatives.[21] Second, with the help of an ally who worked in the personnel department at GBC headquarters, BUILD surreptitiously obtained employment data for the committee's top twenty-five member corporations. According to BUILD's analysis, these data showed that the majority of African-American workers were employed in positions at or near the bottom of the pay scale; only a few were in midlevel and managerial jobs.[22]

In early 1984 Arnie Graf, Vernon Dobson, Douglas Miles, Marian Dixon, and Carol Reckling met with the chair of the GBC's board, Alan Hoblitzell. BUILD leaders told him about the Boston Compact and presented their proposal for the Baltimore Commonwealth, expressing concern about the high unemployment rate among young African Americans.

With a reputation as a social moderate, Hoblitzell was sympathetic to the issue of black youth employment.[23] "I told them this may be something we can rally around," he recalled. "This would help convince youth that something was out there for them, that there would be a job. And it would assist the business community to be responsive to people's needs." Hoblitzell told the BUILD representatives that as the new president of Baltimore's major business organization, he wanted the corporate community, as he put it, to "be aware of and sensitive to the needs of minority groups."[24]

During spring and early summer 1984, Graf, Dixon, Reckling, Dobson, and Miles had several meetings with Hoblitzell and Robert Keller, GBC's executive director, without coming to terms on what could be done to address black youth unemployment. Hoblitzell and Keller insisted that the corporate CEOs would not support any program that smacked of "quotas, track programs, things that seemed to invade the way people ran their businesses."[25] Hoblitzell and BUILD representatives were unable to reach an agreement on the details of the school compact. Miles recalled a crucial meeting with Hoblitzell that fall: "Hoblitzell kept looking at his watch, saying, 'I have to catch a plane. I really don't have time to pin anything down.' He said a final no. Then I looked at him and said, 'Mr. Hoblitzell, you and I stand at a very unique position, a crossroad in the life of this community. We can take the leadership of building one community, or become perpetual enemies. Wouldn't the history of Baltimore read better if a black preacher and a white businessman helped save the city rather than further divide it?'"[26]

During this meeting, Hoblitzell advised Graf, Dobson, Miles, and the other BUILD representatives to put together some ideas and to be prepared to present them to other members of the GBC board. In winter 1984 BUILD presented its Commonwealth proposal to GBC's full board. Several CEOs immediately expressed reservations, reminding their colleagues that they already supported youth and minority employment opportunities through the "Blue Chip In" program. Blue Chip In was established in 1981 in response to the Reagan administration's cutbacks in summer youth employment and job training programs. The GBC's original goal for Blue Chip In was to raise $500,000 from local corporations and to create 200 full- and part-time jobs; however, in its first year, the committee raised $2.2 million and created over 1,700 jobs.[27] Blue Chip In was eventually expanded into a campaign to supplement the federal jobs program, which had been reduced.[28] Because of this involvement, when presented with BUILD's Commonwealth proposal GBC board members responded that member corporations could not be asked to do more.

Moreover, several GBC board members argued that as a regional business group with ties to the entire Baltimore metropolitan area, the committee had to balance corporate donations across varied jurisdictions. It would not be fair, they continued, for Baltimore City to get all the corporate community's philanthropic donations. As a vice-president of C&P Telephone explained, "GBC must balance support between jurisdictions. They work with jurisdictions across the state. They can't give all the money to Baltimore."[29]

Race and Intergroup Social Capital

The GBC's refusal to support BUILD's compact proposal turned into a highly visible battle between African-American leaders and the city's white corporate sector. Tensions, harsh words, and animosity continued for nearly six months. For several months, GBC officials refused to meet with BUILD leaders. According to a BUILD organizer, "GBC tried to stonewall us. They thought that if they could just ignore us the movement would fizzle out just like past efforts had and they wouldn't have to meet with us. They kept trying to stonewall. They knew if they talked with us it would provide us with issue recognition. The GBC knew if they gave us issue recognition they had to meet with us."[30]

A number of respondents believed race played a part in the debate, including one BUILD volunteer active in the Commonwealth discussions: "The GBC refused to hear us out. They didn't see it in their self-interest to help a school system where 80 percent of the students are black. They said essentially that it is not our problem. Racism was the problem. The GBC couldn't bring themselves to help black kids."[31]

BUILD refused to abandon their efforts and instead went on the offensive. First, if the GBC refused to discuss their compact proposal again, Arnie Graf threatened to release to the news media the employment data that BUILD claimed showed the unfair treatment of black workers. "We informed the GBC that we would release our findings to the media unless they talked with us," recalled another BUILD staff member. "They feared this. They knew their hiring and promotion rates as they related to blacks," he added. Release of the data, BUILD leaders surmised, would enlarge the scope of the conflict between African-American church leaders and the corporate community. Second, BUILD organized a series of mass meetings to demonstrate broad support for the Commonwealth and to pressure corporate leaders to act. One such meeting was attended by nearly 800 persons.[32]

When several national newspapers, including the *Washington Post,* focused attention on the confrontation, civic leaders panicked. Such publicity—coming just as the city's downtown revitalization efforts were gaining national attention—could potentially damage efforts to attract new businesses and more tourists. According to a GBC official, "A number of civic leaders were angry because they thought the fight would hurt the city's image. The word would get out that blacks in Baltimore were raising hell with the business community and it could hamper the city's effort to attract new businesses, industry, and tourists."[33]

Alan Hoblitzell wanted very much to end the impasse. The controversy between BUILD and the GBC was occurring during his tenure as president, and he preferred to move on to other issues. Mathias Devito, chairman and CEO of the Rouse Company, came to Hoblitzell's aid. Devito was perhaps one of the most influential members of GBC's board because of his position as head of the development firm founded by James Rouse—a founding member of the GBC who was active in its affairs until his death in 1996.

Significantly, Devito and Rouse had developed a personal relationship with the Reverend Vernon Dobson, who eventually came to depend on the two business leaders to help accomplish many of BUILD's goals.[34] Devito became a key liaison between BUILD leaders and the GBC board members, arguing that Baltimore needed a quality workforce and that the school compact was a step in that direction. He lobbied members to meet with BUILD and develop a Commonwealth program both groups could support. Dobson's relationship with Rouse and Devito paid off. The GBC board eventually voted to direct its executive director, Robert Keller, to meet with Dobson, Miles, Graf, and other BUILD volunteers and hammer out a school compact proposal.

From the outset, business leaders expressed concern about BUILD's proposal to guarantee a job for every high school graduate based only on attendance. They wanted to require more effort from the students and the school system. "The GBC said we will give you jobs if you give us good students," recalled the president of a large firm and at that time the only African-American member of GBC's board.[35] The GBC leaders wanted students to have a grade point average of 3.0 or better and a daily attendance average of 95 percent during their junior and senior years. As Keller recalled years later, "We said 95 percent. Is that practical? Damn right it's practical. What we're saying is they can't learn if they don't show up. Employers say that if they show up it means they can probably read and write and we'll train them."[36]

Keller indicated that the business leaders would agree to a Commonwealth proposal in which eligible students had to achieve a 95 percent average daily attendance rate and an average grade of B or better during their last two years in high school. Further, the GBC proposed dropping the automatic job guarantee, instead offering a guarantee that each student would get at least three job interviews and priority placement from a pool of more than 150 participating employers.[37] The decision to hire the high school graduate would be left to the business firm.

Some BUILD volunteers objected. "We wanted simply a good attendance record. What happened is that we had people saying that we agreed to an 'elitist' program," recalled a BUILD organizer. Despite opposition from several BUILD staffers and volunteers, Gerald Taylor, who replaced Arnie Graf as lead organizer when Graf became regional director of Industrial Areas Foundation projects in the mid-Atlantic region, urged BUILD members to accept the compromise: "I felt our first challenge was establishing a public relationship. . . . I knew if we did we'd have the clout over time to realize our program."[38] Taylor believed that by accepting the GBC's counter proposal, BUILD opened the door for black civic and community leaders to develop a public relationship and a new level of trust with the economic elite, thus providing the bridge for greater intergroup social capital. On April 24, 1985, the Commonwealth Agreement was signed. Its preamble read in part: "The Commonwealth Agreement commits the Baltimore Public Schools, the Greater Baltimore Committee, . . . and BUILD . . . to improve educational opportunities, to prepare students for careers, post secondary education and to improve access for jobs. The Commonwealth Agreement is about a common vision, a common focus, a common wealth—One Greater Baltimore."[39]

For its first three-to-four years the Commonwealth Agreement moved along mainly as an incentive program for high school graduates, offering priority hiring into entry-level jobs. Yet in BUILD's estimation, involving the city government fully could make the agreement even more comprehensive, opening doors to entry-level employment for hundreds of BCPS graduates. BUILD envisioned including the Office of Employment Development (OED), which administers employment and training programs. The OED could coordinate with potential employers to help high school graduates obtain additional training and sharpen their interview skills.

BUILD also hoped the Commonwealth would actively engage the city's mayor, school officials, and a wider segment of the community to support their efforts to reform the entire school system. The formation of the Commonwealth convinced BUILD and the GBC that systemwide school reform offered the best hope for the city's youth. In order to carry out this goal, BUILD needed the full support of Mayor William Donald Schaefer.

Mayor Schaefer's Role in the Commonwealth

Mayor Schaefer's relationship with BUILD leaders, however, was strained. Many of BUILD's earlier demands, such as improved police protection, arson control, decent and affordable public housing, and rat eradication, had been directed at Schaefer and his administration. BUILD leaders were also vocal critics of his administration's emphasis on downtown redevelopment. Schaefer did not take to criticism well. "Anything that raised negatives about Baltimore, he just did not want to hear," explained Douglas Miles. "He didn't even acknowledge that there were homeless in the city."[40]

Schaefer was especially irritated when asked tough questions in public and was particularly uncomfortable attending BUILD-sponsored issue forums. These were usually held in a large black church and attended by hundreds of volunteers. A former school administrator commented on Schaefer's anxiety: "He was afraid of BUILD. They would invite people into their public forums and ask tough questions. . . . They finally got to talk to Mayor Schaefer and he agreed to come to one of the forums. I always went with him when schools were discussed, to help answer questions. The Mayor does not like being asked tough questions in public. To be honest, I think the man was just scared."[41]

Several of BUILD's activist ministers were considered to be political opponents of Mayor Schaefer. Some of them, like Miles and Dobson, had openly and aggressively campaigned for city council candidates and mayoral hopefuls critical of the Schaefer regime. In the 1979 city council races, Miles and a number of other prominent black clergy endorsed Kweisi Mfume, a local radio talk-show host and political neophyte. Miles was one of Mfume's most active supporters, providing the annex of his church for Mfume's headquarters. On the campaign trail, Mfume castigated the Schaefer administration and adopted "Beat the Bosses" as his campaign slogan. "Everybody knew we meant those who controlled city hall and Mayor Schaefer," Mfume recalled.[42] In his autobiography, Mfume credits Miles's outreach to other black ministers as crucial to his upset victory.

In 1983, when William Murphy tried to unseat Schaefer, tensions between BUILD and the mayor reached new heights. Both the Baptist Ministers Conference and the Interdenominational Ministerial Alliance, two of the city's largest organizations of African-American ministers, endorsed Murphy.[43] Vernon Dobson, an IMA member, was a vocal supporter of Murphy, declaring, "I think the [black] Church will have to be enthusiastic in its support of Murphy once the Schaefer record is examined. . . . I feel we have let black people and poor people down because we have been too quiet about Schaefer in the past."[44] During the campaign, BUILD sponsored a mayoral debate between Schaefer and Murphy. Schaefer faced so much tough questioning that he "stormed out" of the debate, saying he was "set up" and "embarrassed" by BUILD.[45] Afterward, Schaefer did not meet with BUILD leaders or attend any of their forums until after his election as governor in 1986.

Predictably, Mayor Schaefer opposed the Commonwealth, undoubtedly in part because of these cumulative tensions. He never forgot that Miles and his ministerial allies helped elect a critic of his downtown redevelopment program to the city council. Nor did Schaefer forget that Dobson, Miles, and other BUILD leaders endorsed and actively campaigned for Murphy. "Schaefer was fighting the Commonwealth," recalled a BUILD organizer. "He didn't like the Common-wealth and he didn't like BUILD. He didn't like it primarily because it was started by Vernon Dobson who along with other BUILD ministers had supported his challengers."[46]

Schaefer did not support the Commonwealth for additional reasons. Publicly, he argued that the city's Blue Chip In program was sufficient. The Commonwealth, he said, was unnecessary. He believed the city was not big enough for two major youth-jobs programs. Moreover, city hall observers maintained that the Common-wealth did not fit Schaefer's style of governance. As an OED administrator ex-plained, "Mayor Schaefer had little tolerance for process and partnerships. He was a can-do mayor. He would get something and simply say let's do it." Further, Schaefer's top concern was downtown redevelopment, not education. Kenneth Wong notes that Schaefer "maintained a low profile in school matters" and "be-came increasingly assertive in land use issues."[47] Schaefer apparently wanted to avoid working with the school system at all costs. In his opinion, heavy involve-ment in school affairs offered few rewards.[48]

Schaefer therefore stood on the sidelines while the GBC and BUILD negotiated the Commonwealth. Moreover, he asked school superintendent Alice Pinderhughes and Linda Harris, head of the city's OED, not to get involved with it. Pinderhughes, who had worked with BUILD in the past and believed in the Commonwealth, ignored Schaefer's directive and quietly worked with both the GBC and BUILD. With over forty years in the school system, Pinderhughes was nearing retirement and had nothing to lose. Harris, however, who recently had been promoted to her post by Schaefer, complied with his demands.

The 1987 Mayoral Election

In November 1986 BUILD held its annual convention, drawing over 2,500 vol-unteers and a host of state and local officials. Among those present was Maryland's new governor-elect, William Donald Schaefer, who had successfully sought the office that year. Still holding a defiant posture toward BUILD, he urged the group to be "realistic" and not to push for short-term gains that, he said, could jeopar-dize the economic development of the city in the long term.[49]

Also in attendance were the two principal candidates for mayor of Baltimore. Schaefer's elevation to the governor's office made way for city council president and longtime Schaefer ally, Clarence "Du" Burns, to assume the mayor's office after December 1986. Burns, the city's first African-American mayor, in 1987 campaigned to retain the office for a full four-year term. His principal opponent was Kurt L. Schmoke, Baltimore's state's attorney.

BUILD leaders used their 1986 convention to present a six-point antipoverty program that they hoped would dominate the issues of the 1987 municipal elections. An expanded Commonwealth Agreement was a central part of the agenda. To show support for their antipoverty program, BUILD leaders planned a petition drive to correspond with the upcoming elections. Following Saul Alinsky's dictum that public officials respond to political strength rather than to moral appeals, BUILD planned to get thousands of signatures from voters who supported the Commonwealth Agreement.

As the 1987 mayoral campaign came to a close, BUILD had collected nearly 55,000 signatures. A few weeks before the election, the Reverend Sig Arneson, a BUILD volunteer, told an audience that included the principal mayoral candidates and other candidates for city offices, "I hope you recognize the significance of what 55,000 signatures means. That represents one out of seven registered voters in Baltimore City. It represents one out of three black residents in the city."[50] "The language of politics is votes," a BUILD organizer explained. "We turned the traditional role of political campaigns around. We went to the two candidates and asked them which one supported the agenda BUILD espoused. Since we are a nonprofit organization we can't endorse political candidates; but we can tell people which candidate supports BUILD's program."[51]

Mayor Burns and Kurt Schmoke had little choice but to sign on to BUILD's plan, and the latter endorsed it without reluctance. Burns initially rejected its agenda for the poor as "unrealistic." Two months later he changed his mind, however, and promised to expand the Commonwealth agreement: "I must admit, when the agenda was first presented to me, I did not believe the goals were realistic. I come to confirm my commitment and the city's commitment to the BUILD municipal agenda."[52]

Many observers attributed Kurt Schmoke's close victory over Burns to his quick endorsement of BUILD's agenda. A few days after he won the election, Schmoke told an audience of about 2,000 BUILD volunteers that "the real winner was BUILD's agenda. And BUILD's agenda is Baltimore's agenda."[53] Schmoke, Gerald Taylor, Carol Reckling, Douglas Miles, and Vernon Dobson began meeting about specifics on education, low-income housing, community policing, and a wide range of other issues. By the time Schmoke took office in December 1987, he and BUILD had developed a solid working relationship. "When the mayor first got into office," recalls a BUILD organizer, "he took leaders of BUILD to his cabinet and told them that we are part of the cabinet too."[54] BUILD was considered part of Baltimore's governing regime.

Shortly after Schmoke's inauguration, BUILD and the GBC asked the mayor to lead the Commonwealth effort. "BUILD and GBC had the agenda," recalled a GBC official. "We told Kurt that we will deliver the Commonwealth to him if he would take the leadership. We took it to him. He is the community's agenda set-ter."[55] The new mayor willingly agreed.

Schmoke Expands the Commonwealth Agreement

Mayor Schmoke believed that preparing youth for the future was the responsibil-ity of all: business, government, nonprofit organizations, and the community-at-large. He also wanted to build on the many summer-jobs projects, school-to-work transition programs, internships, mentorships, and other productive programs functioning independently throughout the city.

In winter 1988, following Schmoke's personal direction and involvement, BUILD, the BCPS, OED, GBC, and the Private Industry Council (the local public-private committee charged with planning and administering federal job-training programs) announced a major expansion of the Commonwealth Agreement, call-ing it the Baltimore Commonwealth. The expanded program was designed to coordinate all career preparation under one umbrella, centralizing the services linking youth to entry-level jobs. To reach this goal, Schmoke vowed that his administration's priority would be to mobilize the entire team for a long-term commitment to changing the odds for the city's youth, resulting in a productive workforce. To facilitate the expanded partnership, the mayor established a Com-monwealth Department within city government. He named a Commonwealth coordinator to provide "the primary source of organizational support to the Com-monwealth Partnership."[56]

The expanded Commonwealth billed itself not just as a program but as a comprehensive strategy. If interviews themselves did not produce a job, for ex-ample, OED staff would evaluate the young person and provide necessary assis-tance, such as interviewing tips, information about other opportunities, or résumé preparation. City government, under the direction of the OED, would also help Commonwealth students obtain summer jobs.

With the expanded program, the Commonwealth offers an array of oppor-tunities designed to provide career-readiness services to the city's youth. Through community service projects, motivational rewards, exposure to college, on-the-job skills building, job opportunities, mentoring support services, and other programs, the Commonwealth can interact with youth at critical stages in their development. Much of the funding for these activities is supported by federal and state job-training revenue.

Race, School Reform, and Black Youth Employment

The expanded Commonwealth, however, did not solve all the problems related to black youth employment. Of the nearly 5,000 students in the 1987 graduating class, only 635 qualified for the program with the prerequisite 95 percent attendance rate and a grade of B or above in both their junior and senior years.[57] Students had a particularly difficult time meeting the attendance standard.[58] The people involved in the program offered two explanations for the continuing challenge of placing the graduates into entry-level employment. Many business elites, in particular, pointed to the inadequacy of the schools. The executives and managers of GBC member corporations continued to complain about the qualifications and caliber of the BCPS graduates. They contended that the students lacked both the hard skills and the soft skills that employers were looking for.

A second explanation was that business leaders, BUILD ministers, and school officials never agreed on a mission for Commonwealth. GBC officials viewed it as a "strategy" by which all those involved could assemble the resources necessary to reform the BCPS. Many corporate leaders saw a stronger school system as a means to fuller employment. Indeed, when negotiations about the components of the Commonwealth were under way, a number of corporate and civic elites expressed this view to Peter Szanton, who was conducting interviews for the *Baltimore 2000* report. According to him, "[Business leaders] wanted the schools to far better prepare Baltimore's young, and especially its poor, for decent jobs. They saw the school system as the only instrument society now has for insuring that young people acquire not merely basic education, but the personal characteristics—self-respect, capacity to work with others, dependability —that employers require and that are not absorbed through family or neighborhood life."[59] GBC officials complained that school administrators never appeared serious about reforming the school system, pointing, for example, to central office administrators' resistance to site-based management. "We had a vision of Commonwealth," recalled a GBC staffer. "The school system never understood; never understood it, or never bothered to embrace it." Consequently, the GBC had difficulty getting its members fully to embrace the Commonwealth.

BUILD, school officials, and OED staffers, perceiving the Commonwealth as a program to extract business resources, in turn pointed to the reluctance of GBC members to hire BCPS graduates. "We have had kids go and interview and what we discover is that often times there is still this mix-match between what businesses want and what the kids have to offer," explained an OED staffer who worked closely with the Commonwealth. Still others believed that employers simply had an aversion to hiring African-American youth. A former high-ranking black school administrator believed race played a factor: "I hate to say this but I think it is racial. The kids still have problems with the GBC. We would send our top kids to the GBC for jobs just to see what would happen. The kids would not get the jobs. They would hire some of the white kids in the suburbs. The people in the decision-making process would blame it on the middle-managers. These are the people I was meeting with. The kids of course never got to talk to the top people." Another black respondent, a school board member who believed that the GBC's initial reluctance to join the Commonwealth resulted from its members' perception that it would largely benefit African-American students, echoed the administrator's assertion: "Racism is not dead in Baltimore," he observed. "GBC does not live and breathe black life. These are black kids we are talking about."

The Commonwealth partnership dissolved in 1993. Although the services created under the project still operate in the OED, the strategic coalition of the GBC, BUILD, school officials, city officials, and other organizations "for all intents and purposes," as one GBC official put it, "doesn't exist anymore." "We're not a larger collaborative that is envisioned by the Commonwealth," explained the GBC staffer. The major educational stakeholders returned to addressing black youth unemployment, working independently.

THE COLLEGEBOUND FOUNDATION

Initial discussions about the Commonwealth concentrated on linking a specified level of attendance and grade point averages with guaranteed job interviews. A major component missing was an initiative to assist graduates who were college-bound.

This oversight was first observed by BUILD.[60] In summer 1986 its leaders sought to remedy this situation, and about a year after the original Commonwealth Agreement was signed, convinced a dozen local colleges (University of Maryland at Baltimore County, Towson University, Goucher College, Johns Hopkins University, and Coppin State College, among others) to set aside financial aid for a group of high school graduates who had earned good grades and had good attendance records. The idea behind these "passport scholarships," as BUILD called them, was to reverse the decline in the number of BCPS graduates who entered college. One year into the program, participating colleges reported that they received more applications from city high schools than in previous years; however, the number of Baltimoreans who actually enrolled did not rise substantially.

One of the problems, organizers conceded, was that BUILD leaders and the students believed the colleges and universities would offer scholarships to cover the full cost of tuition instead of a mixture of loans, work-study jobs, and grants that students would have qualified for anyway because of their socioeconomic status. Moreover, under federal student-aid guidelines, students and their families are expected to pay some of the cost. In many instances, families had to come up with $500 to $1,500 annually to help fill the gaps that financial aid did not cover.[61]

BUILD wanted to reduce (or possibly eliminate) the amount of money families were left to pay for college tuition. In fall 1987 BUILD leaders approached the GBC to persuade corporate leaders to develop a college-assistance program that would help close the financial gap. As a GBC staff member recalled: "BUILD came to GBC and said: Look, we know getting into college is complicated and kids aren't encouraged and they don't think they can go to college. But we know some students who managed to get through that process and then they are short

$500 or $1,000. The families are tapped out; they are already borrowing. If you're so interested in education, put your money where your mouth is and hand out business scholarships."

GBC officials were receptive to BUILD's idea of helping more BCPS graduates continue their education. Increasingly, many of the entry-level positions with promotion potential were jobs that required at least two years of education or training beyond high school. Personnel managers "were seeing students applying for entry-level jobs they now felt needed some post-secondary training. Students were stopping at high school. And there was a feeling—no documentation—that students in Baltimore City were not aspiring to continue with their education," explained another GBC staffer. The employers' perceptions are confirmed by research.[62]

The GBC, however, believed that providing scholarships was only part of the solution. They thought that the students needed to be counseled about the value of going to college and the kinds of courses to take. And students needed hands-on assistance in completing financial-aid forms and college-admission applications. The costs associated with applications and college entrance examinations also created barriers for many students. According to a GBC education staffer, corporate leaders envisioned a program that could address these challenges:

> What you need to do is have people directly in the high schools. They need to tell them why they need to go to college; what courses they need to take; why they need to stay in school. We were hopeful that as students saw people they knew—siblings, neighbors, cousins—go to college that it would raise the level of expectations both on the part of the staff as well as individual students and their families that it would have some small impact in terms of providing hope.

In May 1988 the GBC formed the CollegeBound Foundation. GBC leaders initially proposed establishing an endowment as a way to avoid annual fund-raising and to cut down on the expenses associated with such campaigns. In June the local Abell Foundation challenged the corporate community to put up the money to build the endowment and donated the initial $4 million. By the end of summer the GBC had garnered pledges totaling $25 million. By 1990 approximately $13 million was actually raised. Forming CollegeBound as a 501-C(3) nonprofit foundation gave business leaders complete control of the program, establishing organizational independence from the public sector. Many of CollegeBound Foundation's board members are prominent business executives, and Mayor Schmoke and the school superintendent are ex-officio members.

CollegeBound works with students to encourage them to take the SATs. Counselors help students fill out complicated financial-aid forms and assist in college selection. The program attempts to make students and parents more aware of the financial support available for college, thereby increasing the number of high school students who apply, enroll, attend, and graduate from four-year colleges. Paid advisers (supported by the foundation) go into the high schools to help students learn of scholarship opportunities and to assist them with the often over-whelming application process. During the school year, CollegeBound advisers make group presentations to thousands of high school students and conduct more than 2,500 one-on-one sessions to discuss college options, course requirements, SAT registration, and financial-aid applications.

CollegeBound awards deserving students with financial aid to attend college through its "last-dollar grants." The GBC provides "last dollar scholarships" (averaging about $1,200) to help students bridge the gap between conventional financial-aid sources, such as scholarships and school loans, and their own re-sources. CollegeBound also helps students pay college admission application fees and the fees associated with standardized tests. In summer 1989, eighteen students received last-dollar grants; by 1995 there were 186 students receiving them, each averaging about $1,280.[63]

The strength of CollegeBound, business leaders argue, is not measured in these figures. Instead, the effectiveness of the program can be seen in the increasing number of students applying for financial aid and college admission and leverag-ing the resources to which they are entitled. One evaluation of CollegeBound estimated that counselors reached over 10,000 BCPS high school students through presentations about college options. High school seniors counseled by the pro-gram's advisers were three times more likely to attend college and continue through to the end of their freshman year than those seniors who did not engage in its activities.[64] Significantly, CollegeBound had its greatest impact on students in BCPS' "zone" or neighborhood high schools (the vast majority of CollegeBound youths attend zone schools) who accessed the program's activities.[65]

In an urban setting like Baltimore, where regular employees often view out-siders with suspicion and hostility, CollegeBound staffers underwent a period of initiation and testing.[66] School-based staff harbored "an understandable skepti-cism about the perseverance" of the CollegeBound program. Principals and BCPS guidance counselors questioned the corporate community's commitment, express-ing their concern to outside evaluators of the program in 1995.

All too frequently, explained these informants, programs parachute in, promise the moon, fail to deliver, and then pick up stakes and leave. The hopes of staff are raised, then dashed. As a safeguard against further disappointment, the scar tissue of cynicism builds up. The expectations of administration and guidance counselors become progressively diminished, so the next time an [outside] agency arrives with an offer of help, the response is likely to be indifference or even hostility.[67]

Another obstacle that CollegeBound and school employees had to confront was the concern of regular school counselors about their job security. When CollegeBound began placing advisers in high schools, guidance departments were already beginning to show evidence of a siege mentality. If site-based management were to be fully adopted, for example, principals would be given increased flexibility in personnel matters. If CollegeBound advisers were doing the work of regular school counselors, then principals could eliminate those slots, hiring regular academic staff in their place. Given Baltimore's national reputation as a laboratory for school privatization schemes, it is no surprise that some BCPS employees harbored suspicions that CollegeBound's offer of help operated as part of a strategy to expand private management of school functions.

And these suspicions were exacerbated by the history of racial mistrust that existed between the largely white corporate sector and the predominantly African-American school administrators, principals, guidance counselors, and other school-based employees. CollegeBound has had to navigate these challenges in many (though not all) of the city's high schools.

Despite rapid growth of the CollegeBound Foundation's endowment, by 1990 it became clear that Baltimore-area businesses would have difficulty meeting the $25 million pledged, partly because Maryland was hard hit by a series of economic recessions. Moreover, the 1980s and early 1990s witnessed a number of corporate mergers and buy-outs that brought new corporate leaders to Baltimore who had little allegiance to the program. The shrinking corporate leadership pool became front-page news when Alan Hoblitzell, CEO of Maryland National Bank, and Jack Moseley of USF&G resigned. Their companies were among Baltimore's most generous corporate givers. A *Sun* business reporter described the impact of corporate mergers and the recession on local corporate philanthropy:

> Merger mania, which gripped Wall Street in the 1980s, robbed Baltimore of many home-grown companies and the clout their top executives could wield on issues as diverse as fund raising and stadium-building. In their place is a a group of executives who may feel more loyalty to a distant corporate headquarters than to Baltimore. The remaining pool of powerful, home-grown CEOs is so shallow you can see bottom. Meanwhile, the recession has caused many locally based companies to retreat inward, concentrating more on the bottom line and less on community problems.[68]

Consequently, the corporate supporters of CollegeBound were forced to change their funding strategy and to redefine their financial goal. The foundation now holds annual fund-raising drives similar to the campaign that helps fund the Baltimore Symphony Orchestra. Area businesses are asked to make annual donations. In 1997 the foundation's endowment totaled $11 million.

SUMMARY

As collaborative efforts, Commonwealth and CollegeBound require the participation of a network of key institutional players, including members of the corporate community, government leaders, and leaders of groups such as parents, communities, and nonprofit organizations. The participation of civic elites is essential not only in acquiring important financial resources but also for collaboratively designing and supporting programs to help Baltimore's youth overcome some of the barriers they face in the transition from school to work. Programs like the Commonwealth are important to urban school systems because they open for their students channels to the economic mainstream. As William Wilson has observed, such networks are taken for granted in school systems serving middle-class communities, yet they are atypical in households served by inner-city school systems.[69]

The formation of the Baltimore Commonwealth and CollegeBound illustrates the important link among three of our central concepts: black social capital, intergroup social capital, and urban regimes. The interpersonal and institutional forms of black social capital were clearly depicted by BUILD. By the mid-1980s black leaders such as the Reverend Vernon Dobson and the Reverend Douglas Miles, and hundreds of BUILD volunteers, were brought together through a concern for the limited employment opportunities for African-American youth. Because the long history of shared racial experiences serves to bring African-American elites together and to allow them to rally black community support, black social capital no doubt played a role in the creation of the Baltimore Commonwealth and the CollegeBound Foundation.

Yet formation of these programs also illustrates the dilemmas of black social capital. In Baltimore, if people are seeking to address issues of black youth unemployment and attempting to ease high school graduates' transition from school to work, then most likely they are thrown into contact with white corporate leaders. "Uncle Bubba" (as one longtime African-American minister referred to white business leaders) controls the resources. Though BUILD leaders relied on black social capital to organize in opposition to white domination, creating and implementing the Commonwealth and CollegeBound Foundation required their collaboration with the business community. It is likely that such programs would simply not exist had it not been for the cooperation of Baltimore business leaders such as Alan Hoblitzell, James Rouse, and Mathias Devito. The programs suggest the importance of considering social capital within an intergroup context.

Racial tensions and perceptual legacies linked to race can frustrate formation of intergroup social capital among civic elites. The dialogue between the GBC and black community leaders over the Commonwealth was defined in racial terms by many participants and observers. Many African-American leaders believed that businesses were reluctant to join because the program would ostensibly benefit the graduates of the BCPS whose student enrollment was nearly 80 percent African American. Although tremendous progress has been made, America remains largely divided along racial lines. This is true not only among so-called ordinary citizens but also among civic elites. In Baltimore, as in other big cities, it is still relatively uncommon for blacks and whites to mingle on a daily basis. Building networks of trust and civic engagement within an intergroup context requires frequent interaction with individuals beyond one's own social, ethnic, and racial community.[70] The relationship between James Rouse, Mathias Devito, and the Reverend Vernon Dobson, for example, illustrated the effect of weak ties on inter-group social capital. These kinds of relationships, however, are rare in Baltimore. The comment by Alan Hoblitzell is telling: "The Commonwealth created a vehicle by which we could continue to have a dialogue about the school system and other issues in ways that I never would have expected. It's changed the way of thinking of a lot of businesses in the city. And it's been a way to learn about people. It's just not my normal experience to sit down with a black minister and talk about the issues we do."[71]

The mobilization of black social capital in support of mayoral candidate Kurt Schmoke was another significant step toward the formation of the Baltimore Commonwealth and the CollegeBound Foundation. Schmoke's election in 1987 altered the composition of the city's governing regime, opening city hall to black leaders long ignored during former mayor William Donald Schaefer's tenure. BUILD leaders, for example, became central players. Although Mayor Schmoke was not the initiator of the Commonwealth and CollegeBound, he played an important part in pushing the issue of black youth employment and access to college to the top of the local agenda. Schmoke used the visibility and strategic resources of the mayor's office to encourage the formation of intergroup social capital. He was indispensable in helping facilitate cooperation between corporate-sponsored CollegeBound staff and regular school personnel, assuring school-based personnel that their work was essential to its success, and in directing the school superintendent to work with CollegeBound staffers. Social capital, even robust intergroup social capital, is not enough without the votes, political incorporation, and political leadership to back it up and convert it into policy. The election of Mayor Kurt Schmoke and the subsequent inclusion of BUILD ministers and other African-American civic leaders into the governing regime represents the cross-sector elite component of intergroup social capital.

Yet two factors could potentially weaken the level and extent of intergroup social capital devoted to school reform. First, mergers and buyouts leave many companies in the hands of conglomerates based in other cities, altering the level of corporate attachment to Baltimore and decreasing business support of programs designed to improve it. The recent purchase by out-of-state corporations of USF&G, Maryland's largest insurance company, and of Alex Brown, Incorporated, the century-old brokerage firm, both based in Baltimore, suggests that the effects of potential changes in the city's corporate community are still unfolding. The incentives for local corporate engagement are likely to diminish greatly, radically altering social capital among Baltimore's civic elites.

Second, the tradition of black autonomy in the school system might lower the level of elite social capital committed to school reform. Educators and business leaders have always differed over whether to emphasize the acquisition of basic skills or high-order thinking skills. In Baltimore tensions between educators and business leaders are also exacerbated by race. The corporate sector is dominated by white men; the school system is dominated by African Americans. Only three blacks are among the twenty-nine directors of the GBC board.[72] To put it bluntly, the corporate community's heightened involvement in school affairs has led many blacks to believe that the business community is attempting "to control" their school system. Such disagreements and suspicions clearly take a toll on intergroup social capital.

8

The Defeat of Private Management

It's time we put this concept called capitalism to use in our public schools to educate our populace.
– JOHN GOLLE

We have to watch out for people from outside, especially ones with profit motives, coming to the inside trying to do what we have been trying to do.
– THE REVEREND WILLIAM C. CALHOUN

Baltimore gained national attention in 1992 when it awarded Education Alternatives, Incorporated, a five-year contract to operate and manage nine public schools. It was a remarkable break from traditional school reform efforts, even though contracting in public education is not new. Using private companies to provide accounting, construction, legal services, data processing, food service, pupil transportation, and janitorial services is common. But transferring the management of entire schools or school systems to a private corporation is unusual and risky.

Paul Hill has observed that "'contracting out' has recently joined vouchers and outcomes-based programs among the true hot-button issues in public education."[1] Under private management (or contracting out), schools are independent enterprises; parents choose to send or not to send their children there. Private management is also supposed to increase parental involvement, break the political hold special interests have on public schools, improve relations between individual schools and communities, and provide a quality education more efficiently.

The difficulty officials faced in reforming the BCPS had frustrated Mayor Kurt Schmoke, leading him to try a nontraditional and controversial approach. Five years after taking office and seeing little improvement in general school achievement, Schmoke believed that the BCPS could be reformed only by taking what he called "very drastic steps." "What Tesseract [EAI] is going to end up doing," Schmoke argued, "is going to show that public personnel, using private management techniques, can dramatically improve the performance and quality of education in our schools."[2]

Superintendent Walter Amprey believed differently, at first. He heard about EAI while still an associate superintendent in suburban Baltimore County. As he recalled, his initial reaction was, "Gee, that's ridiculous."[3] After the school board, a nine-member body appointed by Schmoke, selected Amprey to be superintendent about a year later, he did an about-face. EAI "appears to be one of the silver bullets of education," he said, becoming one of its strongest supporters.[4]

Black social capital facilitated the cooperation between the city's African-American leadership and African-American parents to end one of the nation's first and largest school privatization experiments. It was instrumental in rallying opposition to a school reform idea believed to be poorly conceived and economically detrimental to the black community. Baltimore was one of the first major U.S. cities to turn over the management of its schools to a private, for-profit corporation; its experience raises doubts about private management of public education in inner-city schools.

EDUCATIONAL ALTERNATIVES, INCORPORATED

In the early 1990s the leading for-profit education business in the United States was Education Alternatives, Incorporated, a publicly traded firm based in Eagan, Minnesota.[5] EAI is the brainchild of John Golle, its chief executive officer. In 1986 Golle, a former salesman for the Xerox Corporation, purchased a company, USA Schools, from Control Data Corporation and changed the name to EAI. (USA Schools was formed by Control Data in the early 1980s to spark business involvement in school reform.)

Golle also gained the exclusive rights of Control Data's philosophy and teaching system known as the Tesseract Way. The Tesseract method relies heavily on computers, individualized educational plans for each student, and major parental involvement. The model also calls for a second adult in each classroom for additional instruction and lower student-teacher ratios. Tesseract encourages students to work together in flexible, free-flowing groups instead of sitting immobile while a teacher lectures. Parents are required to be actively involved in each student's learning plan. If they won't or can't, other adults in the community are recruited as mentors. According to an EAI promotional brochure: "The Tesseract approach focuses on each child to nurture his or her educational needs. The program's practices focus on parental involvement, active learning, Personalized Education Plans for each child and professional development for teachers. Research has proven that personal attention improves confidence, self-esteem and academic performances."[6]

EAI also contracts with Johnson Controls World Services, a company specializing in building maintenance and management, to maintain the schools' physical plants. KPMG Peat Marwick, an international accounting and consulting firm, joins with EAI to manage the finances of the schools. According to EAI, the three companies combine their capabilities to provide educational, managerial, and financial expertise in the management of public schools, like satellite offices benefiting from the resources of a large, multinational corporation.

EAI forms partnerships with schools and school systems. EAI transforms the learning environment for communities in order to improve student performance in a cost effective way. EAI manages schools and provides educational consulting services. EAI enters into contracts with schools or school districts as an advocate and catalyst for change. As partners with the schools, EAI brings additional investments, best practices from business education, and expertise in management disciplines.[7]

Initially, John Golle planned to open a network of private schools. He opened his first Tesseract school in 1987 in Eagan, Minnesota; a year later, a second opened in Paradise Valley, Arizona. By that point, however, he realized that building a network of private schools would take more money than he could raise, so he decided to go after the public school market.

In 1990 EAI won a consultant contract to implement Tesseract at South Pointe, a new elementary school in Dade County (Miami), Florida, that opened in 1991. Dade County became one of the nation's first school districts to contract out the instructional services of a public school to a private corporation. However, EAI did not operate or manage South Pointe; the contract stipulated that Dade County would continue to operate the school and control most of its $2.3 million budget. EAI's task was to introduce the Tesseract method into the school and to train teachers. As one Dade County school official stressed, "We use the Tesseract model . . . as far as teaching is concerned, but EAI does not have anything to do with any part of the school administration."[8]

EAI agreed to cover the additional costs incurred in implementing its instructional model, including computers, teacher training, and the salaries of the student teachers from the University of Miami, and in turn received a $1.2 million fee.[9] No profit for it was built into the contract; Golle saw the experience as "a way to buy ourselves into the public schools."[10] The Dade County deal made a name for EAI.

SEARCH FOR NEW REFORM

The move to bring EAI to Baltimore was initiated by Mayor Schmoke and Robert Embry of the Abell Foundation. In summer 1990, Embry contacted John Golle, after reading about EAI in a national newspaper.[11] Golle visited Baltimore and sold the idea to Embry, who later informed Schmoke about EAI. Sometime during the 1990–1991 school year, Golle invited Superintendent Richard Hunter to visit the Tesseract school in Minnesota "to see for himself how EAI's Tesseract program was working."[12]

During this period, Hunter was locked in a public battle with Mayor Schmoke, fighting to keep his job, and could not go to Minnesota. In March 1991 Hunter dispatched BCPS' director of Elementary Schools, Charlene Cooper-Boston, and two other school officials to Eagan; they were joined by BTU president Irene Dandridge. The Abell Foundation sponsored the group's trip, which gave the officials several days of concentrated observation. Group members sat in on classes and interviewed teachers, parents, and students.

Two months later, the delegation appeared before the school board to report on its visit. Dandridge told members she was "impressed with the program . . . and asked the board's permission to look at what they can come up with as a proposal."[13] "The Tesseract school would seem to do all the things unions are against," she added. "But we can't be [against it] because the end results are good for kids." Dandridge said the BTU would approve the waivers of union rules that would be necessary for such a project. Cooper-Boston added that the Tesseract school was a fine example of quality instruction: "We were impressed with the school and their basic philosophy that truly focuses on meeting the individual needs of each child. The environment was more interactive. The staff was trained to get the most from the child and the children seemed to feel better because they were in direct control of their own learning capabilities. Plus, the parents are required to actively participate."[14]

Deputy Superintendent Edward Andrews, however, advised board members that it would be "illegal to turn over a public school to a private sector" firm.[15] EAI could either be contracted to run some of the city schools or work as a consultant for the school system. The school board voted to investigate the possibility of contracting with EAI.

Meanwhile, Mayor Schmoke played a critical behind-the-scenes role. Because of the great publicity spawned by his visible struggle with Hunter, Schmoke decided, as a reporter described it, "to put EAI on the back burner for a short period of time until Hunter was cleared out of the way." When Walter Amprey replaced Hunter in August 1991, Schmoke informed Amprey that "among other things that are left over for decision-making is this question of whether Baltimore is going to contract with EAI." Schmoke recalled telling Amprey, "It's your call."[16]

Other sources offer a more complex scenario, one that is more explicit about the political realities of Baltimore. According to a respondent close to the EAI discussion, "Mostly Embry and Schmoke ran [the EAI decision]. When Amprey came on board . . . Schmoke sat him down and said, this is what we are going to be doing. The superintendent probably was told when he was hired—'this is the way things are going to be and if you don't like it maybe you should look elsewhere for a job.' There was a problem with Hunter and Schmoke along those lines. Hunter thought he was in charge."

Schmoke's manner of operating is perhaps less blunt than the respondent suggests, but his dismissal of Richard Hunter indicates that the mayor set policy priorities and expected the superintendent to follow through on them. Amprey, as an experienced and sophisticated observer of Baltimore politics, probably did not need a great deal of direct instruction, and he did change his tune on EAI rather abruptly. Moreover, he seemed quite comfortable with the mayor's leadership in education. As he told reporters a few years later, "What we have here is an almost perfect way of doing things. The mayor calls the shots on the major issues, which he should. I work for him."[17]

In spring 1992 top school officials, including Superintendent Amprey, and three union officials—Sheila Kolman, president of PSASA; Irene Dandridge; and Loretta Johnson, the longtime leader of the school system's paraprofessionals (or teachers' aides) and a vice-president of BTU—visited South Pointe Elementary School in Miami (then the only public school using the Tesseract model). Again, the Abell Foundation paid for the trip.

By all accounts, the Baltimore delegation considered the visit to the Miami EAI school a success. "What we saw in Miami we were very impressed with," explained a BTU official. "We talked to our counterparts in Miami, Dade Teachers' Union, and they were happy with it," she added. Kolman told reporters that she saw "children who are engaged in learning, children who seem to like learning, a wide array of resources, and one positive after another. I don't think children can lose from this."[18] A central office administrator who made the trip corroborated the union leaders' enthusiasm: "I found everything that research says we should be doing not only in place, but in place consistently. . . . So we are riding back in the van and of course, Irene [Dandridge] just loved it. And Loretta [Johnson] was saying 'Oh, how great this is.' Everything was just fine."

By spring 1992 it appeared that several influential education players—the mayor, the new school superintendent, union officials, and the president of the Abell Foundation—were willing to experiment with private management in Baltimore. Cooperation and agreement existed, at least for awhile.

Community Controversy

In early June 1992 Superintendent Amprey announced that school officials had signed a letter of intent with EAI to operate and manage nine BCPS schools.[19] Predictably, the announcement received mixed reaction and generated considerable controversy. Linda Prudente, a spokesperson for the BTU, reiterated the unions' support of EAI, declaring that its leaders were "enthusiastic" about the experiment.[20] The Greater Baltimore Committee, long an advocate of business-management techniques in the operation of the BCPS, supported private management. Business leaders naturally liked the idea of having a business corporation operating schools. *The Sun,* an important molder of elite opinion, applauded Schmoke and Amprey for "being willing to try this new approach."[21] The newspaper carried a front-page story touting the success of EAI at South Pointe, although the Tesseract model had been in place just over a year, and no evaluation had been conducted.[22]

Leaders of BUILD and the Interdenominational Ministerial Alliance, however, asserted that EAI's major concern was not education but profit. Arnold "Arnie" Graf, regional director of BUILD's parent organization, Industrial Areas Foundation, questioned whether privatization was the remedy for the BCPS' problems. "The bottom line in a money-making venture is profit," he asserted.[23] "This is a dangerous road for us to take," said the Reverend William Calhoun, president of IMA.[24] Typically supportive of the Schmoke administration's school reform initiatives, BUILD and IMA became obdurate opponents of the privatization experiment.

Race, Jobs, Politics, and Private Management

The day before city officials were scheduled to approve the EAI contract, BUILD sponsored a public forum to demonstrate its opposition to private management of public schools.[25] With Mayor Schmoke in attendance, over 600 residents crowded into St. Peter Claver Church in the Upton neighborhood, where a real showdown heated up. In a fiery speech, BUILD's cochair, the Reverend Robert Behnke, told the mayor, "We will fight you on this because the whole thing is contrary to public education."[26] Schmoke held firm on his decision to hire EAI, telling the crowd that its demonstrated use of private-management techniques could improve student performance and the quality of education in the BCPS. Schmoke argued that the experiment with EAI was consistent with site-based management, a goal supported by BUILD. Moreover, he suggested that privatization liberated schools from an unwieldy central bureaucracy. Schmoke politely but forcefully told BUILD leaders, "We have different roles. We can't play the same role. We consult . . . but ultimately the responsibility for governing the city is mine."[27] As he recalled in an interview, "I simply said that it is BUILD's job to be an advocate; it is my job to govern."[28]

BUILD and the IMA opposed EAI on philosophical grounds, but underlying worries over jobs, racial control of the BCPS, and BUILD's relationship with city hall fueled their criticism even more.[29] BUILD leaders were concerned about the impact that private management would have on school employees. Despite declining revenues, the school budget was still significant; in 1995 it was over $629 million. With the out-migration of manufacturing jobs and declining employment opportunities in wholesale and retail trade in the city center, the BCPS emerged as a principal employer. Indeed, the public school system was the largest employer in Baltimore City (see Table 8.1). In 1995 the BCPS employed 11,414 workers, compared to the largest private employers, Baltimore Gas and Electric Company, with 8,000 employees, and Johns Hopkins Hospital, with 6,500 workers. As an employer, the BCPS was labor intensive, offering jobs across the entire occupational spectrum.

Table 8.1. Baltimore's Largest Private-Sector Employers, 1995

	Nature of Business	No. of Employees
Baltimore Gas & Electric Company	Electric and gas utility	8,000
Johns Hopkins Hospital	Health care	6,500
Giant Food, Inc.	Retail food/pharmacy	6,139
Bell Atlantic	Telecommunications	6,083
AT&T	Telecommunications	4,000
Nations Bank Corp.	Banking	4,000
Sinai Hospital of Baltimore	Health care	3,001
USF&G Corp.	Insurance	2,287
First Maryland Bancorp	Commercial banking	2,075
Baltimore Sun Co.	Newspaper	1,818
Baltimore City Public Schools		11,414

Source: Greater Baltimore Committee, "Largest Private-Sector Employers in Baltimore Area," Baltimore, 1995.

A racial dimension affected the concerns of many BUILD members as well, primarily because African Americans held over 70 percent of the BCPS' 11,000 jobs. Largely bcause of a diminished industrial base, continued racial discrimination in the private sector, and decades of political patronage, the public schools historically provided an avenue by which African Americans could find employment, and a large sector of the community—particularly the middle class—continues to work in the public schools.[30] Black ministers' concerns about potential job loss are directly linked to the fact that many teachers, principals, administrators, and other personnel are prominent members of their congregations.

Interviews with several African-American ministers, many of them active in BUILD and the IMA, revealed these fears. As one BUILD leader said,

> The fact is that many of our major attractions—civic center, convention center, the Baltimore Arena, . . . operate with employees who are not city employees. Employees now are temporary or part-time, or employees of a contract company. It destroys some of the employment base of the city. Of course, because Tesseract is a move toward privatization of the school system, and as more schools are turned over to Tesseract, Tesseract then has the authority to hire and fire, to reallocate, to reassign employees at will, and that's very threatening to a person. That's their livelihood in the school system.

When asked what BUILD's position would be if a reputable, independent evaluation found that EAI significantly improved student performance in the nine schools, the leader replied, "We'd still be leery of the privatization of a traditional government function." Most of the African-American ministers responded similarly.

Lurking beneath the surface of opposition to EAI was a concern that it meant a shift in racial control of the schools. Although Mayor Schmoke and Superintendent Amprey did not face the vocal opposition from African-American residents that Washington, DC Superintendent Franklin Smith experienced when he sought to promote EAI management of fifteen schools, racial concerns were not absent from the Baltimore case.[31] Given the history of racial politics in the city, especially in local school affairs, the fact that the head of EAI was a white businessman was not lost on many black educators and the larger African-American community. Consider, for instance, the comments of an African-American minister: "I'm against [EAI] because, first of all, it demoralizes and diminishes the talents and effectiveness of teachers that are already present in our school system. . . . Number two, it also says that persons are not quality-equipped to teach and I don't believe that. I don't see some midwestern white corporate firm coming in that knows nothing about our city leading us." Another black respondent, a former teacher and retired administrator in the BCPS, stated emphatically her opposition to EAI in racial terms:

> Walter [Amprey] likes Tesseract. I ain't gonna never want no white folks to come in and run my school system for me, but that's because he and I are different people. He feels good about it, and if he feels good about it, I have to feel good about it for him, not for me. It's helping him achieve his goals. It ain't helping me achieve my goal as a community leader. They ain't gonna put no Tesseract up here in my school, I can tell you that. The school in my community, while I'm president of that neighborhood association, no Tesseract is coming in there, because there's nobody white that can come in there and run my school system with a value system far removed from the people who they serve.

Though race never became a major part of the public debate, John Golle attempted to allay criticism that EAI, whose top executives were white, was profiting at the expense of the African-American community. In 1995, as opposition intensified, EAI hired two African-American executives from the Xerox Corporation and gave them visible roles in the Baltimore experiment. William Goins, a graduate of Morgan State, became the second-in-command at EAI. And Ramon Harris was hired to oversee the day-to-day operation in the city.[32]

Another significant factor influencing BUILD's opposition was the manner in which Mayor Schmoke made the decision to hire EAI. Several African-American leaders expressed surprise over school officials' interest in private management, claiming to have been left out of the discussions. "We all woke up one day and we saw Tesseract was going to be implemented. We were pissed," recalled a Baltimore Urban League official. "And I called the superintendent [and asked him] how in the hell can you implement a program without telling the community."

Leaders of BUILD were deeply troubled. Throughout most of his first term Mayor Schmoke, BUILD, and the IMA had worked closely on the Commonwealth and other education issues. In 1990 BUILD was given further imprimatur when it became the only community group involved in planning site-based management.

However, Schmoke and Amprey moved forward on contracting EAI with virtually no community scrutiny, no debate, and no discussion with BUILD.

For BUILD leaders, Mayor Schmoke's decision to contract with EAI without formally consulting them suggested that he took them for granted. "Tesseract was put into place without any real formal discussion with anyone," an active BUILD minister recalled. Another prominent black minister who was active in BUILD explained that "Tesseract got done behind closed doors. It was not made public until it was made public." Although the GBC was not involved in the decision-making process either, its education liaison, who worked closely with BUILD, contended that those leaders were bothered because they were not a part of the decision-making process: "BUILD has opposed Tesseract. They'll tell you about big bad businesses profiting on the backs of our children and all of that sort of thing. And I think they believe some of that. But their biggest bitch was that they found out the same time we found out that Amprey was committing to a contract that afternoon before it was announced at a 9 A.M. press conference." The Reverend William C. Calhoun was especially bitter, arguing that "we have been to several meetings where there was plenty of opportunity to hold dialogue on the matter. The only thing we've had to go on are the press accounts. They had better not sign that contract until we can sit down and discuss the matter thoroughly."[33]

Schmoke disagreed with this assessment. He reminded BUILD leaders that Irene Dandridge and other BTU leaders had always been aware and supportive of the experiment. In an interview, Schmoke pointed out that he had consulted with the teachers' union:

[The decision] was made in consultation with BTU but not the BUILD leadership. . . . So this was part of our discussion that we had after the decision was made. A major constituent organization of BUILD, which is BTU, was very supportive of Tesseract. The president of the union had been to the schools, knew the corporation that was involved. They were very supportive. . . . The BUILD leadership team was not involved in that loop and so they were upset about that.[34]

Schmoke and Amprey nonetheless calculated that allowing the private-management idea to be debated would have killed the experiment before it got started.[35] "I knew this was the only shot I had," Amprey told a reporter. "I knew we were going to have to put this plane together while we were flying or we weren't going to put it together at all."[36] In an interview, Amprey reiterated that he had to work quietly for EAI to be launched:

It wouldn't get done unless it happened that way. If you really think about it, it wouldn't get done unless it was done by getting people yanked into place [rather] than having people complain about it as it was moving. Anything else becomes just a big football bouncing around. It gets talked about for a few years. . . . It just gets tossed around and beaten to death and made into mush. So you almost are forced to yank an initiative into place.[37]

Not all black leaders and organizations were troubled by the EAI experiment. The Baltimore NAACP, for example, took no official position on Tesseract. The editors of the *Baltimore Afro-American* were also willing to give it a chance. Although expressing concern about EAI's commitment to the school district's Afrocentric curriculum, the editors contended that the Tesseract model was promising. "Based on the past performance of EAI," the paper explained, "we believe this undertaking could be rewarding for the students and certainly, for the company. . . . We applaud this new endeavor because, with the elimination of much of the bureaucracy, the management of the schools may proceed more smoothly."[38]

Such endorsements did little to allay BUILD's concern. The rift generated by the EAI decision altered the way BUILD perceived the mayor and signaled the unraveling of trust and civic engagement between city hall and the black church community.[39] "You get screwed with a smile. That's been our experience," one BUILD minister said of the group's relationship with city hall, clearly expressing the difficulty leaders had in adjusting to Schmoke's firmness. As one BUILD volunteer recalled, "After that incident, the relationship [between Schmoke and BUILD] changed. We were meeting every three weeks—afterwards we didn't meet for two or three months." The stocks of social capital built up between Mayor Schmoke and the black clergy since his election in 1987 appeared to be near default.

The EAI Contract

School and city officials quickly crafted a contract agreement to implement Tesseract by the opening of the 1992–1993 school year. Led by Deputy Superintendent Patsy Blackshear, a team of top school administrators negotiated with EAI officials. John Golle promised school officials that EAI would improve student performance without spending more money than the school system spent per pupil. Hence, for the 1992–1993 school year the contract was worth $26.7 million. School officials arrived at this figure primarily because Golle insisted that EAI receive the systemwide average cost per pupil of $5,549 for each of the 4,815 students projected to attend the nine schools (one middle school and eight elementary schools) during the school year (see Table 8.2). EAI's profits were to come from what was left in the operating account after paying salaries, operating schools, and accounting for start-up investments like facilities improvement, equipment, and teacher training. The five-year contract could be terminated by school officials at any time with a ninety days' notice.

Unlike the arrangement in Dade County, in Baltimore officials contracted with EAI to manage and operate the schools. Under the terms of the contract, the school system retained authority over the assignment of all professional staff, although

Table 8.2. Demographics of EAI Schools, 1993–1994

	Total Enrollment	Mobility Percentage	Percentage Chapter 1	Percentage Free Lunch
Dr. Raynor Browne Elementary	387	54.5%	75.0%	96.2%
Mildred D. Monroe Elementary	272	41.5	50.6	85.8
Harlem Park Elementary	619	49.4	73.1	95.0
Malcolm X Elementary	388	37.4	67.7	93.4
Edgewood Elementary	526	37.5	35.3	80.3
Sarah M. Roach Elementary	439	29.2	28.4	75.0
Mary E. Rodman Elementary	731	18.1	38.9	76.6
Graceland Park–O'Donnell Heights Elementary	381	37.6	70.8	86.1
Harlem Park Middle School	1,251	40.0	n/a	95.4

Source: Maryland State Department of Education, 1994.

EAI could recommend their selection, assignment, and transfer and set final staffing levels. The contract required that EAI abide by the collective bargaining agreements between the city and the unions representing employees. EAI could, however, hire its own paraprofessionals and transfer those employed by the BCPS. Inexplicably, the contract did not set performance standards. It mandated school officials and EAI to "agree to meet and agree" on evaluation and performance criteria for the 1992–1993 school year "as soon as possible" and to meet thirty days prior to each succeeding year to agree on performance criteria for the coming school year.[40]

The contract also specified that EAI, in consultation with each student's parents, prepare a Personal Education Plan (PEP) for each child, since a major component of Tesseract was that students, staff, parents, and the community work, learn, and share together. Periodic surveys to measure parental satisfaction with each school were also required. And the contract included a provision allowing EAI to use the school buildings and other facilities for community activities, including but not limited to preschool, before- and after-school day care, weekend day care, adult education, and community programs.

Subsequent analyses by different observers have criticized school officials' handling of the EAI agreement. Judson Porter, the school system's finance director at the time (he was later demoted), described the contract process with EAI as curious:

I think I was the only financial person who even tried to negotiate anything. It was clear it was an initiative the superintendent wanted to proceed with and negotiations really weren't what you would call hard-bargaining. [The school system] could have gotten a much better deal simply because EAI wanted to get its foot in the door. We were in a position of strength and didn't exercise it. . . . It is really an inverted contract. I've never seen anything like it. It's really strange: You don't put it out to bid; you don't negotiate the best price you can possibly get.[41]

Lois Williams and Lawrence Leak, who conducted the only independent evaluation of EAI in Baltimore, maintained that "beginning a new program without a planning year for the schools was a serious mistake." EAI officials did request a year for planning, but Schmoke and Amprey sought a quick and flashy way to transform urban schools and forged ahead. School officials moved too quickly, "launching a project of a scale and complexity far beyond [EAI's] previous experience."[42] In their painstaking analysis of the contract's budget allowances, other researchers found that BCPS officials could have saved money by using alternative methods for calculating EAI's per pupil allocation. They also faulted city officials for not including accountability and performance standards in the contract.[43]

Schmoke Overrules the Opposition

Financial matters of any importance in city government (contracts, salaries, levying of city taxes, and so on) must come before the Board of Estimates, which is responsible for formulating, determining, and executing the fiscal policy of the city. No municipal department can spend more than $300 without its approval. The EAI contract therefore had to be reviewed.[44] Although the city council president presides over the Board of Estimates and the city comptroller is also a member, the five-member board is dominated by the mayor and his two appointees. Thus, in Baltimore's strong-mayor system, the outcome of the EAI vote was already determined. Nevertheless, in an emotional three-hour debate, critics of the contract used the Board of Estimates publicly to voice concerns about the efficacy of the Tesseract program.

City council president Mary Pat Clarke was the most outspoken local politician to oppose EAI. She argued that the nine schools, in effect, would receive more per pupil funding than other schools in the city. Clarke contended that the calculation for the systemwide "average" of $5,549 per pupil allocated to EAI included high schools and special education services, which cost more to operate than regular elementary schools. Under the proposed contract, she argued, the Tesseract schools would have an unfair financial advantage over other schools. "Give every school the same amount that EAI will get and we will show you that we can beat a Tesseract at its own game," she insisted.[45] Clarke also complained that the contract failed to specify the performance standards EAI would have to meet. The criteria for evaluating the experiment were unclear, she contended, and she voted against granting EAI the contract.

City Comptroller Jacqueline McLean, one of three elected officials on the Board of Estimates, expressed concern about EAI's financial stability. "There are too many questions financially that I would like to have answered before we move ahead," she said.[46] She had obtained unofficial reports about EAI's investment in high-risk derivatives and its use of "unethical" accounting methods to inflate the price of its stock.[47] As the city's chief elected fiscal officer, McLean worried that EAI could encounter financial difficulties that might hamper its ability to fulfill the contract. She also contended that EAI's noncompetitive contract violated the city's minority set-aside ordinance guaranteeing a share of city business to companies owned by minorities and women, an ordinance she had spearheaded while a member of the city council. Moreover, she questioned the wisdom of launching such a massive project so suddenly. McLean joined Clark in voting against the EAI contract.

BTU's Irene Dandridge, who initially had backed the project, argued that the city was moving too fast. "I do not think we have the support of the public because we have rushed it," she told members of the Board of Estimates. She also contended that the language of the contract was "very, very loose."[48] She expressed concern about the fate of the paraprofessionals and other nonprofessional employees not specifically protected in the contract. Although it prohibited EAI from firing teachers or transferring them involuntarily, no such protection was given to the teachers' aides. Those concerns were echoed by leaders of the City Union of Baltimore, Local 44 of the American Federation of State, County, and Municipal Employees, and several unions representing city employees.

Although most of the significant decisions made in city government came before the Board of Estimates, it was created primarily as a sunshine panel, giving all sides an opportunity officially to air their views on the city's fiscal policy. Ultimately, policy is the mayor's decision. Schmoke promised to follow up on the concerns raised by others, but he announced that he was "convinced that the adoption of Tesseract will be in the best interest of the children of the city."[49] The mayor and his two appointees subsequently voted for the contract, which was approved by 3 to 2.

Parental Reaction

Implementing Tesseract was smooth, initially. Parents, teachers, and students praised EAI for transforming the schools' physical environment. The nine schools underwent extensive renovations: the buildings were painted, new carpeting installed, broken window panes replaced, leaky faucets fixed, broken toilets repaired, and rubble-strewn schoolyards cleaned and landscaped. Teachers and principals were pleased with the additional resources EAI provided: bright new tables and chairs in each classroom, a telephone on each teacher's desk, and a working photocopier in each school.

Many parents were excited about the personal education plans and the prospect of more individualized attention for their children; with a second adult promised in each classroom it could be realized. "I like the idea that students aren't only taught at their own grade level but are allowed to advance at their own pace," remarked a parent. And parents, teachers, and principals were pleased that their schools received many more computers, even though they arrived nearly six months into the school year. Indeed, EAI's harshest critics credited it with providing access to computer technology. A spokesperson for the teachers' union observed that EAI "has been able to bring in a multitude of technology. There are computers now in almost every classroom. They have computer labs. I mean that's resources that Baltimore City could not provide. So, when you ask teachers in those schools what they like about the Tesseract program, that's their response—more technology and more supplies."

Although many parents appeared willing to give EAI a chance, the more active parents (especially those involved in PTA) were annoyed that school officials had not informed them about plans to hire the company. The PTA president at Sarah Roach Elementary School was angered at the pace of change. "Parents aren't sure what Tesseract is all about, but the school district seems to be forcing it on us."[50] An officer of the City-Wide PTA complained that "this all happened too fast. There was confusion, secrecy, and lack of communication. The parents, who are supposed to be such an important part of this Tesseract process, felt left out. I think a lot of this could have been avoided if they had delayed implementation by six months or a year."[51] The president of Rayner Brown Elementary School questioned the school system's wisdom in going beyond local officials: "I think we could do it ourselves, instead of hiring a private firm to come," she told reporters.[52] A parent active in the City-Wide PTA criticized the volume of education programs and experiments under way in the schools: "My concern here is that you have all these programs. We had some problems last year with Tesseract. The choice was made before it got down to the parents. I personally feel that our students are being used in many ways as guinea pigs, because we have a lot of programs that have been brought into the city: Tesseract, Enterprise Schools, Sylvan Learning, [and] Calvert."

EAI began encountering problems at the beginning of the school year, when it instituted two cost-savings policies that angered some parents. First, it transferred ninety teachers' aides—people who lived nearby and were among the few who held jobs in those neighborhoods—from the Tesseract schools and replaced them with less experienced, and less costly, recent college graduates (many of them from outside Baltimore).

The practice of having neighborhood people work as teachers' aides is a holdover from the 1960s when Mayor Thomas D'Alesandro, looking for ways to expand his support among African-American voters, began using federal Title I monies to hire people from the surrounding communities to work in the classrooms. Over the past thirty years, the program provided thousands of jobs and brought the schools closer to the neighborhoods.[53] Parent activists supported the practice, considering the teachers' aides a trusted part of the school community that could not be replaced by the new interns. "We really haven't seen them do anything but bring some new teachers' interns in and get rid of our aides. I think the parents were mad about that," recalled the co-president of Graceland Elementary School's PTA.[54] EAI officials argued that the interns, all of whom were college graduates, were better qualified than the unionized teachers' aides, who could not be dismissed, according to the contract.

EAI officials quickly lost the support of parents with learning-disabled children in their second cost-saving measure: the reassignment of special-needs students to regular classrooms. The students' placements were made without parental consent. Staffing reports showed that half the special education teachers were removed from Harlem Park Middle School by the 1993–1994 school year. By the second contract year, the reassignment of special education students allowed EAI to cut fifteen of thirty teachers. These two actions, transferring the paraprofessionals and mainstreaming the students with learning disabilities, led many parents to question whether EAI had the best interests of the students at heart.

Union Opposition

Although its president, Irene Dandridge, had initially endorsed the EAI experiment, BTU changed course before the ink dried on the contract, becoming perhaps the most organized, vociferous, and determined opponent of Tesseract. Why the sudden conversion? First, BUILD leaders pulled the union in line after its officials supported EAI without prior approval, especially from the ministers. Some local observers believed Dandridge's endorsement of the experiment was simply the manifestation of a rift between BTU and the BUILD leadership. BUILD quickly repaired the rift by convincing the union's leadership that EAI was not in the school system's, or the black community's, best interest.

Second, BTU officers grew concerned about the long-term job security of its members. The episode concerning the teachers' aides, combined with EAI's earlier decision to reassign union custodians from the nine schools and replace them with nonunion janitors, convinced union officers that the firm's strategy was to save money and make a profit by replacing relatively expensive union members with less costly nonunion personnel. The BTU also questioned the wisdom of replacing experienced teacher's aides with college interns who were willing to work for less money and no health benefits. Loretta Johnson, vice-president of BTU, charged that "what [EAI] wanted to do was bring in these interns, whose job description was the same, give them lower pay, and that's how they would make their profit."[55]

The teachers' union objected and filed a grievance, claiming that the teachers' aides should not be transferred and should get their positions back from the interns. In protest, hundreds of teachers picketed city hall and boycotted training sessions introducing them to Tesseract's teaching methods.[56] Mayor Schmoke eventually had to step in to negotiate an agreement that left some union aides in the nine schools (some EAI classrooms then had three aides) and found jobs elsewhere in the school system for the rest. The compromise also affected the budgets of schools not involved in the experiment as they were forced to use paraprofessionals who transferred from EAI schools.

The BTU's battle with EAI, Superintendent Amprey, and Mayor Schmoke intensified. The union filed a lawsuit claiming that the contractual agreement with EAI violated the city charter because it had been approved without competitive bidding and without considering the city's minority set-aside provisions. The BTU organized numerous protest marches on city hall and the school headquarters.[57] It encouraged its parent organization, the American Federation of Teachers, to launch a nationwide effort to discredit EAI.[58] When Amprey announced that he was considering the expansion of Tesseract to three more schools, Dandridge called for his resignation. "We believe Dr. Amprey has just gone absolutely crazy with this whole idea of privatization," she declared.[59] Indeed, the teachers' opposition escalated into a bitter and oftentimes personal contention with Superintendent Amprey, who was closely identified with the experiment.

In the only independent evaluation of EAI in Baltimore, Williams and Leak stressed "the importance of securing the support of a school's faculty in the initiation of any program of change." As they observed, "It is difficult for any program of school reform to be successful without the full support of teachers."[60] In an interview, a spokesperson for BTU echoed this observation:

> If we can't sell it to the teachers, it's not going to be sold anywhere else. Those are the people that have to implement it. If they don't buy into the program, it's not going anywhere, and that's what we have tried to stress to the superintendent, to the business community, [Robert] Embry, what have you. If you don't get the support of the teachers, it's not going to succeed, because those are the front-line troops. Those are the people who have to carry it out. If those people don't buy into it, if they don't understand it, if they're not willing partners, then you're not going to have a successful program.

By filing a grievance and a lawsuit, the BTU launched an aggressive and ultimately successful campaign to kill the private-management experiment. As a vocal and well-organized group, the union was able to keep their battle over Tesseract in the news and force community leaders to take a position on the experiment, thus, with its allies, expanding the scope of the conflict.

City Politics

The Baltimore City Council has relatively few powers, with little formal authority and virtually no policy-setting role in education. In school affairs, the council's role is more one of oversight and of monitoring school officials and education policy. However, city council members can apply public pressure to persuade the mayor and superintendent to change policies they deem detrimental to a particular constituent group.

Parents, teachers, and other education activists turn to council members when a school policy is proposed that they believe would adversely affect their children, schools, programs, or jobs.[61] Parents, for example, have persuaded city councillors to see to it that their children are assigned into or out of a particular attendance zone. And Barclay parents and supporters of the Stadium School certainly lobbied city councillors to support their cause. "At some of the comprehensive schools," an education reporter observes, "no public function occurs without the council members from the district being invited; no call from those council members [to a principal] goes unreturned for long."[62] According to a central office administrator, "Everyone is so paranoid in education they always have political allies. . . . The union folks have worked through their political allies. Many are members of the [city] council." In school affairs, members of the city council provide constituent service to parents, teachers, and other educational stakeholders just as they would in other municipal matters. As their campaign to derail the private management experiment intensified, the BTU and other opponents of EAI turned to the city council. In Mary Pat Clarke they found a willing and visible leader to crusade against Tesseract.

Mary Pat Clarke emerged from the neighborhood activism of the 1960s and 1970s. A white liberal, she rose to political office campaigning as a grassroots activist and forming partnerships with black candidates. She won a seat on the city council in 1975, representing a racially mixed district on the city's east side, and was reelected in 1979. Determined to move up, she ran unsuccessfully for council president in 1983, losing to Clarence "Du" Burns. In 1987, after Burns had ascended to the mayor's office, Clarke won the vacant presidency, defeating two candidates and demonstrating her citywide appeal.

As council president, Clarke built upon and strengthened her reputation as being responsive to constituents' needs.[63] A self-styled populist, she cultivated a solid rapport with voters, constantly appearing in the neighborhoods, hugging children, scribbling down problems on her note pad, marching with church organizations, and pushing city bureaucracy into motion. During her nearly two decades on the council, she was known as an independent and tireless champion of community causes. Her independence and populist bent, however, earned her the enmity of the corporate and political establishment, especially when she opposed the development of Harborplace, the festival marketplace and centerpiece of the downtown Inner Harbor.

During her eight years as city council president, Clarke positioned herself as the leader of the anti-Schmoke wing of the nineteen-member council. When the mayor proposed a policy, Mary Pat Clarke was likely to oppose it. "A lot of times she will take a position opposite of the mayor just to show that there's a difference between her and the mayor and it could be anything," explained a BTU official. A city council member who served with her echoed these sentiments, maintaining that Clarke found it politically expedient to oppose Schmoke:

Mary Pat Clarke, as far as I'm concerned, is what's wrong with populism. She's in the position as president of city council where she has absolutely no responsibility, no authority, but she's in a position where she's very visible as a citywide elected official. Now the mayor obviously has a lot of authority, a lot of responsibility, and if things don't go well, he's going to get blamed for it. So, you've got a situation where if the mayor says it's black, Mary Pat's going to say it's white, because she wants to be the mayor. Which is a real nice position to be in, when you don't have to take blame for your positions, and you can always take credit. . . . She opposes everything, I mean, you name it. She's in favor of bizarre things. She'll cherry pick issues that are popular in segments of the community. We had a battle over the budget recently because of Mary Pat. She proposed a five cents tax cut when it was a totally inappropriate time to do it because she knew that the mayor was opposed to it, and because all the taxpayer coalition people would rally around her. She does the same thing with environmental issues, just issue by issue she will do that.

In September 1993, a full two years before election day, Clarke announced that she would challenge Mayor Schmoke in the 1995 Democratic mayoral primary.[64] Clarke's persistent opposition to EAI fueled what local observers viewed as a long-shot campaign. In March 1994 she testified before the school board, reaffirming her complaint that the schools operated by EAI had an unfair advantage because their per pupil funding exceeded that of most other city schools.[65] In May, after Superintendent Amprey announced his intentions to expand EAI's role to at least four more schools, Clarke convened a council hearing to air testimony about EAI's role in Baltimore. Amprey and EAI chairman Golle were asked to explain the funding disparities between Tesseract schools and other city schools. The meeting was attended by over 100 EAI opponents who packed the council chambers, many wearing "NO EAI" buttons.[66] It was a raucous meeting, often interrupted with applause, jeers, and shouts from parents, teachers, and members of several city unions. In the end, a majority of council members voted to urge Mayor Schmoke not to expand EAI to other schools before an outside evaluation was conducted.[67]

The council then passed a charter amendment proposal establishing an Office of Contract Compliance to oversee privatization efforts.[68] If adopted by the council and approved by voters, the amendment would require city officials to demonstrate that the contracting-out of municipal services would result in significant savings. Given the controversy surrounding the Tesseract program, the true intent of the proposal was to stop the trend of contracting-out government operations. Mayor Schmoke vetoed it. In his veto message, he indicated that the bill would establish "a new layer of unnecessary and potentially costly bureaucracy" and "impede the timely and innovative reorganization of city services."[69] Clarke was unable to get the supermajority needed to override the veto.

The city council's activities and the media publicity they generated had an immediate impact. It reenergized the BTU and their allies. Two weeks after the council's public hearing, the union led a protest march from city hall to North Avenue. The rally was attended by over 250 protesters, many of them chanting, "The superintendent must go."[70] Later, in an open letter sent to the school districts' teachers, the superintendent appealed for their support:

> Recent events have made it clear to me that we must communicate with each other more frequently and more openly. All of my life I have been a teacher or a student and sometimes both. You, our teachers, have one of our society's most critical—and criticized—professions. We know we cannot exist or succeed as a school system without you, your skills, and your talents. . . . While arguments about privatization have dominated the news, we must not allow such issues to impede our comprehensive efforts to make the systematic changes we need.[71]

The pressure from the unions and their allies was so great that eventually Amprey was forced to back down. Four days after sending his letter, the superintendent announced that he had abandoned plans to expand EAI's role. "I think there's a message coming from a lot of people in the city that's saying, 'Wait a minute, let's slow down,'" he told reporters.[72]

The End of EAI

EAI's demise became apparent by fall 1994. In June it had reported "dramatic gains" in standardized test scores of students at the Tesseract schools. Then in October 1994, the *Sun* released an analysis challenging the claim, suggesting that EAI had overstated test score gains. The new test data showed that standardized scores rose throughout the school system but declined at schools run by EAI. Initially, EAI officials intimated that someone in the school system's testing office might have sabotaged the results.[73] Golle and Amprey blamed the discrepancies on honest clerical errors, however.

The test scores controversy intensified criticism of the experiment from all sides. The BTU called for an immediate end to the contract. City council members fumed. "This is an outrage," declared Councillor Lawrence Bell. "I think EAI has proceeded under false pretenses. There is a tremendous credibility gap; they have not been forthcoming, and they have misled us," he added. Mary Pat Clarke demanded that Mayor Schmoke end the experiment immediately: "This system cannot afford to squander its credibility and resources on a pilot project to the detriment of the schoolchildren. It seems that the course of action that makes sense is an immediate termination."[74] Even those council members who stopped short of calling for an immediate end to private management expressed reservations about renewing the contract.

Superintendent Amprey, trying to minimize the importance of standardized test scores, argued that EAI critics had placed far too much emphasis on them. Yet with an election year looming, Schmoke was forced to announce that EAI's fate depended primarily on student test scores and the results of an independent evaluation. "Ultimately," he declared, "the success or failure of Tesseract is going to be determined for most people by the academic performance of the children. . . . Our system has been judged for so long by how our kids do on these tests that we cannot ignore the fact that test scores are going to be a significant determinant in the success or failure."[75]

In August 1995 the first outside evaluation of the EAI experiment was completed. The report, conducted by the University of Maryland, Baltimore County, found that the Tesseract schools showed little difference from comparable city-run schools on test results, attendance, parental involvement, or even cleanliness.[76] Three years into the experiment, student scores on the Comprehensive Test of Basic Skills were about the same as in 1992, the year of EAI's arrival, for the Tesseract schools, the control schools, and the city schools as a whole. Significantly, the evaluators found that Baltimore City was spending about 11 percent more (approximately $628) per student in the Tesseract schools than in comparison schools.[77] The report asserted that "the promise that EAI could improve instruction without spending more than Baltimore City was spending on schools has been discredited."[78]

The evaluation was released one month before the Democratic mayoral primary. Despite the controversy, Mayor Schmoke defeated Mary Pat Clarke by a comfortable margin. Notwithstanding his victory, Schmoke criticized EAI but then sought a renegotiated contract. He offered to continue the contract "at a rate 16 percent less than EAI was projected to receive under the average per pupil cost formula."[79] Golle refused. Referring to the evaluation's fiscal analysis, Schmoke then asserted that the city could not afford to keep EAI. Superintendent Amprey told reporters, "We have only so many dollars."[80] EAI's management of the Tesseract schools ended on March 4, 1996, a year and three months short of the original five-year contract.

SUMMARY

Baltimore's experience with private management of public schools illustrates the strength of black social capital. In this instance, the goal of the African-American leadership was to discredit, derail, and ultimately end a school reform initiative perceived to threaten the economic and social fabric of the black community. BUILD, IMA, black parent activists, and the BTU mobilized to end Tesseract.

The BTU's concern over private management is easy to understand: private contractors might hire teachers who were not part of the union and might establish wage and working conditions that threatened existing collective bargaining agreements. Many African-American parent activists were also worried about potential job loss in the black community. EAI's strategy to reduce costs and make a profit was to lower the salary and benefits of support staff: secretaries, food-service workers, and custodians. According to Alex Molnar, "In many instances, these represent an important source of income for the very families that provide stability in their communities and decent home environment for their children. People of color often dominate such job classifications as teacher aide, custodian, and secretary. . . . By signing a contract with EAI or Edison, a school district is in effect assuring a transfer of wealth from minority workers in the community to white investors somewhere else."[81] In short, African-American leaders drew on the city's large endowment of black social capital once EAI was perceived as a threat.

Baltimore's experience with EAI also reveals the dilemmas of black social capital. In this instance, the common bonds, networks, and loyalty within the African-American community established parameters around individual efforts to broaden and promote intergroup social capital. As Clarence N. Stone has argued, "In an intergroup context, the effort of any individual to extend trust and engage in reciprocal considerations is subject to challenge by others who assert *group loyalty* as the pivotal consideration."[82] Superintendent Walter Amprey, hired as a reformer, became the pariah in an intense and sometimes personal battle with opponents of EAI. Moreover, throughout much of Mayor Schmoke's initial four-year term, he and African-American ministers had worked closely on a number of issues, including reforming the BCPS. The trust and loyalty that had developed between BUILD and city hall over the years then came into question. In interviews conducted during the height of the EAI controversy, several BUILD ministers asserted that Mayor Schmoke was not a "dependable" ally. "It's a tentativeness to his being an ally," explained one. Another agreed, adding that Schmoke is "dependable in that he remains true to form. In private he will assure us. In public, he will hesitate. In practice, he will generally side with the business community. He's dependable to say one thing and do something else."

Baltimore's experience with private management, however, illustrates the durability of black social capital. The EAI experiment created a lot of dissension, dividing the city's reform coalition and splitting the black community. Yet these divisions did not deplete or destroy the common bonds, loyalty, or trust among the city's black leadership. Black social capital remained strong, as indicated by the firm support the African-American community, including leaders of BUILD and the BTU, gave Kurt Schmoke in his successful 1995 campaign against challenger Mary Pat Clarke. "Many black political and religious leaders who had not endorsed Schmoke or hadn't shown much enthusiasm for his campaign were pleading the mayor's case to voters, emphasizing that the black community could not relinquish a position that it had worked so hard to get."[83] The result was an unexpectedly large African-American voter turnout and a "stunning" Schmoke victory margin. In sum, the EAI controversy, and the divisions it engendered within the black community, reveals the organic nature of black social capital. Just as picking a flower does not destroy the garden in which it is rooted, dividing a coalition organized around a specific issue does not necessarily imply the erosion or depletion of the underlying social capital.

9
School Reform and the City–State Connection

Soon, the battle lines were drawn, city against suburbs. . . . A Montgomery–P.G. coalition is Baltimore's nightmare. Together, we control forty-six House votes, the city controls only thirty. And together, 1,590,809 people live in Montgomery and P.G.; only 675,401 live in Baltimore City. When united, Maryland's DC suburbs are too big to be ignored, dismissed, or sent to bed with no supper.
– Blair Lee

Maryland and Baltimore leaders have traditionally enjoyed cooperative relations. Maryland has what Daniel Elazar calls an "individualistic" political culture, meaning state government is viewed as a means to respond to public demands, and new programs are initiated mainly in response to vocal support from constituents.[1] Although Maryland's politics may be undergoing significant transition, the state remains Democratic, and Baltimore overwhelmingly so. Hence, the two have a party-based foundation for city–state cooperation.

In the late 1980s, when Baltimore's efforts to implement systemic school reform moved in fits and starts, Maryland's education officials launched an ambitious and aggressive campaign to institutionalize reform at the state level. Although calls for reform were directed at the twenty-four Maryland school districts, state officials focused much more narrowly on Baltimore's. Ultimately, the state's school improvement and accountability program led the city's officials to protest what they considered encroachment on local autonomy, and they challenged the new reforms as unfair for a school system with inadequate resources. These events led to a long and bitter struggle over explosive issues of funding and accountability. In 1997, over the vocal protest of many Baltimore leaders, Maryland officials significantly expanded their authority in the city's schools, curtailing Mayor Schmoke's influence in the BCPS. Underlying this struggle was race, the omnipresent subtext. To contextualize these developments, it is important to begin with a brief synopsis of the political environment in which Maryland's state educational policies are formulated.

STATE EDUCATION POLITICS

School districts are creatures of the state because public education is a state responsibility, mandated by state constitutions. Although the "passion for local control" remains strong in American cities, the rate of state involvement in local school affairs is increasing dramatically. Recent examples include state expansion into education finance, accountability requirements, programs for children with special needs, and local academic standards.[2]

Maryland law assigns broad responsibilities for public education to the Maryland State Board of Education (MSBE), which sets policies and standards for prekindergarten through high school. It exercises general control and supervision over each of the state's twenty-four school systems. MSBE members are appointed by the governor, serve staggered four-year terms, and may serve two full terms. Board members also appoint the state superintendent of schools, who manages and administers the day-to-day operations of the Maryland State Department of Education (MSDE).

During my research, the state board was dominated by members appointed by Gov. William Donald Schaefer, including Robert C. Embry Jr., a trusted associate and friend, who later served as its president. Nancy S. Grasmick, a Baltimore native, was appointed state superintendent in 1991. Reportedly, Grasmick and her husband "were part of a small circle close to Governor Schaefer," and she "assumed the superintendency amid whispers that she got her job because she was politically well-connected."[3] Although the MSDE became a more activist agency under Grasmick's and Embry's leadership, the central players to be examined are the governor and the influential members of the Maryland legislature, not the elites who make education policy a full-time occupation.

SCHOOL PERFORMANCE AND STATE ACCOUNTABILITY

Over 60 percent of the BCPS' budget (approximately $400,000 in 1995) is supported by state funds. By the late 1980s and early 1990s, Maryland education officials, and more than a few state legislators, insisted that school districts provide concrete evidence that the large sums of state funds invested in the schools were actually paying off.

In August 1987 Governor Schaefer asked one of his longtime advisers and a respected Baltimore business leader, Walter Sondheim, to chair the Governor's Commission on School Performance. Examining ways to measure the performance of public schools and developing strategies to improve student achievement were the commission's mandate. Two years later, the Sondheim Commission issued recommendations to establish accountability and to effect school improvement efforts.[4] Principal measures included

- the establishment of a more comprehensive assessment system at the state and local levels to identify excellence, uncover problem areas, and point the way toward improvement;
- the creation of a system that would collect and report student achievement information for schools, school systems, and the entire state;
- replacement of the state's current testing programs;
- the establishment of a statewide school improvement program directed and supported by a high-level unit in the MSDE devoted solely to school improvement;
- direct intervention by state education officials to reconstitute failing schools by suspending local policies found detrimental to improvement efforts.

In 1991, in response to the Sondheim Commission's report, the MSBE adopted the Maryland School Performance Assessment Program, comprising a battery of annual statewide tests given to third-, fifth-, and eight-graders to measure their skills and knowledge in reading, writing, language arts, mathematics, science, and social studies. The tests differ dramatically from standard multiple-choice exams like the California Achievement Test. First, they are not "norm based." That is, they do not measure student performance merely by comparing it to the "norm" established by a designated set of students. Instead, the new tests are "criterion-referenced," measuring students against objective rather than relative standards and determining how well students mastered the skills and knowledge the state has decided are important. MSPAP tests also require students to apply learned skills in ways that demand problem solving, decision making, and reasoning abilities. For example, some math and science items require students to work in small groups to solve problems.

The key feature of MSPAP, however, is not the way it measures student performance. The program is not designed to evaluate individual students but to assess individual schools and to hold them accountable for their teaching performance. The MSDE established standards for school performance using MSPAP tests, dropout rates, yearly promotion rates, and attendance. In addition, officials began examining student completion of entrance requirements established by the University of Maryland System. A school that performs well is one that achieves satisfactory or above on each measure. The MSPAP intentionally holds schools to very high standards, so high that state officials do not expect even top-rated school systems to meet them until the year 2000. Beginning in 1992, the MSDE issued its annual *Maryland School Performance Report* for each school, school system, and the state. The school performance reports—report cards of a sort—reveal which schools are making progress toward achieving satisfactory performance and which are not.

By the early 1990s twenty or more states had adopted takeover laws or intervention procedures for school districts unable or unwilling to adhere to state standards.[5] In July 1995, after school reform efforts failed to raise student performance, New Jersey's Department of Education ousted Newark's elected school board and took control of the school district.[6] In late 1993 Maryland joined New Jersey and the small group of states having intervention policies in schools with low MSPAP performance or lack of progress. The Public School Standards regulation, better known as "reconstitution," allows the MSDE to replace principals and other administrators, directly oversee a school, contract with a private corporation to manage failing schools, or permit other private institutions to operate targeted schools. Targeted schools must develop a school reform plan within three months and submit it to the MSBE for approval or face state intervention.

From the start, Baltimore school officials, teachers' union leaders, school activists, and some parents expressed concern about MSPAP, fearing that BCPS schools would be singled out as underperforming. Parents, clergy, community activists, and city politicians opposed the new assessment program, arguing that Maryland was requiring school improvement without adequate financial support. As one parent explained, "We are not against the testing, but we are against the way the tests [could be] used politically to denigrate the city and to justify withholding of funds from city schools."[7] The Maryland State Teachers Association and the Baltimore Teachers Union denounced reconstitution as a scheme to "turn public schools over to private operators."[8] Publicly, Maryland's local superintendents endorsed the takeover measure, though privately many complained about the state's meddling in local affairs.

MSPAP, however, won the crucial support of Governor Schaefer, who strongly endorsed the idea of putting schools under the control of the state when local authorities did not appear up to the task. A number of key legislators agreed with the MSDE's emphasis on holding schools accountable but cautioned that state takeovers of schools would be expensive.

Baltimore's business leaders welcomed the state's aggressive stand. As early as 1991, the Greater Baltimore Committee recommended "an extraordinary State assumption of the management" of failing schools, believing such action could serve as a wake-up call for the city.[9] One respondent, a Baltimore banker, explained: "Whether [a state takeover] would ever happen is in question, but I certainly think there's a high degree of concern that it could happen. You've got somebody saying you have to measure up on certain basic standards, and if you don't we're going to take some other serious action."

Institutionalizing State-level Reforms

When the reconstitution measure took effect in January 1994, two Baltimore schools, Frederick Douglass High and Patterson High, were the only ones in the state targeted for state intervention.[10] Both schools ranked among Maryland's lowest in the proportion of students meeting MSPAP standards. The threat of state takeover created a firestorm. Parents, students, teachers, elected officials, and community activists mobilized to respond.

At Douglass, whose distinguished alumni included Supreme Court Justice Thurgood Marshall, entertainer Cab Calloway, former congressman Parren Mitchell, and NAACP president Kweisi Mfume, community leaders formed the Save Our School Coalition to prevent the takeover.[11] Mitchell, an organizer and vocal member of the coalition, called the threat an "unfair example of an insidious plot to show that everything that is black-run has a flaw."[12] Mitchell's statement was an ominous sign of the contentious and politically volatile role that race played as state-level officials sought to institutionalize reform in the majority-black school district.

At Patterson, nearly 400 students boycotted classes after Superintendent Walter Amprey announced his negotiations with Hyde School of Maine, a private boarding school that stressed character building and parental involvement, to manage the beleaguered school. Carrying placards reading "NO HYDE FOR PATTERSON. SAVE OUR HIDE," the students threatened to march on city hall. When the founder of the Hyde School appeared at a public hearing in the school auditorium, parents and students reportedly "booed, shouted, and cursed" as he spoke.[13] The proposal was denounced by parents, school activists, and union officials as a thinly veiled attempt to put more city schools in private hands. Amprey was forced to abandon the negotiations, opting for a reconstitution plan that included the removal of Patterson's entire staff, requiring teachers and other staff members to reapply and compete for their jobs, and dividing the school into separate academic and career-preparation programs. The MSDE eventually approved the plan and a similar one for Douglass High.

In January 1995 tensions between Baltimore and state education officials intensified when elementary and middle schools in Maryland came under the reconstitution provisions. Again, only Baltimore schools (Arnett Brown Middle, Calverton Middle, and Furman Templeton Elementary) were targeted. This time, city officials vowed to fight. Superintendent Amprey described the state process of identifying low-achieving schools as "cosmetic and wholly political."[14] Other BCPS administrators maintained that the reconstitution procedure was flawed because it did not take into account such factors as poverty. School administrators questioned how the state could pass judgment on the three schools with so few resources and such disadvantaged students. Calverton, for example, had recently reopened its library after it was closed for two years for lack of resources. At Templeton, 99.7 percent of the 504 students were poor enough to qualify for a free meal. Acknowledging that reform was necessary, Mayor Schmoke contended that Amprey's approach to school improvement was moving the system in the right direction, but he also insisted that the city's major need was more funding.

For nearly two weeks the BCPS resisted a state order to reconstitute the three schools, even barring an MSDE monitoring team from visiting them. Baltimore officials argued that the teachers, administrators, and parents in the schools had already started their own reforms and needed more time to see the results. They viewed the reconstitution process as trampling on the long tradition of local school autonomy. Irene Dandridge of BTU stated the matter bluntly, demanding that state officials "butt out. Let us make our own improvements. I think it's high time that the city rejected the notion that the state knows better how to fix the city's schools."[15]

State education officials refused to "butt out." Between 1994 and 1997, all but two of the fifty-two schools the state designated as reconstitution-eligible were in Baltimore. State Superintendent Nancy Grasmick declared that the public and the legislature were demanding accountability. Poverty was no excuse. "All children can learn" became her standard refrain. Grasmick (and a growing number of Maryland legislators) believed that the large percentage of BCPS' schools targeted for state intervention indicated a problem larger than an individual school. Money, she added, was not necessarily the answer; there were systemic problems.

To Sue or Not to Sue?

Rumors of Baltimore's filing another lawsuit over education funding had circulated since 1986, following BUILD's unsuccessful lobby of state legislators for equitable school funding.[16] Mayor Schmoke had flirted with the idea of a court challenge since his election in 1987. However, as the young mayor of the state's largest city, he reportedly had ambitions eventually to run for governor or for the U.S. Senate. Schmoke considered the courts a last resort, believing a lawsuit would alienate important constituencies outside Baltimore and jeopardize other fiscal requests to the legislature.

In May 1992, however, Schmoke announced that the city would join with the Maryland American Civil Liberties Union (ACLU), taking the state to court over school funding. "We've gone through a number of legislative sessions and we think that we've given enough time for this to be worked out," he declared.[17] "We need some kind of judicial intervention to get some kind of meaningful reform."[18] Schmoke's action was applauded by a number of local groups. Even the editors of the *Sun* acknowledged that "a political solution seems unlikely" and "a legal challenge may be the only way to solve the problem" of the disparity in educational spending.[19] The city hired a respected Washington, DC law firm, which had worked on school funding cases in Kentucky and West Virginia, to develop the city's legal argument.

Several Baltimore legislators, however, criticized the threat of a lawsuit, maintaining that recent legislative sessions had been good to the city, providing a steady increase in state education aid and state assumption of operating costs for a number of institutions, including the zoo, the city jail, and City Community College. Similarly, state officials and legislators outside Baltimore, especially in the suburban counties, questioned the timing of a lawsuit; a Montgomery County legislator called it "a slap in the face."[20] Delegate Timothy Maloney of Prince George's County, who chaired an important education subcommittee of the House Appropriations Committee, sent Schmoke a sharply worded letter recounting the state's efforts to provide financial assistance to Baltimore and urging him to reconsider his decision:

> The timing of this announcement could not have been more unfortunate. . . . Only five weeks earlier, the General Assembly finished work on an extraordinary program of assistance for Baltimore City. Many delegates—from both rural and suburban counties throughout the state—made significant political sacrifices to support the City this session. These relationships are now jeopardized by this suit. . . . It is unrealistic to expect effective cooperation among diverse jurisdictions during the prosecution of this lawsuit.[21]

In 1979, when he was mayor of Baltimore, William Donald Schaefer had unsuccessfully sued the state over the same issue. Governor Schaefer sympathized with Schmoke, agreeing that the cash-strapped city needed more financial support for its schools. Schaefer, however, urged Schmoke not to pursue another lawsuit. The legislature, Schaefer contended, was now much more attuned to the problems of the city. The governor encouraged Baltimore leaders to continue working through the political process to remedy the school funding problems. To move the process along, Schaefer appointed a twenty-two-member commission of legislators and prominent citizens to review Maryland's school funding formula and to recommend changes. He asked the commission, chaired by Donald Hutchinson, president of the Maryland Business Roundtable and later executive director of the GBC, to report back in time for the 1994 legislative session. Schmoke, not sanguine about going to court anyway, agreed to drop the lawsuit, vowing to revisit it should the commission's work, and any subsequent action by the legislature, prove inadequate.

Local education activists questioned Schmoke's change of course, doubting that any significant measures would result from the new commission. "We have had education commission after education commission in Maryland. And I don't really see anything occurring from another one," remarked the president of the Baltimore NAACP.[22] Some likened Schmoke's backtracking on the lawsuit to his protracted decision over the fate of former Superintendent Richard Hunter, concluding that the mayor was too indecisive and cautious. Others questioned whether Schmoke was placing his personal political ambitions above the welfare of the city's schoolchildren; a former school board member noted that he "had been promised by the Mayor that we would vigorously pursue equity funding for Baltimore City through the courts." The board member surmised that Schmoke's ambition to capture a statewide office figured in his decision not to push the lawsuit. "I think the reason they were not prepared [to push the lawsuit] was that the Mayor was contemplating at the time running for state office. I know that and he knew it, and this is why he backed away from it." Disappointed by the mayor's announcement, the board member asked Schmoke not to reappoint him to a second term. In his resignation letter, he expressed his "increasing disenchantment with the intrusive political climate" within the BCPS and deep disappointment "with the political realities that surround decision making in public education in Baltimore City."[23]

Race, Class, and the Politics of School Funding

The Governor's Commission on School Funding, or the Hutchinson Commission, as it came to be known, released its final report in January 1994, just in time for the beginning of the General Assembly session. The commission substantiated Baltimore's claims that the BCPS could not be expected to meet state standards without more resources, and it reached three basic conclusions. First, the single best predictor of school results is the proportion of students living in or near poverty. Second, Baltimore City had the highest percentage of poor students. Third, high poverty schools should be targeted for increased state funding.[24]

The Hutchinson Commission recommended a substantial increase of state funds to the BCPS and other poor school systems for five years, beginning in 1994. Full implementation of the recommendations would increase state aid to education by an additional $571 million over the funding formula in place in 1994, amounting to an accumulated five-year rise in overall state spending, totaling approximately $1.2 billion, and at least $500 million (over five years) in additional state support for the BCPS.

The commission's funding proposal received a cold reception in the legislature. Opponents contended that it was too costly and would require legislators to approve a major tax increase during an election year. Many legislators complained that the commission did not incorporate any strong accountability standards into its funding scheme. With a sizable proportion of the proposed aid directed to Baltimore and growing sentiment in the legislature that more state oversight of the BCPS was necessary, the report's recommendations were pronounced "dead on arrival."

The most vociferous critics of the proposal were legislators and leaders from Montgomery County. In the past, Montgomery had supported Baltimore on a number of critical social and educational programs for a variety of parochial and politically expedient reasons. But fundamentally, its support was based primarily on the liberal-to-moderate political philosophy of an electorate with a substantial population of federal and other government employees.[25] This philosophy recognizes the positive role of government and its special responsibility to direct its resources to help people in need, especially in the crisis neighborhoods and schools of inner-city Baltimore.

By the early 1990s, however, the situation had changed. Maryland experienced an economic recession and Montgomery, like other jurisdictions, suffered. A tightening budget has changed the way Montgomery County's leadership thought about education. Citing a growing minority student population (Montgomery schools were 78 percent white in 1980 and 56 percent white in 1995) and a rise in the number of high poverty schools (from six in 1988 to nineteen in 1993), Montgomery officials began accusing state officials of inattention to the county's needs.[26] As one county councilman explained, "It's time Baltimore and the rest of the state saw us for what we are. We are no longer the deep-pocket county. We may still be the economic engine of the state, but unless the rest of the state understands how much we have changed, they could end up killing the goose that laid the golden egg, and then what?"[27]

Montgomery County leaders were skeptical about the goal of the funding commission from its inception, worrying that in his last year in office, Governor Schaefer would alter the state funding formula in a last-ditch effort to shift more money to his favorite city's schools. The editors of the *Silver Spring Gazette,* a popular county daily, noted that "we are among those skeptics who believe that the Governor's Commission on School Funding is a thinly veiled, last gasp by William Donald Schaefer to grab more money for Baltimore City's mismanaged schools from the pockets of Montgomery County taxpayers. . . . In school funding as in every state program, the city is like a spoiled child: It wants the rest of the state to send money, but it wants no oversight, no strings attached."[28]

Legislators from Montgomery County claimed that under the commission's funding plan, their school system would lose state aid that was already projected under the current law. They complained that the proposal would essentially help Baltimore City students at their school system's expense, costing their schools an estimated $21 million in anticipated funding over five years. In an interview, a Montgomery County legislator contended that "the Hutchinson Commission came up with an educational funding reform that would help the city at the expense of Montgomery County. I don't want to play that game. Education funding is the area my constituents care most about and where they get the least of the [state's] money. The Hutchinson Commission targeted our sacred cows." The four Montgomery County representatives on the commission signed a minority report, denouncing the proposal as a costly money grab by Baltimore City:

> Make no mistake about it, the substantive long-term recommendations of the majority are not affordable and necessarily will translate into a major tax increase. . . . The majority would have several school systems lose state aid that is now programmed under current law. Such a policy is totally unacceptable. Education reform cannot mean helping some children at the expense of others. . . . [Moreover] the lack of accountability provisions in the majority report is one of its most glaring weaknesses. We must know by now that throwing money at problems, without programmatic change and accountability standards, is not the answer.[29]

Political leaders from Prince George's County were also opposed to the Hutchinson plan. Although home to many solidly middle-class black neighbor-

hoods and more affluent than Baltimore City, Prince George's is the least affluent of the major Washington, DC suburbs.[30] Enrolling more than 113,500 students,
it contains Maryland's largest school system. With African-American student
enrollment at about 69 percent, Prince George's has the largest concentration of
minority students after Baltimore. In 1995 it also had the second largest number
of students (50,421) receiving free or reduced-price meals. And by 1991the positive image Prince George's schools had received in the 1980s had begun to fade.
A 1993 commission of prominent business leaders concluded that the county's
"schools are failing, our children are falling behind." Between 1990 and 1994
the percent of local residents believing the schools were getting better fell from
46 to 15 percent. When the Hutchinson Commission report was released, Prince
George's leaders "were under fire because of students' poor showing on key performance assessments and crowded schools and limited funds to make improvements in neighborhood schools."[31] In near unanimity, Prince George's political
leaders, including the county's first African-American chief executive, Wayne
Curry, opposed the Hutchinson proposal, believing it would hurt their chances to
get more state aid for their struggling school system.

The Hutchinson Commission's recommendations thus went nowhere. The
struggle at the state level over funding and school reform soon became a sub-
urban/inner-city conflict, laced with a noticeable dose of racial politics. As legislators, business leaders, and other civic leaders from across the state (including a
few in Baltimore) questioned giving more aid to Baltimore schools, especially
without significant state oversight, a number of Baltimore advocates suspected
that the debate was not over funding or reform, but over race. A number of black
and white respondents perceived that legislators' criticism of the BCPS implied
that the black administrators were simply incompetent or that the BCPS students
were unable to achieve.[32] "The major challenge," according to an education funding
advocate, "is getting past this racist attitude that lets people dismiss this problem
as not affecting them. That it's 'those kids' and that's not 'our kids.' It's 'those
kids.'"

Many Baltimore respondents speculated that suburban legislators selected
racially tinged language ("pouring money down a black hole," for example) when
presenting funding and accountability issues, playing on white anxieties and feeding white hostility to increasing state aid to the majority-black city. A white Montgomery County legislator acknowledged that what he called "Baltimore bashing"
played well to many suburban voters. "If I were running against me," he explained,
"I could beat me by Baltimore bashing. The way to beat an incumbent from Montgomery County is to say, 'That sucker has been down there twelve years voting
to send our money to Baltimore City.' All I have to do is bash. It's popularly known
as 'Baltimore bashing.'"

The demographic profile of Maryland's political landscape, the state's history of racial discrimination, and limited state resources allowed the politics of
racial mobilization to take hold, paralyzing state and city leaders' ability to insti-

tutionalize reform at the state level. Yet the opposition of African-American elected officials from suburban Prince George's County demonstrates the complicated role of class and race in Maryland politics and illustrates the potential weakness of that county as a state-level ally of black leaders in Baltimore.

HOWARD "PETE" RAWLINGS AND THE CRESAP STUDY

According to education researchers Catherine Marshall, Douglas Mitchell, and Frederick Wirt, individual legislators who are knowledgeable, who have the respect of the legislature, who can influence budget items, and who "guide the votes of other legislators" are often "powerful enough to make or break education policy."[33] Delegate Howard "Pete" Rawlings fits this description. During the struggle over school reform, accountability, and funding of the BCPS, Rawlings emerged as the central and most influential insider helping craft legislation that ended the stalemate between Baltimore and state officials.

Rawlings, an African American, was elected in 1978 to represent an inner-city Baltimore district. A graduate of Douglass High School, he earned a master's degree in mathematics and later became an instructor and administrator at Baltimore City Community College. In Annapolis, Rawlings earned a reputation as a staunch advocate for the poor and for Baltimore City, battling for equal opportunity for African Americans in state employment, pushing for increased participation of black firms in garnering state contracts, and working to open Maryland's universities and colleges to minority students.[34] In 1992 he worked his way to one of the legislature's most powerful posts, chair of the House of Delegates' Appropriations Committee.

Rawlings was also an advocate for Baltimore schools. Like many of its leaders, he believed that more state funds were necessary to provide the city's children with an adequate education. As chair of an influential budget-writing committee, he was in a position to argue for more financial support for the BCPS. However, when he pressed his colleagues in the legislature, they complained that school officials were already mismanaging millions of state dollars.

Rawlings became committed to ending the impasse. In early 1990 he personally convened a small, confidential group with "firsthand knowledge of the school system" to assess the "organizational culture" of the BCPS. The group found a system lacking a "sense of urgency," "individual initiative," and "teamwork." The BCPS, according to the group, was hampered by "excessive bureaucratic control and influence" and "an unacceptable degree of turf protection." The group concluded that failure to address these matters would "doom the BCPS to another decade of stagnation."[35]

These findings confirmed Rawlings's suspicions about the management of the BCPS and convinced him, as he indicated in a sternly worded letter to Mayor Schmoke, Superintendent Richard Hunter, and the school board, that "the infusion of additional resources and new programs alone will not bring about the long-term positive benefits we all desire. The culture of the administrative organization must be altered."[36]

Rawlings's history of advocacy, his position as chair of an influential funding committee, and his race put him in a unique position to demand more efficient management practices from BCPS administrators. As he put it, "You can't call me a racist. You can't accuse me of not being knowledgeable of city public schools. Because I'm in a position to raise these questions, it peels away some of the issues that cloud the focus." Rawlings became more forceful in insisting that school administrators change their management practices, observing that BCPS leaders "have deluded themselves and convinced others in the community that they are doing a good job."[37]

After complaining that nothing happened to his group's report, in spring 1991 Rawlings asked the Associated Black Charities to commission an independent study of BCPS management. Rawlings believed that a comprehensive examination of school system operations would reveal the possibility of improving the level of student achievement if the system were managed more efficiently. During the 1991–1992 school year, the international management consulting firm, Towers/Perrin/Cresap, conducted an extensive management study of the BCPS.[38] The Cresap Study, undertaken in cooperation with the school board and Superintendent Walter Amprey, proved to be a scathing indictment when it was released in June 1992.[39] It supported Rawlings's and other legislators' contentions that more state money without strong state oversight was a waste of resources.

The report stated that although some individual schools performed quite well and had high staff morale, the overall system was afflicted with a "culture of complacency."[40] It also found that many top administrators were former teachers and principals who "lack technical skills, training and experience in their current capacity."[41] It criticized the school system for using inadequate employee evaluation instruments. "Personal relationships rather than competence, experience, or performance" were found as key factors in determining who received promotions.[42] The practice of hiring maintenance workers and other "non-educational personnel" from lists provided by city hall highlighted another personnel problem where school principals lacked control.[43] The consultants also found that union contracts contained "onerous" provisions severely hampering effective operations.[44] The report uncovered what it called an established "culture" and "entrenched" attitudes in the system that did not encourage "effective management."[45]

The Cresap consultants made 101 recommendations (strongly encouraging implementation of fifty-three) for improving the efficiency and effectiveness of the BCPS. The central recommendation was the implementation of site-based management, recasting the BCPS into a "network of enterprise schools."[46] The report also urged the BCPS to redesign its personnel practices, financial management and budgeting capabilities, and management information systems.

Rawlings used the Cresap Study to aggressively pursue significant management changes in the BCPS. When the legislature convened in January 1993, he attached a provision to the 1994 budget bill requiring that the MSDE and the BCPS enter into a three-year agreement to monitor and evaluate the implementation of the Cresap recommendations. If the city failed to comply, the provision would allow the state to withhold 2 percent of its education allocation. The House of Delegates adopted the provision. Although the final version of the 1994 budget bill removed the withholding provision, it kept the requirement mandating state education officials and BCPS administrators to monitor the implementation of the Cresap recommendations for three years. Superintendent Walter Amprey and State Superintendent Nancy Grasmick selected a third party, MGT of America, to conduct an independent evaluation of BCPS' progress in implementing the Cresap recommendations. Amprey and Grasmick agreed to report back to the legislature.

Meanwhile, in early December 1994 Mayor Schmoke threatened again to take legal action to force the state to provide the BCPS with adequate funding. In announcing the planned lawsuit, Schmoke expressed frustration over efforts to get more state money for the BCPS: "We've rallied, we've lobbied, we've had a governor's commission that essentially confirmed all that we have been saying, which is that targeted investments in low-performance schools make a big difference. . . . We think we have made our case in a lot of different forums, yet we still have this financial disparity."[47]

Five days later, the Maryland chapter of the American Civil Liberties Union filed the case *Bradford v. Maryland State Board of Education* on behalf of parents of students in twelve BCPS schools, claiming they were being denied a fundamental right to an adequate education. As part of its legal strategy, the ACLU planned to show that BCPS schools did not receive enough funding for them to meet the state's new MSPAP standards. This strategy differed from that of the plaintiffs in the 1979 lawsuit, in which the court ruled that disparities in funding alone were not unconstitutional. The *Bradford* suit did not argue that spending was unequal but that the lack of sufficient money denied the children's right to an "adequate" education.[48] Similar lawsuits succeeded in other states, including New Jersey.

Democratic governor Parris Glendening, who took office in January 1995 and was actively supported by Schmoke, asked the mayor to delay the lawsuit. As the former executive of Prince George's County, Glendening believed he could convince his former associates from neighboring Montgomery County to work together to resolve the funding issue. Mayor Schmoke, wishing to craft a political solution, again agreed to abandon the lawsuit.[49] His decision, however, had no effect on the ACLU's legal challenge.

Meanwhile, the 1995 legislative session was a replay of the 1994 session. Baltimore actually lost ground when MGT America reported to the legislature that after three years little had changed in the BCPS. The system continued to be "top down," site-based management (enterprise schools) still lacked an effective implementation plan, and some central office administrators were reportedly blocking the policy. Key union contract provisions deemed burdensome had not been renegotiated. And "ineffective principals and teachers" were still reported to be a barrier to school improvement.[50]

Rawlings described the report as "devastating in terms of undermining the confidence that was building with regard to the school system."[51] It convinced him that Schmoke and Amprey were unwilling to tackle the big issues concerning efficiency and management. When Amprey was invited to a legislative hearing to respond, Rawlings found him to be "defensive and indignant." Rawlings added that "many legislative members left feeling that the management of the BCPS had little intention, from the beginning, of ever implementing the recommended reforms." He then observed, "Like many of my colleagues, I believe poor management practices significantly contribute to the unacceptable level of student performance."[52]

In response to what he considered the BCPS' lack of cooperation, Rawlings attached another provision to the 1996 state budget, withholding $5.8 million (estimated to be 25 percent of the expenditures for salaries, wages, and benefits for BCPS administrators) from Baltimore's share of state education aid. The funds would be released only if the BCPS reduced by 5 percent the salaries of those administrators named in the MGT report as failing fully to implement the Cresap recommendations. Both houses of the Maryland legislature passed the withholding provision.

State Takeover or Partnership?

On September 15, 1995, Mayor Schmoke finally carried out his threat and filed a legal claim in Baltimore Circuit Court aimed at forcing the state to provide tens of millions of dollars more a year in education funding for the BCPS.[53] Baltimore's principal legal argument was the same as the ACLU's lawsuit: the city was unable to provide a constitutionally adequate education because it was given insufficient resources. The city's lawsuit also sought to prohibit the MSDE from ordering reforms in any more schools through reconstitution and to force the legislature to release the nearly $6 million in funding it had withheld. State Superintendent Grasmick quickly countersued, claiming that the BCPS had mismanaged the school system.

The lawsuits launched a flurry of activity in both the state house and city hall. The main sticking points between Mayor Schmoke and state officials were funding, reform, and accountability. Both sides hoped that the issues could be settled out of court. In a series of secret meetings held shortly after the lawsuits were filed, Schmoke and Grasmick discussed plans to alter management of the BCPS and to settle the lawsuits. These talks, reportedly held for several weeks, resulted in the two officials agreeing to a "partnership" that would significantly increase the state's role in the management of the BCPS in exchange for additional education aid. The partnership would abolish the city school board and the superintendency, replacing them with a board appointed jointly by the governor and the mayor, with a CEO appointed by the new school board. The city would also have to agree to a series of management reforms, including overhauling the school system's personnel procedures and renegotiating union contracts.

By spring 1996, the major players, including Schmoke, Glendening, Grasmick, Rawlings, and state senator Barbara Hoffman (chair of the budget committee), appeared to have reached an agreement allowing increased state oversight of the BCPS in exchange for an infusion of additional state dollars. As part of the agreement, Glendening vetoed House Bill 608, Rawlings's withholding provision. In his veto letter to House Speaker Casper Taylor, Glendening noted that Mayor Schmoke had entered into a "City–State agreement," allowing Maryland "full oversight of all functions relating to the Baltimore City Schools."[54] A similar letter was sent to Schmoke.[55]

As word spread of the pending partnership agreement, however, Mayor Schmoke wavered. In a series of uncharacteristically biting and sharply worded letters to Governor Glendening, Schmoke contended that he had not committed to entering into a partnership agreement, implying that the BCPS' problems were caused by a lack of financial resources, not by mismanagement:

> I will not agree to something I do not believe in. There is no reason why Baltimore City should be subjected to a different level of state control of its schools than is applied to all other subdivisions in the State. I have confidence in the leadership of the Baltimore City Public Schools. I will not hand over control of our children's future to those who rationalize the State's refusal to provide adequate resources and try to affix blame somewhere other than where its belongs. The problem is not management. It is money.[56]

In another defiant letter to the governor, Schmoke implied that state leaders' persistent call for restructuring the BCPS's management was at best offensive and at worst racist: "The idea that management is the primary problem is insulting and paternalistic, and to my mind gains currency, in certain circles, because it is politically expedient and appeals to popular stereotypes."[57] Those who negotiated the partnership agreement were dismayed by Schmoke's assertion that he had not agreed to the management changes. The mayor's chief lobbyist in Annapolis, Henry W. Bogdan, had sat in on the negotiations and recalled, "There was agreement that a city–state partnership tied to future state funding increases was the only practical solution."[58]

Perhaps two factors figured into Schmoke's apparent reversal. First, he was uncomfortable with key specifics of the proposal. Second, he faced pressure from powerful community leaders to resist relinquishing local autonomy to the state. As part of the city–state agreement, state officials proposed giving Baltimore $150 million in additional education aid (on top of the approximately $400 million already provided) over a five-year period if the city agreed to substantial restructuring of the BCPS. Schmoke argued that the additional state funds were significantly less than the $500 million the Hutchinson Commission considered essential because of the high concentration of poor students in the schools.[59] Further, he opposed the provision stripping away his power in personnel and procurement decisions in the BCPS. Under the proposed partnership, the new school board would have complete control of all BCPS personnel and procurement. Under the existing structure, the city's Board of Estimates, controlled by the mayor, approved all contracts and appointments of all noneducational personnel. In a critical editorial, the *Sun* observed that Schmoke wanted to retain this mayoral "money pot."[60]

Schmoke was also influenced by local politics. The most vocal opposition to the city–state partnership was from members of Baltimore's powerful black clergy, especially members of IMA and BUILD. These ministers jealously guarded black administrative control of the BCPS. The church community considered the proposal an "outrageous" state "takeover," threatening the long tradition of black control of the BCPS.[61] According to the Reverend Roger Gench, cochair of BUILD, "racial prejudice and stereotypes [were] behind" the agreement.[62]

Other groups opposed the city–state agreement as well. The Baltimore Board of School Commissioners passed a resolution condemning those who would "destroy the school system through the withholding of funds, disguised partnership proposals, takeover attempts and court actions."[63] The resolution called the agreement a thinly disguised takeover of the city's schools. The BTU, Baltimore City-Wide PTA, and PSASA also denounced the partnership as usurpation of local control.

Mayor Schmoke's forceful letters (which were widely circulated by his public relations office) to Glendening could have been an attempt to appear recalcitrant, to leave the impression among politically powerful school interests that he was fighting the good fight and would not relinquish local control easily. Otherwise, it was a duel Schmoke had already lost. Glendening and state leaders took a firm position with city officials, designating a deadline for Schmoke to agree to the partnership. The city's lawsuit was scheduled to go to court in early November 1996. Not knowing what to expect from a court ruling, or how long it would take to reach a final judgment (an appeal of the case was expected), everyone involved preferred a political solution instead of a judicial one.

After a couple of weeks of intense negotiations, Glendening increased the amount of additional state aid to $254 million over five years—$30 million in fiscal year 1998, $50 million each in fiscal years 1999 and 2000, at least $50 million each in fiscal years 2001 and 2002, and an addition $24-million increase for capital improvements. With time running out, Schmoke was ready to sign on. On November 27, 1996, Schmoke and Glendening announced that the parties had reached a settlement. At a news conference, reportedly near tears and his voice cracking with emotion, Schmoke announced that he had entered a partnership with the state: "When I came into office, I said it was my goal to make this the city that reads. It became clearer and clearer to me that our community could not achieve that goal without a partnership with the state. I can tell you from the bottom of my heart, everything tells me this is the right thing to do. The clear winners of the settlement are the schoolchildren of Baltimore City." He hoped future generations would remember the agreement as "the day that the adults stopped fighting one another and joined and started fighting for the children."[64]

Some parents, educators, and school administrators, however, noting that the Hutchinson Commission had recommended additional state aid of up to $140 million a year, wondered whether the $254 million over five years was enough to improve the schools significantly. As one school activist explained, "We lost control and we got $50 million a year. I think they traded too much."[65]

The agreement was incorporated into a consent decree designed to settle the education funding lawsuits.[66] The major components included (1) establishing a new Board of School Commissioners (the nine members would be jointly appointed by the governor and the mayor from a list of "qualified" applicants submitted by the MSBE; (2) giving the restructured school board "complete control of all personnel and procurement," including the negotiation of union contracts; (3) restructuring the top management of the BCPS, including replacing the superintendent with a chief executive officer who would be responsible for its overall administration; (4) requiring the new school board to develop and implement (with the approval of state officials) a "master plan to increase student achievement" that incorporated key recommendations from the 1992 Cresap Study; and (5) establishing an evaluation system that would report the progress of reform in the BCPS to the Circuit Court of Baltimore City, the MSBE, the General Assembly, and the public.

The Legislature Supports the Partnership

The final step in adopting the partnership and settling the lawsuits was to gain approval of the spending plan by the legislature. Given that a number of groups opposed the plan, its passage was not ensured. Montgomery County officials tried to derail the agreement, petitioning the Maryland Court of Appeals to void it because they had not been allowed to intervene in the consent decree. They argued that their officials should have been party to the agreement because the county's school budget would be affected by any increase in aid to Baltimore. The court denied their request.

Despite the court's ruling, Montgomery County officials sought other ways to prevent legislative approval. They joined leaders in Prince George's County to use their growing numbers in the legislature to force Glendening substantially to increase educational aid to the rest of the state.[67] Their counterproposal requested an additional $44 million in school aid in fiscal year 1998, and $108 million each year for four years, with Montgomery and Prince George's Counties getting the biggest share. Moreover, political leaders in the county questioned if more money would solve the problems afflicting Baltimore's troubled school district. "It's like putting millions of dollars into a one-wing airplane. One-wing airplanes don't fly. It's just good money after bad," declared a Montgomery County legislator.[68]

The assertive opposition of suburban leaders caused great dissension. The president of the senate chastised Montgomery and Prince George's officials for being parochial: "They are acting like hogs feeding at the trough."[69] The debate in the legislature turned especially bitter after the chair of the senate budget committee, Barbara Hoffman, raised the issue of race as she discussed Montgomery County's opposition to the proposal. Hoffman, who is white, told reporters that the county legislators' opposition "comes across as racist."[70] "What [many legislators] really say to you, privately, is that you have a population that can't learn. That infuriates me. There's a lot of racism in that. There's a lot of racism aimed at the students and the faculty."[71] Hoffman later apologized.

Leaders of the growing suburban counties were not the only opponents of the city–state partnership. The BTU and other city unions came to Annapolis to lobby against the measure. The BTU opposed the provisions allowing the new school board to reopen contract talks and to reach new work agreements with unions. Moreover, BTU and PSASA leaders objected to the requirement that certain central administration supervisors reapply to the new school board for their old positions.[72]

Black community leaders, parent groups, and black ministers from Baltimore were perhaps the loudest critics of the proposal, arguing that the African-American community was giving up its rights to influence school operations. Many of these community leaders opposed sharing power with white state officials.[73] The Reverend Arnold Howard, president of the IMA, noted that the ministers opposed the partnership because they believed that the additional funds were "not enough" to warrant state oversight of the city's largest municipal department.[74] The Reverend Frank Reid, pastor of Bethel A.M.E. Church (and Mayor Schmoke's stepbrother), also spoke out against the agreement. Paraphrasing a verse from Scripture, Reid asked, "What does it profit a city to gain $254 million and lose its soul?"[75] In an open letter to state legislators, the ministers and community leaders denounced the school-aid package as "anti-democratic" and as revealing "racial paternalism":

> We will not accept Baltimore becoming a colony of the state, with its citizens having no say in the education of their children. African Americans, in particular, have fought a long, hard battle for equality. Over the years, too many paid the ultimate price for community empowerment. We will not stand and allow the gains those people sacrificed and died for to be given away. We have earned the dream of quality education for our children, and local autonomy in decision-making.[76]

Delegate Rawlings lambasted the ministers for putting adult concerns before the concerns of children. "These folks are being led and fed information by people who do not have the interest of Baltimore children at heart. The interest of the children should be the bottom line."[77]

None of the opposition, however, was able to stop the momentum toward institutionalizing state-level reform in the BCPS. In early April 1997, following days of intense behind-the-scenes negotiations, the House of Delegates voted 78 to 61 (just seven votes more than needed for a clear majority) to approve the city–state partnership. Legislative leaders incorporated a provision to add $33 million in education aid for other school systems around the state (including $6 million for Montgomery County and $8 million for Prince George's Counties). Only three of Montgomery County's twenty delegates supported the measure, and no legislator from Prince George's County voted in favor of it. Three Baltimore legislators voted against it. Two days later, the Maryland Senate easily passed the agreement, 33 to 13. On April 10, 1997, Governor Glendening signed the legislation into law.

SUMMARY

Governors and legislators have direct influence on the operation of local school systems, and the fight over state education budgets has become an annual drama in state capitals, where funding for cash-strapped central cities has become a major issue. The struggle between Baltimore and the General Assembly illustrates how difficult it is to transfer social capital into an intergroup context. The state legislature had become increasingly insistent that Baltimore change its management practices and be held accountable for the millions of state dollars it received to operate the BCPS. Often these demands led to political and racial clashes between city and suburb. Local politicians and activists in Montgomery County and in Baltimore have learned to use race to promote solidarity for their positions. By their own admission, elected officials in Montgomery County understand that "Baltimore bashing" plays on white anxieties and helps solidify support among suburban voters. Further, Parren Mitchell, Mayor Schmoke, prominent black clergy, and other city leaders have rallied opposition to state accountability standards based on African-American resentment of white domination and exclusion. Racial politics thus can hamper the formation of intergroup social capital between central city and state officials.

The role of legislative leadership is also important, as the part Delegate Rawlings played illustrates. Rawlings was convinced that without strong accountability standards the BCPS would never master its organizational quagmire and the state would never significantly expand the funds needed to address the challenges of educating Maryland's largest concentration of poor children. Rawlings personally developed a strategy to make more state funding conditional on the city's conceding to greater accountability for its schools' performance. When it became clear that because of its "culture," the BCPS and its allies were unwilling to alter the structural and administrative practices deemed detrimental to school improvement (for example, provisions in union contracts that hampered effective operations and personnel practices that encouraged patronage appointments), Rawlings risked giving up some of Baltimore's independence. He braved the criticism of black city leaders who accused him of selling the city's soul in order to pave the way for the BCPS to receive additional state funding in exchange for unprecedented management changes and tough accountability standards. Rawlings's formal authority as a powerful member of the state legislature put him in a position to promote cooperation among city officials, business groups, neighborhood organizations, church leaders, and state officials.

The significance of resources must not be overlooked. For more than a decade, Mayor Schmoke, the GBC, education specialists at Johns Hopkins and other universities, BUILD, CPHA, and various parent, community, and civic organizations worked collectively and individually toward school reform. These local groups were joined in the late 1980s and early 1990s by state education officials who sought to institutionalize reform at the state level. The MSDE adopted an aggressive school assessment program, combined with a stringent takeover provision, designed to hold individual schools accountable for their students' performance. Yet these groups have been unable to demonstrate that significant improvements have come about in student achievement: educational improvement is likely to occur only if substantial resources are committed. Even Nancy Grasmick, the tough, determined, and reform-minded state superintendent, embraced the belief that the BCPS could not provide an adequate education to students without an infusion of more resources. Although a committed believer in the idea that "all children can learn," Grasmick was a strong advocate for funneling additional funds into the BCPS. As a member of the Governor's Commission on School Funding, she is credited with shaping its final report to direct more state education aid to Baltimore. The funding plan of the city–state partnership, however, falls considerably short of the funding recommended by the commission.

10

Lessons from the Baltimore Experience

To ignore the intimate connections between school and community in the reform and restructuring of urban schooling is to condemn such attempts to almost certain failure.
– KENNETH A. SIROTNIK

Perhaps not since Floyd Hunter coined the phrase "community power structure" in his 1953 analysis of decision makers in Atlanta have both academicians and ordinary citizens embraced a concept as they have that of social capital.[1] Hunter's study served as the archetype for an entire school of community power studies that persisted well into the 1970s. Black-power activists, referring to the disproportionate influence of whites in the affairs of their communities, adopted the term "white power structure."[2] In the late 1990s social capital has become a multidimensional concept widely used by academics as a theoretical paradigm and employed by Pres. Bill Clinton, former House Speaker Newt Gingrich, neighborhood activists, and local community leaders as a technique for solving social problems. Advocates from all points on the political spectrum have seized upon the concept.

As popular as the idea of social capital has been, few studies have applied the concept at the local level. Yet when the theory is applied to school reform in Baltimore lessons are learned and key findings result. My analysis begins with a discussion of the important role of governmental institutions and actors in the city's school reform effort. I stress the need for social capital theorists to find a more prominent role for state authority. I also caution against viewing the reinvigoration of local associational life as a panacea for school reform; when it comes to improving American's inner-city schools, social capital is no substitution for financial capital. I then consider how the prevailing political culture encouraged the formation of black social capital while creating institutional barriers restrict-

185

ing the growth of intergroup social capital. Thus an examination of the past decade of school reform efforts by Baltimore leaders can help to clarify the role of
social capital and to establish promising avenues for future discussion and research.

GOVERNMENTAL INSTITUTIONS

Robert Putnam's work on social capital emphasizes informal relationships: how
"our relations with one another" can facilitate cooperation.[3] In their recent three-
city analysis, John Portz, Lana Stein, and Robin Jones stressed the crucial role
institutions play in triggering "civic capacity," a concept similar to social capital,
when it is vested in the positional power of a mayor, superintendent, or in other
public officials. They found that "institutions provide the foundation for civic
capacity. . . . Institutions provide the empirical context through which collective
actions are conceived and implemented."[4]

Putnam's work on social capital has little to say about the influence of institutions on social capital. Yet in this book I have shown that formal institutions
lodged in city and state governments advanced intergroup social capital. I have
argued that big-city mayors play a central role in urban regimes, placing them in
a critical position for promoting intergroup social capital, given their visibility
and access to significant resources. As the city's first elected African-American
mayor, Kurt Schmoke included key leaders and organizations in the African-
American community in discussions and issues surrounding public education,
worked with predominantly white business leaders on promoting private-sector
involvement in the BCPS, encouraged community leaders and neighborhood activists to take ownership of their neighborhood schools (e.g., during the Barclay
and Stadium School movements), and negotiated with state officials on issues such
as funding and accountability.

On taking office in 1987, Mayor Schmoke vowed to make Baltimore "the
city that reads" and to keep education high on his administration's agenda. The
strong-mayor structure of city government facilitated his efforts to reform the BCPS.
Until very recently, the school system was an agency of city government operated by a school board whose members were appointed by the mayor. Although
significant school improvement has been difficult, Schmoke's institutional power
allowed him to focus attention on the challenges facing the BCPS. Without his
support the Barclay-Calvert collaboration and the Stadium School would not have
been realized. Schmoke's insistence that school personnel work with College
Bound advisers allowed private-sector volunteers to assist in counseling and
preparing students for college. His dismissal of Superintendent Richard Hunter
indicated that the mayor set a broad course and expected the superintendent to
follow it. Moreover, Baltimore's experiment with EAI could not have happened
without Schmoke's endorsement. The mayor's high-profile involvement and will-

ingness to apply the political weight of his office allowed the challenges facing the city's schools to remain high on the agenda.

Baltimore Delegate Howard "Pete" Rawlings also played a pivotal role as chair of the Maryland House of Delegates' Appropriations Committee. As principal author of the legislation creating the city–state partnership, Rawlings developed a strategy to bring much-needed management reform to the BCPS and significantly to expand the state funds targeted for the city's schools. Far from being a "sell-out," as some opponents of the partnership labeled him at the time, Rawlings used his institutional power in the legislature to remove many of the bureaucratic practices deemed detrimental to school improvement, to direct additional state dollars to the city's cash-strapped schools, and to broaden the spectrum of civic leaders and school volunteers actively engaged in the school reform movement.[5]

Gertrude Williams, the determined principal of the Barclay School, provides another example of a person in a position of official authority who facilitated cooperation among parents, community groups, church leaders, teachers, and community leaders. After becoming principal of Barclay in 1971, Williams worked closely with parents, encouraging and cajoling them to become actively involved in their children's education and in the life of the school. She has reached out to small businesses in the Remington, Abell, Greenmount, and Charles Village communities not only for volunteers but also for garnering precious resources to purchase equipment and to send students on field trips. Barclay's strong relationship with college students at Johns Hopkins University (many of whom tutor Barclay students) is a direct result of the leadership Williams displayed as principal of the neighborhood school.

Schmoke's influence over the direction of Baltimore's schools was greatly diminished by the state legislature in 1997. Wilbur Rich and other sympathetic observers of inner-city schools welcome state takeovers, arguing that "more state regulations and inspections could potentially protect the learning opportunities of poor children."[6] Granting that political dynamics were involved in Maryland's decision to expand its authority over the BCPS, the city–state partnership will most likely lead Schmoke and future mayors to shy away from more direct involvement in the schools. Indeed, a year after passage of the legislation, observers noted a shift in Schmoke's attention away from schools and toward downtown redevelopment.[7]

The Baltimore case illustrates the need to forge clearer conceptual links between social capital theory and more traditional political science theories about voting, representation, political incorporation, and political leadership. The central roles of Schmoke and Rawlings, for instance, suggest that when black social capital is combined with conventional electoral activity, resulting in black political empowerment, African Americans are in a better position to use governmental institutions to advance their causes. Politicizing black social capital and transforming it into a force for policy change is an important step. In responding to an issue like inner-city school reform, neighborhood groups, voluntary associations, religious organizations, labor unions, business groups, and other informal associations are certainly significant, but so are governmental institutions and actors.

FINANCIAL RESOURCES

During Baltimore's decade-long effort to reform its public schools, the interplay between social capital and resources has come to the fore. Challenges facing the city included the financial difficulties brought on by deindustrialization and suburbanization. Pursuing a policy priority such as urban school reform requires not only high stocks of social capital but also financial resources. The Baltimore experience suggests that in cash-strapped cities, social capital must be combined with sufficient resources.

Baltimore's effort to institute site-based management throughout its schools provides a good example. Implementation of SBM collapsed because central office administrators refused to relinquish more authority to individual schools. Moreover, principals, teachers, and other school-based staff did not demand or push for the process. Ironically, many central office administrators, teachers, principals, staff, parent activists, and church leaders enjoy bonds of personalism (another dimension of social capital); hence theoretically, SBM could work in the BCPS. Setting aside other issues concerning the program (for example, it is hard enough for inner-city schools to maintain functional PTAs, let alone involve teachers and parents in real local governance), I would argue that SBM failed because the plan of implementation was designed without significant infusions of additional funds.

In Baltimore, the average school has a budget of approximately $2.6 million, much of it committed to salaries, building operations, and materials. Giving principals and teachers more authority to control budgets sounds like a great idea; however, it does not change the reality of the allocations. Salaries and other essentials have to be paid, leaving very little in funds for principals and teachers to draw upon to launch innovative, school-based programs. School-based staff members were asked to take on more responsibilities without additional resources. Viewed from this perspective, it is little wonder that Baltimore's principals and teachers were not enthusiastic about SBM.

The Barclay-Calvert collaboration illustrates what social capital combined with financial resources can accomplish in the area of urban school reform. The Barclay School benefited from the leadership of Gertrude Williams and the relatively high reserves of social capital represented by its active steering committee of teachers, staff, parents (including parents of former Barclay students), and community leaders. However, the funding (over $500,000) and other support provided by the Abell Foundation were equally critical to the academic achievement of the students. As the independent evaluator explained, it is impossible to overemphasize the significance of the foundation's role:

> One of the gifts of Abell's involvement in the program has been the knowledge shared among the staff that 'things will work out.' Calvert materials *arrive on time*. Back-up materials *are* made available. Training and backup support have consistently been of high quality and have not been taken away during any of the school district's regular crises. . . . Stable, targeted, long-term funding eliminates one of the greatest inhibitors to change in teaching practice—an often well-founded skepticism among teachers.[8]

Baltimore officials have argued for years that the state should provide the city with more resources, that the educational needs of the largely poor students outstrip the city's revenue capacity. Indeed, this was the recommendation of the Governor's Commission on School Funding. Although many suburban leaders vociferously (and correctly) argued that poor management in the BCPS results in waste, the vast majority of knowledgeable observers agree that Maryland should do more. A recent federal study, for example, showed that the amount of state funding marked for high-poverty school districts in Maryland was among the smallest in the nation.[9] For every dollar Maryland provided in education aid for each student in a district, it designated only an additional four cents per poor student, well below the national average of sixty-two cents per poor student, and more than eight times below amounts provided by Mississippi and South Carolina.

In *Making Democracy Work*, Robert Putnam defines social capital in part by quoting James S. Coleman, whom Putnam credits as an originator of the concept.

> Like other forms of capital, social capital is productive, making possible the achievement of certain ends that would not be attainable in its absence. . . . For example, a group whose members manifest trustworthiness and place extensive trust in one another will be able to accomplish much more than a comparable group lacking that trustworthiness and trust. . . . In a farming community . . . where one farmer got his hay baled by another and where tools are extensively borrowed and lent, *the social capital allows each farmer to get his work done with less physical capital in the form of tools and equipment.*[10]

Although Putnam's intent is to foster political and economic development, his emphasis on social capital proffers a potentially dangerous view of government's role in helping provide the financial capital needed to address housing, public safety, health care, education, and other social issues: an almost nonexistent one. Fiscal conservatives and government minimalists have seized upon his notion of social capital to argue that the solution to modern social ills lies in dismantling the state.[11] Conservative social capital enthusiasts would love to substitute "soft" social capital for "hard" financial capital.

Many on the left view the social capital concept with suspicion when it is offered as a cheaper alternative to or substitute for the financial capital required to accomplish reform. "It is absurd," writes Adolph Reed Jr., "to present neighborhood and church initiatives as appropriate responses to the effects of government-supported disinvestment, labor market segmentation, widespread and well-documented patterns of discrimination in employment and housing."[12] The compensation for the inadequate funding of inner-city public schools should not be left to neighborhood improvement organizations, parent associations, community-based organizations, church groups, and other voluntary associations. Although the Barclay/Calvert collaboration and the support given it by the Abell Foundation deserves applause, it simultaneously acknowledges that government has not legitimately provided citizens of the Remington, Abell, Greenmount, and Charles Village communities with a level of resources that meets the needs of their children. Blending additional federal and state resources with the stocks of social capital found in many cities should go a long way in improving central-city schools.

POLITICAL CULTURE

My research in Baltimore suggests that a city's capacity to activate the intergroup social capital needed to carry out school reform is a by-product of local political culture. Unfortunately, political culture variables have been underemphasized or ignored altogether by most urban scholars, including those employing urban regime theory. A benefit of the social capital concept is its emphasis on political culture. Putnam's work on regional governments in Italy reminds us that citizens' political relations to and association with local governmental institutions are shaped by the predominant political culture. His findings are consistent with Barbara Ferman's comparative analysis of Chicago and Pittsburgh, showing that political culture helps shape the direction of a city's politics and local policy.[13]

Since the mid-nineteenth century, a tradition emphasizing an identification of politics and government with material exchange and patronage has dominated Baltimore's political culture. This patronage culture not only helped shape the nature of political cooperation in the city, but it also gave rise to an expectation that the public school system is an employment regime. The school system represents a bundle of material benefits, and for over 100 years city officials and citizens have viewed it as an institution ripe for political patronage.

Steven Erie, in his study of Irish Americans and machine politics, points out that one of the problems with patronage politics is that it advanced the group's pursuit of some goals but limited its capacity to address others. Erie argues, for example, that patronage politics facilitated the Irish-American's quest to infiltrate and take over city governments but did little to aid their group efforts toward economic assimilation. Their political machine's emphasis on blue-collar public employment could do only so much for advancing the goal of Irish-American group mobility.[14]

Baltimore's dominant political culture promotes pursuit of particular, narrow benefits. It does not foster cooperation toward broad community goals such as management reform of the school system. During Mayor William Donald Schaefer's regime (1971–1986), the schools came under the administrative control of the black community, for the first time offering African Americans command over jobs and other economic opportunities. For Schaefer, this arrangement encouraged cooperation between the white-controlled city government and the majority-black population, expanding his tenure as mayor and opening avenues for middle-class African Americans to further their economic and professional development. It did little to improve the school system.

Roland Patterson, the city's first African-American superintendent, attempted to go against the grain of the dominant political culture. Determined to reshape the system, Patterson decried the pervasiveness of political influence in the BCPS, accused the city's leadership of indifference to educational needs, and recruited personnel from outside the system to fill both new and established administrative positions. Predictably, he found himself besieged on all sides, meeting strong opposition from the city's white political leadership and garnering lukewarm support from influential middle-class African-American leaders, who felt their consultation was needed. Four years after arriving in Baltimore, Patterson was fired by the city's first majority-black school board.

Kurt Schmoke's leadership in school affairs and his efforts toward reform were also constrained by the city's dominant political culture. In 1990, when interim superintendent Edward Andrews pressured several principals to resign, retire, or accept reassignment to a lesser post, Mayor Schmoke summoned him to city hall and asked him to back off. Schmoke cut short the city's experiment with private management after black church leaders and union officials, fearing the loss of jobs, mobilized to end it. Schmoke again wavered on the city–state partnership after other African-American leaders complained that he was relinquishing procurement contracts, employment opportunities, and other material rewards accrued from black control of the school system.

The other major component of Baltimore's political culture is its tradition of racial segregation and division. "History," Putnam perceptively observed, "smooths some paths and closes others off."[15] Race was the prime factor in the shaping of Baltimore's institutional and physical development. It certainly was not the only element involved, and it was not part of every decision, but it was a consistent and significant component in many important policy decisions. From birth in a hospital designated for African Americans to burial in a black cemetery, black Baltimoreans lived an almost entirely separate existence bounded on all sides by racial discrimination. The city is very much the product of a past that emphasized racial issues.

By the 1980s Baltimore had shed most of its southern orientation; however, segregation and state-sanctioned racial discrimination are not a distant memory unconnected to the present. Given a history of white domination and control, today's African-American leaders view recent gains, especially black administrative control of the school system, as long in coming. Past experiences encourage these leaders to cooperate with each other and to guard against losing what power they do have. For many of them, widespread identification with the past struggles of the black community is a source of power.[16] The distrust these struggles have engendered and the insensitivity of whites to past black experiences hamper the formation of significant intergroup social capital.

INTERGROUP CONTEXT

Black Baltimoreans' response to a city being shaped by segregation was to form their own organizations, develop businesses and colleges to serve the African-American community, construct black churches, create black neighborhoods, and promote solidarity within the African-American community. Black leaders developed solid internal attachments based on past experiences, cultivating interpersonal trust among themselves. Black Baltimore developed high stocks of what I call black social capital.

The African-American leaders' relatively high endowments of social capital, however, put them in a dilemma. Historically, the strength of the black community's leadership was based on internal solidarity in opposition to whites. Today, as population decline, revenue shortfalls, white flight, political isolation, and other negative consequences of deindustrialization and suburbanization continue, black leaders have to work with white corporate leaders and white suburban voters to assemble the financial resources necessary for effective operation of the city's largely black school system. Although past experiences make African-American authority over the school system particularly valued, in the context of a declining central city such control is increasingly dependent on the resources not under their command. The need for activating intergroup social capital is unquestionable.

Transferring social capital within the African-American community into an intergroup context has been a formidable challenge. In the early 1980s, BUILD leaders linked lack of school reform and employment discrimination as barriers to black youth employment. Ultimately they had to work with the Greater Baltimore Committee to address their concerns fully. Initially, BUILD's attempt to form the Baltimore Commonwealth was rebuffed by corporate leaders, who refused to meet with BUILD leaders. Black church leaders complained that corporate leaders were unwilling to commit to the school compact program because the beneficiaries would be the school system's African-American graduates. Still, no matter what tactics BUILD leaders employed, any program purporting to make jobs available to local high school graduates had to have the resources and cooperation of the business community. BUILD's formation reveals two sides of social capital: first, African-American clergy had developed huge reserves of black social capital; second, its transfer into an intergroup context is a difficult process.[17]

The challenge of activating intergroup social capital and facilitating cooperation across various communities is also evident in the relationship between the corporate sector and the black-led school system. Educators and business leaders have always differed over whether to emphasize the acquisition of basic skills or high-order thinking skills. And in Baltimore, tensions between educators and business leaders are exacerbated by race. The corporate sector is dominated by white men; the school system is dominated by African Americans. To put it bluntly, the corporate community's heightened involvement in school affairs has led many blacks to believe that it is attempting "to control" their school system, a sentiment expressed by a black school administrator and amplified by other black respondents:

> The bottom line, in my view, [is that] the corporate community wants to control the school system. In most large urban school districts, in every case where you have a majority-black population, the corporate community controls what takes place. When one is black, it becomes extremely difficult to become superintendent of schools in Baltimore City . . . without getting the approbation of the business community that is white.

Respondents from the business sector acknowledge that they are aware of and are often made to feel uncomfortable by those blacks who question the motives of corporate involvement in the schools. A GBC official explained:

> There is a racial overlay to a lot of things that happen in this city. We have a school system that is more than 80 percent African American. GBC—while we're really reaching to expand our membership to include far more African Americans—I suspect for the next fifty years we will be perceived as a white organization. And so there is at least a tension that will always be there of: "Is whitey trying to tell us what to do? Is whitey trying to take over our school?" So that's a friction we have to get over. . . . To be totally candid, you can't ignore it, because I think it helps decide how things get done in this community.

Some black school officials and many African-American leaders are also suspicious of the significant role Abell Foundation president Robert Embry plays in the BCPS. Although many of the reform projects it supports (the Barclay-Calvert collaboration, for example) are considered successful, some school activists are apprehensive about the foundation and its president's influence in school affairs.

Advocates of systemic education reform frequently include public-private partnerships on the list of initiatives that they believe are critical if urban school systems are to be turned around. In Baltimore, blacks hold most of the key public policy positions within the local government and school systems, but the major positions within the corporate community are occupied by whites. Hence race remains an important variable in educational politics. To be sure, the way in which race expresses itself has changed since desegregation defined local school politics. Nevertheless, race is a critical social and political variable, constraining the development and sustenance of social capital within an intergroup context.

Richard DeLeon's study of San Francisco illustrates how diverse racial and ethnic "progressives" were unable to establish a stable progressive regime.[18] African Americans in particular confronted difficult obstacles while cooperating with San Francisco's progressive elements and chose racial solidarity as the more efficient vehicle for fighting political battles. "Cross-cutting cleavages, divided loyalties, and compound identities . . . corrode the bonds of shared values and grind things to a halt."[19] Latinos, Asian Americans, white progressives, and African Americans were unable to transfer their intragroup social capital into an intergroup context.[20]

Putnam and other scholars employing the social capital concept have little to say about race. Yet the Baltimore experience shows that in American urban politics, where divisions based on race and class are prevalent, achieving cooperation among white business elites, white suburban legislators, state education officials and African-American educators, church leaders, elected officials, and community activists is a significant challenge to social capital. Given the history of racial segregation, discrimination, and African-American resentment of white domination and exclusion in Baltimore and other American cities, blacks' mistrust of whites (and whites' insensitivity) presents a particular challenge to building social capital across community sectors. If social capital is about trust and reciprocity, actors on the Baltimore scene must be able to overcome the divisive character of race.

FUTURE DIRECTIONS FOR RESEARCH

From our examination of Baltimore we are able to generate preliminary findings on the role of social capital in urban regimes and urban school reform. It would be useful to discover whether studies of other cities would uncover similar findings. For example, the formal authority that Baltimore's mayor has in school affairs is an anomaly. Nevertheless, this authority allowed Mayor Schmoke to use his institutional power to exert significant leadership over the direction of school reform. Given that big-city mayors typically do not have such authority, in what other local governmental institutions can one expect to find the level of leadership that can facilitate cooperation across community sectors? For instance, in Detroit, the late Mayor Coleman Young (perhaps one of the most powerful mayors in the city's history) had no formal authority over the school system, and although considered "a friend to Detroit schools," he never played more than a limited role in school affairs.[21] When Young suggested that the schools should be placed under city control, school leaders dismissed it. Given the political autonomy of school districts, can we expect school board presidents or school superintendents—who usually do not have the visibility that a mayor has—successfully to use their institutional power to activate social capital and promote community cooperation for systemic school reform? What are the limitations of formal authority in promoting social capital? Comparative studies examining multiple cities could provide considerable knowledge about the role of institutions in facilitating social capital at the local level.

Examination need not be limited to formal, governmental institutions. The Barclay School movement illustrated the potential role of institutions such as PTAs. Barclay's steering committee of parents, parents of former students, teachers, and community leaders operates like a typical PTA. How can the success and cohesion of this steering committee be replicated across school communities? What role should the government, private sector, or foundations play in promoting social capital among parents within particular communities and intergroup social capital across parental groups?

Moreover, foundations can have enormous influence in school affairs. The Abell Foundation plays a significant role in school reform, supporting a number of successful education-related programs. However, Abell's active involvement in the schools generated resentment, especially among African-American school administrators and community activists. More research is needed on foundations and school reform. One promising avenue of research is an examination of local foundation efforts to encourage community leaders, university researchers, civic leaders, principals, and teachers to collaborate on school issues. How can local foundations promote cross-sector collaboration?

I have argued that linking urban regime theory and social capital theory allows an analysis of intergroup social capital formation among elites, and I have examined social capital within the context of Baltimore's political and economic elites. The job now is for researchers to design studies that emphasize intergroup social capital, urban politics, and school reform at the mass level. Is systemwide school reform restricted to the efforts of leaders and other elites through the formation among them of interpersonal trust and intergroup social capital? Or does such reform require deeper, more broad-based social capital among the mass of average citizens?

Gary Orfield has recently bemoaned America's drift toward increasing school segregation and its grave consequences. Students in highly segregated schools, he argues, usually are economically disadvantaged and often "lack family connections, money, and networks that allow them to move into the mainstream economy." The vast majority of these students are African Americans and Latinos who, according to Orfield, "are literally cut off from routes that lead to job and college opportunities" and denied "access to middle-class schools, and to the world beyond them."[22] If interactions with people beyond our social network (i.e., "weak ties") are "indispensable to individuals' opportunities," minority students in highly segregated school districts are at a disadvantage.[23]

This backward slide toward resegregation suggests the need for research that explores the types of school reform policies most likely to foster intergroup social capital. Mark Schneider and his colleagues recently argued that school choice can build social capital.[24] They found that choice promoted social capital among parents in two majority-white, middle-class suburban school districts and among minority parents in two inner-city communities. But their research design focused on the interpersonal forms of social capital within two largely minority school districts and within two predominantly white, suburban districts. It does not speak to cross-sector formations of mutual trust and networks of cooperation that bridge the black-white divide, or intergroup social capital. Future research should examine the effect of school choice (including school voucher programs) on promoting intergroup social capital.

Similarly, we need to learn more about charter schools within the context of social capital. Both the Clinton administration and the Republican-controlled Congress have supported charter schools, which also have strong Democratic and Republican support at the state level. The bipartisan appeal of this concept has fed the movement's steady growth; twenty-five states and the District of Columbia have enacted legislation for such schools.[25] Can charter schools promote social capital between whites and African Americans? Evidence from Baltimore's Stadium School offers some hope. However, North Carolina's early experience with charter schools raises serious doubt.[26] Since charter legislation was enacted in 1996, a disproportionate number of African-American students have enrolled in the state's thirty-four charter schools; thirteen have black student enrollments of more than 85 percent. In Durham all but two white parents pulled their children from a charter school after realizing they would be a distinct minority there.

Gunnar Myrdal, in his seminal study of race in American society, was one of the first scholars to acknowledge the dilemmas of black social capital. Myrdal observed that, like Americans generally, African Americans were joiners. In the late 1930s, African Americans were members of civic improvement societies and voluntary associations. Indeed, Myrdal shows that "Negroes are more inclined to join associations than are whites." Blacks, he added, "have relatively more associations than do whites." However, Myrdal points out that "membership in their own segregated associations does not help Negroes to success in the larger American society."[27] His observation points to the dilemma of black social capital: interpersonal social capital within a racially defined community does not necessarily translate into the kind of intergroup social capital required to accomplish broad-based tasks. During the time of Myrdal's research, powerful forces of racism and white supremacy no doubt limited the capacity of black social capital to facilitate African Americans' efforts to improve the "race." Recent formulations of the social capital concept refer mainly to one side of the coin—intragroup cooperation and trust. That groups can achieve their purposes better than individuals is a self-evident proposition. The more significant issue raised from the perspective of social capital is whether the operation of such groups and associations also contributes to the building of a society in which cooperation among all its members for all sorts of purposes—not just within the groups themselves—is facilitated.

Notes

1. SOCIAL CAPITAL, URBAN REGIMES, AND SCHOOL REFORM

1. A differentiation should be made between the effectiveness of public education generally and urban school systems specifically. A case can be made that schools in general are performing at least as well as they have in the past (Karl L. Alexander, "Public Schools and the Public Good," *Social Forces* 76 [September 1997]: 1–30). See also David C. Berliner and Bruce J. Biddle, *The Manufactured Crisis: Myths, Fraud and the Attack on America's Public Schools* (Reading, MA: Addison-Wesley, 1995), and Jeffrey R. Henig, *Rethinking School Choice: Limits of the Market Metaphor* (Princeton: Princeton University Press, 1994). Urban school districts are, however, a different matter; many clearly are in decline. See, for example, Jeffrey Mirel, *The Rise and Fall of an Urban School System: Detroit, 1907–1981* (Ann Arbor: University of Michigan Press, 1993), and John L. Rury and Frank A. Cassell, eds., *Seeds of Crisis: Public Schooling in Milwaukee Since 1920* (Madison: University of Wisconsin Press, 1993).

2. Steve Farkas and Jean Johnson, *Given the Circumstances: Teachers Talk About Public Education Today* (New York: Public Agenda Foundation, 1996).

3. Ramona L. Burton, "A Study of Disparities Among School Facilities in North Carolina: Effects of Race and Economic Status," *Educational Policy* 13, 2 (May 1999): 280–95; Jonathan Kozol, *Savage Inequalities: Children in America's Schools* (New York: Crown Publishers, 1991); General Accounting Office, *School Facilities: Condition of America's Schools* (Washington, DC: U.S. Printing Office, 1995), and also *School Facilities: Profiles of School Condition by State* (Washington, DC: U.S. Printing Office, 1996).

4. Jeffrey Henig, Richard C. Hula, Marion Orr, and Desiree Pedescleaux, *The Color of School Reform: Race, Politics, and the Challenge of Urban Education* (Princeton: Princeton University Press, 1999); Jean Anyon, *Ghetto Schooling: A Political Economy of Urban Educational Reform* (New York: Teachers College Press, 1997); Wilbur C. Rich, *Black Mayors and School Politics: The Failure of Reform in Detroit, Gary, and Newark* (New York: Garland Press, 1996).

5. Peter L. Szanton, *Baltimore 2000: A Choice of Futures* (Baltimore: Morris Goldseker Foundation, 1986).

6. Ibid., pp. 10, 34.

7. I have chosen to use the terms "black" and "African American" interchangeably. Good arguments have been made for the use of both, as each suggests different emphases in regard to racial and global identity and the American experience. Indeed, the black/African-American communities in the United States remain divided over their preference. For a discussion of racial nomenclature, see Ruth W. Grant and Marion Orr, "Language, Race and Politics: From 'Black' to 'African-American,'" *Politics and Society* 24 (June 1996): 137–53; Ben Martin, "From Negro to Black to African American: The Power of Names and Naming," *Political Science Quarterly* 106 (1991): 83–107; and Robert C. Smith, *Racism in the Post–Civil Rights* Era (Albany: State University of New York Press, 1995), 100–104.

8. Fellicia Hunter, "Mayor Says Schools' Woes Still 'Serious,'" *Sun*, October 20, 1996.

9. The first systematic contemporary analysis of social capital was published in 1980 by Pierre Bourdieu, a French sociologist; six years later, an English translation appeared in an edited volume on the sociology of education. See Pierre Bourdieu, "La Capital Social: Notes Provisoires," *Aches. Rech. Sci. Soc.* 31 (1980): 3–6, and idem, "The Forms of Capital," in *Handbook of Theory and Research for the Sociology of Education,* ed. John G. Richardson (Westport, CT: Greenwood Press, 1986), pp. 241–58.

10. Robert D. Putnam, *Making Democracy Work* (Princeton: Princeton University Press, 1993). Putnam credits sociologist James Coleman and economist Glenn Loury with developing the term "social capital." Curiously, Putnam does not mention Bourdieu, although the former's analysis of social capital closely parallels that of the latter. See Glenn C. Loury, "Why Should We Care About Group Inequality?" *Social Philosophy and Policy* 5 (autumn 1987): 249–71; James S. Coleman, *Foundations of Social Theory* (Cambridge: Harvard University Press, 1990), especially pp. 300–321.

11. Putnam, *Making Democracy Work,* p. 167.

12. See especially Robert D. Putnam, "The Prosperous Community: Social Capital and Public Life," *American Prospect* 13 (spring 1993): 35–42, "Bowling Alone: America's Declining Social Capital," *Journal of Democracy* 6 (January 1995): 65–78, and "Bowling Alone, Revisited," *Responsive Community* (spring 1995): 18–33; and "Tuning In, Tuning Out: The Strange Disappearance of Social Capital in America," *PS: Political Science and Politics* 28 (December 1995): 664–83.

13. Not all agree with this assessment. See Seymour Martin Lipset, "Malaise and Resiliency in America," *Journal of Democracy* 6 (July 1995): 14–15, and Everett Ladd, "The Data Just Don't Show Erosion Of America's 'Social Capital,'" *Public Perspective* (1996): 4–22.

14. Putnam, "Tuning In, Tuning Out."

15. Ibid., p. 666.

16. Putnam, "Bowling Alone," p. 73.

17. Putnam, "Prosperous Community," p. 39.

18. Ibid., pp. 39–41.

19. Putnam, *Making Democracy Work,* pp. 63–82.

20. Ibid., p. 81.

21. Ibid., p. 170.

22. Ibid., p. 115.

23. Ibid., p. 183.

24. Ibid., p. 162.

25. Three critical essays appear in *Politics and Society* 24 (March 1996): 5–56; see also the series of articles in *American Behavioral Scientist* 40 (March/April 1997): 550–61.

26. Margaret Levi, "Social Capital and Unsocial Capital: A Review Essay of Robert Putnam's *Making Democracy Work,*" *Politics and Society* 24 (March 1996): 45–55.

27. Sheri Berman, "Civil Society and Political Institutionalization," *American Behavioral Scientist* 40 (March/April 1997): 565 (emphasis in original).

28. Coleman, *Foundations of Social Theory,* p. 302.

29. Thomas J. Sugrue, *The Origins of the Urban Crisis: Race and Inequality in Postwar Detroit* (Princeton: Princeton University Press, 1996), especially pp. 209–58.

30. Levi, "Social and Unsocial Capital," p. 50.

31. Margaret Levi, "Trusting the State," paper presented at Russell Sage Foundation/Russell Sage Workshop on "Trust and Social Structure," Seattle, WA, September 1995, p. 16.

32. Levi, "Social and Unsocial Capital," pp. 46–47.

33. Ibid., p. 50.

34. Filippo Sabetti, "Path Dependency and Civic Culture: Some Lessons from Italy About Interpreting Social Experiments," *Politics and Society* 24 (March 1996): 22.

35. Sidney Tarrow, "Making Social Science Work Across Space and Time: A Critical Reflection on Robert Putnam's *Making Democracy Work,*" *American Political Science Review* 90 (June 1996): 395.

36. Rosenstone and Hansen's analysis of the role of political leaders in generating citizen activity suggests that declining voting rates in the United States may be the result of political leaders' strategic decisions not to contact and mobilize potential voters. See Steven J. Rosenstone and John Mark Hansen, *Mobilization, Participation, and Democracy in America* (New York: Macmillan, 1993), especially chapters 2, 4, and 6.

37. Tarrow, "Making Social Science Work Across Space and Time," p. 395.

38. John Brehm and Wendy Rahn, "Individual-Level Evidence for the Causes and Consequences of Social Capital," *American Journal of Political Science* 41 (July, 1997): 999–1023.

39. Ibid., p. 1017.

40. Ibid., p. 1009.

41. Mark Schneider, Paul Teske, Melissa Marschall, Michael Mintrom, and Christine Roch, "Institutional Arrangements and the Creation of Social Capital: The Effects of Public School Choice," *American Political Science Review* 91 (March 1997): 82–93.

42. Jeffrey Berry, Kent Portney, and Ken Thomson, *The Rebirth of Urban Democracy* (Washington, DC: Brookings Institution, 1993).

43. Mark Schneider et al., "Institutional Arrangements and the Creation of Social Capital," p. 91.

44. Steven Rathgeb Smith, "Social Capital, Community Coalitions and the Role of Institutions," paper presented at the annual meeting of the American Political Science Association, New York City, September 1–4, 1994.

45. For an exception, see Dennis Shirley, *Community Organizing for School Reform* (Austin: University of Texas Press, 1997).

46. In his seminal study, *An American Dilemma,* Gunnar Myrdal characterized African-American participation in voluntary associations during this period as "pathological,"

observing that black social capital accomplished so little because of African-Americans' caste position. See *An American Dilemma* (New York: Harper and Row, 1944), pp. 952–54.

47. Marc V. Levine, *The Reconquest of Montreal: Language Policy and Social Change in a Bilingual City* (Philadelphia: Temple University Press, 1988).

48. Mark S. Granovetter, "The Strength of Weak Ties," *American Journal of Sociology* 78, 6 (May 1973): 1360–80.

49. Kenneth Newton, "Social Capital and Democracy," *American Behavioral Scientist* 40 (March/April 1997): 578.

50. Granovetter, "Strength of Weak Ties," p. 1360.

51. Ibid., p. 1373.

52. Russell Hardin, *One for All: The Logic of Group Conflict* (Princeton: Princeton University Press, 1995), p. 19.

53. Eric M. Uslaner and Richard S. Conley, "Civic Engagement and Particularized Trust: The Ties That Bind People to Their Ethnic Communities," paper presented at the annual meeting of the American Political Science Association, Boston, September 3–6, 1998, pp. 27–28.

54. Clarence N. Stone, "The Politics of Urban School Reform: Civic Capacity, Social Capital and the Intergroup Context," paper presented at the annual meeting of the American Political Science Association, San Francisco, August 29–September 1, 1996; see also his "Civic Capacity and Urban School Reform," in *Changing Urban Education*, ed. Clarence N. Stone (Lawrence: University Press of Kansas, 1998), p. 268.

55. I am indebted to Richard DeLeon for framing the concept in this particular way.

56. Clarence N. Stone, *Regime Politics: Governing Atlanta, 1946–1988* (Lawrence: University Press of Kansas, 1989), p. 3.

57. In addition to Stone's work, see Stephen L. Elkin, *City and Regime in the American Republic* (Chicago: University of Chicago Press, 1987); Marion Orr and Gerry Stoker, "Urban Regimes and Leadership in Detroit," *Urban Affairs Quarterly* 30 (December 1994): 48–73; Gerry Stoker, "Regime Theory and Urban Politics," in *Theories of Urban Politics*, ed. David Judge, Gerry Stoker, and Harold Wolman (Thousand Oaks, CA: Sage Publishers, 1995); David L. Imbroscio, "Reformulating Urban Regime Theory: The Division of Labor Between State and Market Reconsidered," *Journal of Urban Affairs* 20 (1998): 233–48.

58. Stone, *Regime Politics*, p. 9.

59. Clarence N. Stone, Marion E. Orr, and David Imbroscio, "The Reshaping of Urban Leadership in U.S. Cities: A Regime Analysis," in *Urban Life in Transition*, ed. M. Gottdiener and Chris G. Pickvance (Newbury Park, CA: Sage Publications, 1991).

60. Charles H. Levine, *Racial Conflict and the American Mayor* (Lexington, MA: Lexington Books, 1974); Jeffrey Pressman, "Preconditions of Mayoral Leadership," *American Political Science Review* 66 (June 1979): 511–24; John P. Kotter and Paul R. Lawrence, *Mayors in Action: Five Approaches to Urban Governance* (New York: John Wiley and Sons, 1974); Clarence N. Stone, "Political Leadership in Urban Politics," in Judge et al., eds., *Theories of Urban Politics*, pp. 96–116; Wilbur C. Rich, *Coleman Young and Detroit Politics: From Social Activist to Power Broker* (Detroit: Wayne State University Press, 1989).

61. Adolph Reed Jr., "The Black Urban Regime: Structural Origins and Constraints," in *Power, Community and the City*, ed. Michael Smith (New Brunswick, N.J.: Transaction Books, 1988), pp. 138–89.

62. Stone, *Regime Politics*, pp. 77–158.

63. Bryan D. Jones and Lynn W. Bachelor, *The Sustaining Hand: Community Leadership and Corporate Power* (Lawrence: University Press of Kansas, 1986), 203–4.

64. Buzz Bissinger, *A Prayer for the City* (New York: Random House, 1997).

65. Rufus P. Browning, Dale Rogers Marshall, and David H. Tabb, *Protest Is Not Enough* (Berkeley: University of California Press, 1984).

66. See, among others, Albert Karnig and Susan Welch, *Black Representation and Urban Policy* (Chicago: University of Chicago Press, 1980); Edmond Keller, "The Impact of Black Mayors on Urban Policy," *Annals of the Academy of Political and Social Sciences* 439 (September 1978): 40–52; Monte Piliawsky, "The Impact of Black Mayors on the Black Community: The Case of New Orleans' Ernest Morial," *Review of Black Political Economy* 13 (fall 1985): 5–23; Grace Saltzstein, "Black Mayors and Police Policies," *Journal of Politics* 51 (August 1989): 525–44; Leonard Cole, *Blacks in Power* (Princeton: Princeton University Press, 1976); Peter Eisinger, "Black Employment in Municipal Jobs: The Impact of Black Political Power," *American Political Science Review* 76 (December 1982): 380–92; Milton D. Morris, *Black Electoral Participation and the Distribution of Public Benefits* (Washington, DC: Brookings Institution, 1982); and Kenneth R. Mladenka, "Blacks and Hispanics in Urban Politics," *American Political Science Review* 83 (March 1989): 165–91. Even in the cities and towns of the old Confederacy, black incorporation into local governments brought about a more equitable distribution of services, such as fire protection, garbage collection, and public recreation. See, for example, James W. Button, *Blacks and Social Change* (Princeton: Princeton University Press, 1989); Lawrence J. Hanks, *The Struggle for Black Political Empowerment in Three Georgia Counties* (Knoxville: University of Tennessee Press, 1987); and William Keech, *The Impact of Negro Voting: The Role of the Vote in the Quest for Equality* (Chicago: Rand McNally, 1968).

67. See, for example, Rich, *Coleman Young and Detroit Politics*.

68. Stone, *Regime Politics*, p. 8.

69. Meredith Ramsay, *Community, Culture, and Economic Development: The Social Roots of Local Action* (Albany: State University of New York Press, 1996), p. 14.

70. In 1996 a series of social capital questions were slated for inclusion in the National Election Study, a nationwide American election survey conducted by the University of Michigan. Respondents were asked about their "trust" in government and fellow citizens and were also asked a battery of questions concerning their associational involvement. See "Questions on Social Capital Slated for Inclusion in 1996 National Election Study," June 10, 1996 (in author's file). I am indebted to Prof. Hanes Walton Jr. of the University of Michigan for providing me with these questions.

71. For a thorough and insightful discussion of the origins and definitions of social capital, see Alejandro Portes, "Social Capital: Its Origin and Applications in Modern Sociology," *Annual Review of Sociology* 24 (1998): 1–24.

72. My definition is an adaptation of Stone's, who defined social capital as "an ability to gain social ends by cooperation, with minimal reliance on direct payments or coercion." Unlike Putnam's formulation, however, Stone's definition does not incorporate the crucial role of history and past experiences. See Stone, "Civic Capacity and Urban School Reform," p. 268.

73. Coleman, *Foundations of Social Theory*, p. 311.

74. Hanes Walton Jr. and Marion Orr, "African-American Mayors and National Urban Policy: The Fiscal Politics of Urban Federalism," in *African American Power*

and Politics, ed. Hanes Walton Jr. (New York: Columbia University Press, 1997), pp. 341–51.

75. Bob Edwards and Michael W. Foley, "Social Capital and the Political Economy of Our Discontent," *American Behavioral Scientist* 40 (March/April 1997): 669–78.

76. On whites' insensitivity to African-American past experiences, see Jennifer L. Hochschild, *Facing Up to the American Dream: Race, Class, and the Soul of the Nation* (Princeton: Princeton University Press, 1995).

77. "Civic Capacity and Urban Education," funded by Education and Human Resources Directorate of the National Science Foundation, Grant no. RED 9350139; Clarence N. Stone is the principal investigator. I also relied heavily on my own earlier research on Baltimore, "Black Political Incorporation—Phase Two: Baltimore and Detroit" (Ph.D. diss., University of Maryland, 1992).

78. Floyd Hunter, *Community Power Structure* (Chapel Hill: University of North Carolina Press, 1953); Robert A. Dahl, *Who Governs?* (New Haven: Yale University Press, 1961); Todd Swanstrom, *The Crisis of Growth Politics: Cleveland, Kucinich, and the Challenge of Urban Populism* (Philadelphia: Temple University Press, 1985); Clarence N. Stone, *Regime Politics: Governing Atlanta, 1946–1988* (Lawrence: University Press of Kansas, 1989); Dianne M. Pinderhughes, *Race and Ethnicity in Chicago Politics* (Urbana: University of Illinois Press, 1987); John H. Mollenkopf, *A Phoenix in the Ashes: The Rise and Fall of the Koch Coalition in New York City Politics* (Princeton: Princeton University Press, 1992); Richard E. DeLeon, *Left Coast City: Progressive Politics in San Francisco, 1975–1991* (Lawrence: University Press of Kansas, 1992); and Raphael J. Sonenshein, *Politics in Black and White: Race and Power in Los Angeles* (Princeton: Princeton University Press, 1993).

79. Richard E. DeLeon, "Research Methods in Urban Politics and Policy," in *Handbook of Research on Urban Politics and Policy in the United States,* ed. Ronald K. Vogel (Westport, CT: Greenwood Press, 1997), pp. 17–30.

80. Gary King, Robert O. Keohane, and Sidney Verba, *Designing Social Inquiry* (Princeton: Princeton University Press, 1994), p. 44.

81. Hanes Walton Jr., *African-American Power and Politics: The Political Context Variable* (New York: Columbia University Press, 1997), p. 41.

82. King, Keohane, and Verba, *Designing Social Inquiry,* pp. 221 and 52.

2. THE FORMATION OF BLACK SOCIAL CAPITAL IN BALTIMORE

1. Ira De A. Reid, *The Negro Community of Baltimore* (Baltimore: Baltimore Urban League, 1935), p. 46.

2. Gary Browne, *Baltimore in the Nation: 1789–1861* (Chapel Hill: University of North Carolina Press, 1980).

3. Ibid., p. xxii.

4. Paul Kantor, *The Dependent City* (Glenview, IL: Scott, Foresman and Company, 1988), p. 52.

5. Elizabeth Fee, "Evergreen House and the Garrett Family: A Railroad Fortune," in *The Baltimore Book: New Views of Local History,* ed. Elizabeth Fee, Linda Shopes, and Linda Zeidman (Philadelphia: Temple University Press, 1991), pp. 17–37.

6. Browne, *Baltimore in the Nation,* p. 160.

7. Jo Ann Argersinger, "The City That Tries to Suit Everybody: Baltimore's Clothing Industry," in Fee et al., eds., *Baltimore Book,* pp. 81–101.

8. Barbara Jeane Fields, *Slavery and Freedom on the Middle Ground: Maryland During the Nineteenth Century* (New Haven: Yale University Press, 1985), pp. 40–62.

9. Ibid., pp. 48 and 57.

10. Ibid., p. 50.

11. Linda Shopes, "Fells Point: Community and Conflict in a Working-Class Neighborhood," in Fee et al., eds., *Baltimore Book,* pp. 124–25.

12. Leroy G. Graham, *Baltimore: Nineteenth Century Black Capital* (Washington, DC: University Press of America, 1982), and Christopher Phillips, *Freedom's Port: The African American Community of Baltimore, 1790–1860* (Urbana: University of Illinois Press, 1997).

13. Phillips, *Freedom's Port,* p. 153.

14. Fields, *Slavery and Freedom on the Middle Ground.*

15. Phillips, *Freedom's Port,* p. 23.

16. Francis Beirne, *Amiable Baltimoreans* (New York: Dutton and Company, 1951), pp. 269–70.

17. Phillips, *Freedom's Port,* pp. 120–40.

18. C. Eric Lincoln and Lawrence H. Mamiya, *The Black Church in the African American Experience* (Durham, NC: Duke University Press, 1990), p. 48.

19. Harold A. McDougall, *Black Baltimore: A New Theory of Community* (Philadelphia: Temple University Press, 1993), p. 28.

20. Phillips, *Freedom's Port,* p. 143.

21. As early as 1839, and again in 1850, a group of blacks petitioned the mayor concerning the policy of taxing free people of color for the support of public schools. The mayor refused to change the policy. See Bettye C. Thomas, "Public Education and Black Protest in Baltimore: 1865–1900," *Maryland Historical Magazine* 71 (fall 1976): 381–91.

22. Bettye Gardner, "Ante-bellum Black Education in Baltimore," *Maryland Historical Magazine* 71 (fall 1976): 360–66.

23. Phillips, *Freedom's Port,* p. 164.

24. Ibid.

25. Ibid., p. 171.

26. Ibid., p. 172.

27. Lincoln and Mamiya, *The Black Church in the African American Experience,* p. 8.

28. For brief but informative discussions of the Jacobs bill, see Robert J. Brugger, *Maryland: A Middle Temperament* (Baltimore: Johns Hopkins University Press, 1988), pp. 266–69; Phillips, *Freedom's Port,* pp. 207–8; and Fields, *Slavery and Freedom on the Middle Ground,* pp. 76–82.

29. Phillips, *Freedom's Port,* p. 233.

30. The issue divided Maryland's white communities. The nonslaveholders knew that free blacks would leave the state rather than return again to bondage; thus the Jacobs bill would deprive them of the services of the free population and compel them to hire the surplus slave population. Although the counties of the Eastern Shore and southern Maryland (slaveholding areas) controlled the legislature, nonslaveholding northern Maryland had more than twice their number of voters.

31. J. Clay Smith Jr., *Emancipation: The Making of the Black Lawyer, 1844–1944* (Philadelphia: University of Pennsylvania Press, 1993), pp. 142–44.

32. For an informative biography of the Reverend Harvey Johnson, see Azzie Briscoe Koger, "Dr. Harvey Johnson: Minister and Pioneer Civic Leader," 1957, on file in the Enoch Pratt Free Library, Baltimore; see also, "Dr. Johnson Buried," *Baltimore Afro-American* (January 19, 1923), and Eugenia Collier, "House Built on Rock: Union Baptist Church," *Negro History Bulletin* 47 (October–December 1984): 3–7.

33. Roderick Ryon, "Old West Baltimore," *Maryland Historical Magazine* 77 (spring 1982): 59.

34. Smith, *Emancipation: The Making of the Black Lawyer*, pp. 144–45.

35. Thomas, "Public Education and Black Protest in Baltimore," p. 383.

36. Ibid., p. 385.

37. Denton L. Watson, *Lion in the Lobby: Clarence Mitchell, Jr.'s Struggle for the Passage of Civil Rights Laws* (New York: William Morrow and Company, 1990), p. 81.

38. Maryland Commission on Interracial Problems and Relations, *An American City in Transition* (Baltimore: Commission on Human Relations, 1955), pp. 206–7.

39. Charles S. Johnson, "Negroes at Work in Baltimore, Maryland," *Opportunity: A Journal of Negro Life* 1 (June 1923): 12–19.

40. Roderick N. Ryon, "An Ambiguous Legacy: Baltimore Blacks and the CIO, 1936–1941," *Journal of Negro History* 65 (winter 1980): 18–33.

41. Joseph Garonzik, "The Racial and Ethnic Make-up of Baltimore Neighborhoods, 1850–1870," *Maryland Historical Magazine* 71 (fall 1976): 392–402.

42. Cynthia Neverdon-Morton, "Black Housing Patterns in Baltimore City, 1885–1953," *Maryland Historian* 16 (spring/summer 1985): 25–39, and Karen Olson, "Old West Baltimore: Segregation, African-American Culture, and the Struggle for Equality," in Fee et al., eds., *Baltimore Book*, p. 57.

43. Neverdon-Morton, "Black Housing Patterns in Baltimore City."

44. Garrett Power, "Apartheid Baltimore Style: The Residential Segregation Ordinances of 1910–1913," *Maryland Law Review* 42 (1983): 289–328.

45. Unscrupulous realtors took advantage of this situation. Blockbusting became particularly prevalent during the period of the segregation ordinances. White realtors bought old houses and divided them into so-called "apartments," charging rents so high that in many cases, black tenants were forced into subletting. Several slumlord dynasties were initiated by investment in black housing during this era. Morris Goldseker, a Jewish immigrant, began working in real estate in the 1920s, eventually starting his own business, which concentrated on the purchase of old properties at depressed prices in declining sections of the city. By the 1960s, the Goldseker Company was one of the largest real estate firms in Baltimore. Morris Goldseker died in 1973; according to the terms of his will, the Goldseker Foundation was established three years later. See W. Edward Orser, *Blockbusting in Baltimore: The Edmondson Village Story* (Lexington: University Press of Kentucky, 1994).

46. William J. Wilson, *The Truly Disadvantaged* (Chicago: University of Chicago Press, 1987), p. 49.

47. Quoted in Power, "Apartheid Baltimore Style," p. 309.

48. Watson, *Lion in the Lobby*, p. 63.

49. Phillips, *Freedom's Port*, p. 143.

50. Ryon, "Old West Baltimore," pp. 56–57.

51. Ibid., p. 57.

52. Heyward Farrar, *The Baltimore Afro-American: 1892–1950* (Westport, CT: Greenwood Press, 1998).

53. McDougall, *Black Baltimore,* p. 44.

54. Margaret Law Callcott, *The Negro in Maryland Politics, 1870–1912* (Baltimore: Johns Hopkins University Press, 1969), p. 135.

55. Reid, *The Negro Community of Baltimore,* pp. 41–42.

56. Ibid.

57. Brugger, *Maryland: A Middle Temperament,* p. 520.

58. Lenora Heilig Nast, Laurence N. Krause, and R. C. Monk, eds., *Baltimore: A Living Renaissance* (Baltimore: Historic Baltimore Society, 1982), p. 118.

59. Ryon, "Old West Baltimore," p. 59.

60. Watson, *Lion in the Lobby,* discusses the lynching of George Armwood; see especially pp. 31–48.

61. George Callcott, *Maryland and America: 1940–1980* (Baltimore: Johns Hopkins University Press, 1984), p. 146.

62. Genna Rae McNeil, "Youth Initiative in the African American Struggle for Racial Justice and Constitutional Rights: The City-Wide Young People's Forum of Baltimore, 1931–1941," In *African Americans and the Living Constitution,* ed. John Hope Franklin and Genna Rae McNeil (Washington, DC: Smithsonian Institution Press, 1995), pp. 56–80.

63. Callcott, *Maryland and America,* p. 56.

64. Carl Schoettler, "Tale of Two Warriors," *Sun* (February 1, 1998).

65. Callcott, *Maryland and America,* p. 56.

66. Ibid., pp. 145–46.

67. The Development Training Institute, *An Action Plan for Improving Neighborhood Organizations and Community Self-Help in Baltimore* (Baltimore: Morris Goldseker Foundation, 1989), p. 6.

68. McDougall, *Black Baltimore,* pp. 98–106.

69. Ibid., p. 62.

70. Ibid., p. 80.

71. Ibid., pp. 65–73.

72. Ibid., pp. 80–87.

73. Ibid., p. 90.

74. This discussion of BUILD relies heavily on my earlier research on Baltimore. See Marion Orr, "Black Political Incorporation—Phase Two: Baltimore and Detroit" (Ph.D. diss., University of Maryland, 1992), pp. 340–52, and idem, "Urban Regimes and Human Capital Policies: A Study of Baltimore," *Journal of Urban Affairs* 14 (1992): 173–87.

75. Harry Boyte, *Commonwealth: A Return to Citizen Politics* (New York: Free Press, 1989), p. 110.

76. On Alinsky and the IAF, see Sanford Horwitt, *Let Them Call Me Rebel: Saul Alinsky, His Life and Legacy* (New York: Knopf, 1989); Saul D. Alinsky, *Rules for Radicals: A Pragmatic Primer for Realistic Radicals* (New York: Vintage Books, 1972); and Robert Bailey Jr., *Radicals in Urban Politics: The Alinsky Approach* (Chicago: University of Chicago Press, 1974). On the IAF, see Mary Beth Rogers, *Cold Anger: A Story of Faith and Power Politics* (Denton: University of North Texas Press, 1990); Timothy Ross, "Grass Roots Action in East Brooklyn: A Community Organization Takes up School Reform,"

in *Changing Urban Education,* ed. Clarence N. Stone (Lawrence: University Press of Kansas, 1998), pp. 118–38; Jim Rooney, *Organizing the South Bronx* (Albany: State University of New York Press, 1995); and Mark Russell Warren, "Social Capital and Community Empowerment: Religion and Political Organization in the Texas Industrial Areas Foundation" (Ph.D. diss., Harvard University, 1995).

77. Boyte, *Commonwealth,* p. 115.

78. Quoted in Orr, "Black Political Incorporation—Phase Two," p. 342.

79. Boyte, *Commonwealth,* p. 116.

80. Quoted in Orr, "Black Political Incorporation—Phase Two," p. 342.

81. Boyte, *Commonwealth,* p. 116.

82. Ibid.

83. Quoted in Orr, "Black Political Incorporation—Phase Two," p. 343.

84. Boyte, *Commonwealth,* p. 117.

85. Ibid., p. 118.

86. Quoted in Orr, "Black Political Incorporation—Phase Two," p. 344.

87. Quoted in Orr, "Urban Regimes and Human Capital Policies," p. 177.

88. Ibid.

89. Richard C. Hula, Cynthia Y. Jackson, and Marion Orr, "Urban Politics, Governing Nonprofits, and Community Revitalization," *Urban Affairs Review* 32 (March 1997): 459–89.

90. McDougall, *Black Baltimore,* pp. 128–29.

91. Ibid., p. 180.

92. Robert D. Putnam, *Making Democracy Work* (Princeton: Princeton University Press, 1993), p. 175.

3. PATRONAGE CULTURE AND THE POLITICS OF BIRACIAL COOPERATION

1. Charles Johnson, "Negroes at Work in Baltimore, Maryland," *Opportunity: A Journal of Negro Life* 1 (June 1923): 12.

2. Margaret L. Callcott, *The Negro in Maryland Politics, 1870–1912* (Baltimore: Johns Hopkins University Press, 1969).

3. On Cummings, see J. Clay Smith Jr., *Emancipation: The Making of the Black Lawyer, 1844–1944* (Philadelphia: University of Pennsylvania Press, 1993), pp. 145–47.

4. For a detailed discussion of these early black councillors, see the excellent study by Suzanne E. Greene, "Black Republicans on the Baltimore City Council, 1890–1931," *Maryland Historical Magazine* 74 (September 1979): 203–22.

5. Ibid., p. 208.

6. Frank Kent, *The Story of Maryland Politics* (Baltimore: Thomas and Evans, 1911), pp. 17–23; Paul Winchester, *Men of Maryland Since the Civil War* (Baltimore: Maryland County Press Syndicate, 1923), pp. 103–10.

7. On Boss Rasin, see Mary Anne Dunn, "The Life of Isaac Freeman Rasin, Democratic Leader of Baltimore from 1870–1907" (master's thesis, Catholic University, 1949); Winchester, *Men of Maryland Since the Civil War,* pp. 103–10; Kent, *The Story of Maryland Politics,* pp. 17–23; James Crooks, *Politics and Progress: The Rise of Urban Progressivism in Baltimore, 1875–1911* (Baton Rouge: Louisiana State University Press, 1968), pp. 9–47; and Callcott, *The Negro in Maryland Politics,* pp. 35–38.

8. Callcott, *The Negro in Maryland Politics,* p. 36.

9. Robert Brugger, *Maryland: A Middle Temperament* (Baltimore: Johns Hopkins University Press, 1988), p. 386.

10. On the importance of the relationship between state-level political organization and central-city political machines, see Steven Erie, *Rainbow's End: Irish Americans and the Dilemmas of Urban Machine Politics, 1840–1985* (Berkeley: University of California Press, 1988).

11. John R. Lambert, *Arthur Pue Gorman* (Baton Rouge: Louisiana State University Press, 1953), p. 32.

12. Kent, *The Story of Maryland Politics,* p. 335; Lambert, *Arthur Pue Gorman,* pp. 323–60.

13. Callcott, *The Negro in Maryland Politics,* p. 99.

14. Ibid., pp. 101–38.

15. Kent, *The Story of Maryland Politics,* p. 133.

16. Ibid., p. 336.

17. Callcott, *The Negro in Maryland Politics,* p. 27.

18. Ibid., p. 56.

19. Henry Bains, "Five Kinds of Politics: A Historical and Comparative Analysis of the Making of Legislators in Five Maryland Communities" (Ph.D. diss., Harvard University, 1970), pp. 823–25.

20. Ibid., p. 825.

21. Kent, *The Story of Maryland Politics,* p. 17.

22. Ibid., p. 308.

23. Greene, "Black Republicans on the Baltimore City Council," p. 214.

24. In the new Fourth District, in West Baltimore, Republican registration outnumbered Democrats by about 5,000 voters. The white population, however, exceeded that of blacks by approximately 1,100. Evidently, a considerable number of the white Republicans voted on color lines rather than on political party lines. For an account of the 1923 council elections and an indication of the general surprise at the results, see *Sun,* "Negroes Lose Council Seats," May 9, 1923.

25. Verda F. Welcome with James M. Abraham, *My Life and Times* (Englewood Cliffs, NJ: Henry House Publishers, 1991), p. 44.

26. Ibid., p. 44, and Bain, "Five Kinds of Politics," p. 825.

27. In 1951 Adams's underworld activities were so notorious that he was called to testify before Sen. Estes Kefauver's Committee to Investigate Interstate Crime. For many years he was the target of numerous investigations. In 1987 Adams was arrested on federal money-laundering charges. The U.S. Supreme Court eventually overturned his conviction. For information on Adams, see the vertical file under his name at Enoch Pratt Public Library, Baltimore. See also Thomas B. Edsall, *Power and Money* (New York: Norton, 1988), pp. 32–37, and Welcome, *My Life and Times,* pp. 143–45.

28. Nancy J. Weiss, *Farewell to the Party of Lincoln: Black Politics in the Age of FDR* (Princeton: Princeton University Press, 1983).

29. Harvey Wheeler, "Yesterday's Robin Hood: The Rise and Fall of Baltimore's Trenton Democratic Club," *American Quarterly* (winter 1955): 332–44. Other accounts of the life and political career of Jack Pollack can be found in the vertical file under his name at the Enoch Pratt Public Library, Baltimore.

30. Joseph Arnold, "The Last of the Good Old Days: Politics in Baltimore, 1920–

1950," *Maryland Historical Magazine* 71 (1971): 443–48. Although there are no precise numbers, it is possible that nearly 100 district- or ward-level clubs existed in the decades immediately after Rasin's death. John "Sonny" Mahon, John S. "Frank" Kelly, and William "Uncle Willie" Curran were prominent club politicians in the decades immediately following Rasin's death. Thomas D'Alesandro Jr. (a future mayor and member of Congress) was a club leader in the Little Italy community in southeast Baltimore. The list of past district "bosslets" would include such men (with few exceptions, most district-level bosses were men) as J. Joseph Curran Sr., Julian "Chicken" Carrick, Hugo Ricuitti, William "Sweetie" Adelson, Harry "Soft Shoes" McGuirk, and Dominic "Mimi" DiPietro.

31. Quoted in G. James Fleming, *An All-Negro Ticket in Baltimore* (New York: McGraw-Hill, 1962), p. 3.

32. Wheeler, "Yesterday's Robin Hood," p. 339.

33. Welcome, *My Life and Times,* p. 94.

34. Bud Russo, "The Rise of Clarence 'Du' Burns: From Collecting Cardboard to City Council President," *Baltimore Chronicle,* March 5, 1986.

35. Ibid.

36. Fleming, *An All-Negro Ticket in Baltimore.*

37. Ibid., p. 6.

38. Welcome, *My Life and Times,* p. 146.

39. Ibid., p. 37.

40. Ibid., pp. 221–22.

41. Edsall, *Power and Money,* p. 37.

42. Kevin O'Keeffe, *Baltimore Politics, 1971–1986: The Schaefer Years and the Struggle for Succession* (Washington, DC: Georgetown University Press, 1986), p. 15.

43. Sharon Perlman Krefetz, *Welfare Policy Making and City Politics* (New York: Praeger Publishers, 1976), pp. 31–32.

44. Ibid., p. 34. A split among the key factions of the Democratic party was an important factor that aided McKeldin's election.

45. Robert Marc Goldberg, "Party Competition and Black Politics in Baltimore and Philadelphia" (Ph.D. diss., Brandeis University, 1984), pp. 147–49.

46. Ibid., p. 35.

47. Goldberg, "Party Competition and Black Politics in Baltimore and Philadelphia," pp. 149–50.

48. Ibid., p. 156.

49. Ibid., p. 157, and see Peter Bachrach and Morton S. Baratz, *Power and Poverty: Theory and Practice* (New York: Oxford University Press, 1970), p. 81.

50. Mike Bowler, *Lessons of Change: Baltimore Schools in the Modern Era,* a report prepared for the Fund for Educational Excellence, Baltimore, 1991, p. 11.

51. Ibid., p. 13.

52. Quoted in Mike Bowler, "Board Stands up to Be Counted," *Sun,* February 21, 1996.

53. William Ryan, *Blaming the Victim* (New York: Pantheon Books, 1971), pp. 55–59; Estelle Fuchs, "How Teachers Learn to Help Children Fail," *Transaction* 5 (September 1968): 45–49; and Robert Rosenthal and Lenore Jacobson, *Pygmalion in the Classroom* (New York: Holt, Rinehart and Winston, 1968).

54. Nora Frenkiel, "A Last Hurrah: Tommy D'Alesandro Found There Was Life After Big-City Politics," *Sun,* August 26, 1990.

55. Quoted in Marion Orr, "Urban Regimes and Human Capital Policies: A Study of Baltimore," *Journal of Urban Affairs* 14, 2 (1992): 180–81.

56. Mike Bowler, "Patterson Is Hired by School Board," *Sun,* July 17, 1971.

57. On Schaefer's election, see Marion Orr, "The Struggle for Black Empowerment in Baltimore: Electoral Control and Governing Coalitions," in *Racial Politics in American Cities,* ed. Rufus P. Browning, Dale Rogers Marshall, and David Tabb, 2d ed. (New York: Longman Press, 1997), pp. 201–19, and G. James Fleming, *Baltimore's Failure to Elect a Black Mayor in 1971* (Washington, DC: Joint Center for Political Studies, 1972).

58. Athelia Knight and Barbara Vobejda, "Steamroller Style Propels Schaefer," *Washington Post,* September 3, 1986.

59. O'Keeffe, *Baltimore Politics, 1971–1986,* p. 10.

60. Kweisi Mfume, *No Free Ride: From the Mean Streets to the Mainstream* (New York: Ballantine Books, 1996), p. 249.

61. John Feinstein, "Schaefer Is Proud of 'His' Baltimore," *Washington Post,* September 6, 1983.

62. Bowler, *Lessons of Change,* p. 14.

63. Kenneth K. Wong, *City Choices: Housing and Education* (Albany: State University of New York Press, 1990), p. 87.

64. Patterson's tenure is discussed in Hugh J. Scott, *The Black Superintendent: Messiah or Scapegoat?* (Washington, DC: Howard University Press, 1980), pp. 102–18, and Barbara L. Jackson, *Balancing Act: The Political Role of the Urban School Superintendent* (Washington, DC: Joint Center for Political and Economic Studies, 1996).

65. Bowler, *Lessons of Change,* p. 13.

66. Scott, *The Black Superintendent,* p. 112.

67. Verda Welcome, *My Life and Times,* p. 235.

68. Scott, *The Black Superintendent,* p. 107.

69. Edward Berkowitz, "Baltimore's Public Schools in a Time of Transition," *Maryland Historical Magazine* 92 (winter 1997): 423.

70. Ibid.

71. Richard Ben Cramer and Antero Pietila, "Board's Whites Try to Fire Patterson," *Sun,* August 9, 1974.

72. Editorial, "Fresh Start for the School Board," *Sun,* January 4, 1975.

73. In my interviews with key civic leaders, top educational administrators, business executives, and other school activists, some white leaders denied the existence of such an agreement. However, many black educators and other black respondents acknowledged that such an agreement was made. Of course, this type of "distributional" arrangement is familiar to students of American urban politics. Steve Erie, in his study of the Irish political machines, discussed how machine bosses extended their longevity by distributing a variety of public-sector jobs to their fellow Irishmen, who typically got police and fire jobs; teaching jobs went to the Jews, and the Italians received positions in sanitation. See Erie, *Rainbow's End,* and Dianne M. Pinderhughes, *Race and Ethnicity in Chicago Politics: A Reexamination of Pluralist Theory* (Urbana: University of Illinois Press, 1987).

74. Wong, *City Choices,* p. 119.

75. Bowler, *Lessons of Change,* p. 18.

76. Wong, *City Choices,* p. 115.

77. Marc Levine, "Downtown Redevelopment as an Urban Growth Strategy: A Critical Appraisal of the Baltimore Renaissance," *Journal of Urban Affairs* 9 (fall 1987): 103–23.

78. Barbara Vobejda and Gwen Ifill, "Education Issue May Spell Trouble for Schaefer," *Washington Post,* July 28, 1986.

79. Wong, *City Choices,* pp. 113–114.

80. Veronica D. DiConti, *Interest Groups and Education Reform* (Lanham, MD: University Press of America, 1996), p. 115.

81. Mayor Schaefer and his supporters were quick to point out that the state government failed to adequately support the city's schools that enrolled the highest proportion of disadvantaged students in Maryland's twenty-four school districts. In 1979 the city sued the state in an effort to revamp Maryland's local school-aid formulas and to increase funding for Baltimore. The city lost, but the legislature subsequently adopted a new funding formula that brought more state funds to the city's schools. On the disparities in state funding for Maryland school districts, see Robert E. Slavin, "Funding Inequities Among Maryland School Districts: What Do They Mean in Practice?" paper, Center for Research on Effective Schooling for Disadvantaged Students, Johns Hopkins University, Baltimore, 1991, and the Abell Foundation, "A Growing Inequality: A Report on the Financial Condition of the Baltimore City Public Schools" (Baltimore: Abell Foundation, 1989).

82. Slavin, "Funding Inequities Among Maryland School Districts," pp. 11–18.

83. Peter L. Szanton, *Baltimore 2000: A Choice of Futures* (Baltimore: Morris Goldseker Foundation, 1986), p. 41.

84. Will Englund, "Tightly Knit Group of Survivors Controls Power," *Sun,* May 3, 1988.

85. Curiously, no other department of city government is as thoroughly managed by African Americans. Excluding the education department, African Americans constitute only 50 percent of the municipal workforce. In 1994, 36 percent of the administrative and 37 percent of the professional positions in the Baltimore city government were held by African Americans. There remains a number of city departments that have yet to be headed by an African American. For data on the racial composition of Baltimore's municipal workforce, see Marion Orr, "The Struggle for Black Empowerment," pp. 211–13.

86. I borrowed the term "bonds of personalism" from Alan Rosenthal, *Pedagogues and Power: Teacher Groups in School Politics* (Syracuse, NY: Syracuse University Press, 1969).

87. Coppin State and Morgan State graduates are still heavily recruited and hired by the BCPS. Approximately 35 percent of teachers hired in 1996 and 1997 from colleges and universities in Maryland were graduates of Coppin and Morgan. See Liz Bowie, "Teacher Recruiting Criticized," *Sun,* February 10, 1999.

88. Englund, "Tightly Knit Group of Survivors Controls Power."

89. The pastor of Bethel A.M.E., Dr. Frank M. Reid, is Kurt Schmoke's stepbrother. The Reverend Vernon Dobson, pastor of Union Baptist Church, was active in the civil rights movement in Baltimore and a founding member of BUILD. See Harold McDougall, *Black Baltimore: A Theory of Community* (Philadelphia: Temple University Press, 1993), pp. 123–26, and Eugenia Collier, "House Built on Rock: Union Baptist Church," *Negro History Bulletin* 47, 4 (October–December, 1984): 3–7.

90. Orr, "The Struggle for Black Empowerment in Baltimore."

91. O'Keeffe, *Baltimore Politics in 1971–1986,* pp. 63–90.

92. Quoted in Richard C. Hula, "The Two Baltimores," in *Leadership and Urban Regeneration,* ed. Dennis Judd and Michael Parkinson (Newbury Park, CA: Sage, 1990), p. 209.

93. Quoted in Marion Orr, "Urban Regimes and Human Capital Policies: A Study of Baltimore," *Journal of Urban Affairs* 14 (1992): 182.

94. Katharine Lyall, "A Bicycle Built-for-Two: Public-Private Partnership in Baltimore," in *Public-Private Partnership in American Cities: Seven Case Studies,* ed. R. Scott Fosler and Renee A. Berger (Lexington, MA: Lexington Books, 1982).

95. Marc V. Levine, "Downtown Redevelopment as an Urban Growth Strategy: A Critical Appraisal of the Baltimore Renaissance," *Journal of Urban Affairs* 9 (1987): 103–23.

96. Lyall, "A Bicycle Built-for-Two," and Frances M. Froelicher, "CPHA's Impact, 1941–1969: A Personal Appraisal," in *Baltimore: A Living Renaissance,* ed. Lenora H. Nast, Laurence Krause, and R.C. Monk (Baltimore: Historic Baltimore Society, 1982).

97. Lyall, "A Bicycle Built-for-Two," p. 21.

98. Citizens Planning and Housing Association, *Annual Report, 1995–1996,* Baltimore: CPHA, 1996.

4. THE POLITICAL ECONOMY AND CITY SCHOOLS, 1950-1990

1. Jo Ann Argersinger, "The City That Tries to Suit Everybody: Baltimore's Clothing Industry," in *The Baltimore Book: New Views of Local History,* ed. Elizabeth Fee, Linda Shopes, and Linda Zeidman (Philadelphia: Temple University Press, 1991), pp. 81–101.

2. Sherry Olson, *Baltimore: The Building of an American City* (Baltimore: Johns Hopkins University Press, 1980).

3. Jo Ann Argersinger, *Toward a New Deal in Baltimore* (Chapel Hill: University of North Carolina Press, 1988), p. 2.

4. Ibid., p. 5.

5. Sherry Olson, *Baltimore* (Cambridge, MA: Ballinger, 1976), pp. 3–10.

6. Olson, *Baltimore: The Building of an American City,* p. 334.

7. Argersinger, *Toward a New Deal in Baltimore,* p. 8.

8. Olson, *Baltimore: The Building of an American City,* p. 334.

9. Argersinger, *Toward a New Deal in Baltimore,* pp. 30–54.

10. George Callcott, *Maryland and America, 1940–1980* (Baltimore: Johns Hopkins University Press, 1985), p. 43.

11. Task Force on Population Migration, "The Impact of Population Decline on Baltimore," a report to Mayor William Donald Schaefer, May 1978, p. 32.

12. Baltimore is not alone in this respect. In other major school districts, African Americans are predominant among instructional staff, administrative personnel, and nonprofessional positions. See Wilbur C. Rich, *Black Mayors and School Politics* (New York: Garland Press, 1996); Jean Anyon, *Ghetto Schooling: A Political Economy of Urban Educational Reform* (New York: Teachers College Press, 1997); Jeffrey R. Henig, Richard C. Hula, Marion Orr, and Desiree Pedescleaux, *The Color of School Reform* (Princeton: Princeton University Press, 1999); and Caroline Hendrie, "Politics of Jobs in City Schools Hinder Reform," *Education Week* (March 26, 1997): 5–7.

13. Maryland State Department of Education, *Professional Staff by Assignment, Race/Ethnicity, and Gender, Maryland Public Schools* (Baltimore: MD State Dept. of Education, 1993).

14. Marilyn Gittell and T. Edward Hollander, *Six Urban School Districts: A Comparative Study of Institutional Response* (New York: Praeger, 1968), Table 20, p. 234.

15. Marion Orr, "Race, Jobs, and Politics: The Challenge of School Reform in Baltimore," in *Changing Urban Education,* ed. Clarence N. Stone (Lawrence: University Press of Kansas, 1998), pp. 93–117.

16. National Education Association, *Baltimore, Maryland, Change and Contrast: The Children and the Public Schools* (NEA, Commission on Professional Rights and Responsibilities, Washington, DC, May 1967), p. 32.

17. See David Harvey, "A View from Federal Hill," in Elizabeth Fee et al., eds., *Baltimore Book,* p. 236.

18. Richard Hula, "The Two Baltimores," in *Leadership and Urban Regeneration,* ed. Dennis Judd and Michael Parkinson (Newbury Park, CA: Sage Publications), p. 193.

19. Marc V. Levine, "Downtown Redevelopment as an Urban Growth Strategy: A Critical Appraisal of the Baltimore Renaissance," *Journal of Urban Affairs* 9 (fall, 1987): 103–23.

20. John D. Kasarda, "Urban Industrial Transition and the Underclass," *Annals of the American Academy of Political and Social Sciences* 501 (January 1989): 33 and 35.

21. See, especially, William J. Wilson, *The Truly Disadvantaged: The Inner City, the Underclass, and Public Policy* (Chicago: University of Chicago Press, 1987), and his more recent *When Work Disappears: The World of the New Urban Poor* (New York: Knopf, 1996).

22. Barry Bluestone and Bennett Harrison, *The Deindustrialization of America: Plant Closings, Community Abandonment, and the Dismantling of Basic Industry* (New York: Basic Books, 1982).

23. Martin Carnoy, *Faded Dreams: The Politics and Economics of Race in America* (New York: Cambridge University Press, 1994), p. 87.

24. Levine, "Downtown Redevelopment as an Urban Growth Strategy"; Charles Christian and Gavin Keith, "The Decline of Manufacturing Jobs and the Growing Underclass in Baltimore," in *Blacks in Maryland,* report by the Bureau of Governmental Research, University of Maryland, n.d.; and Hula, "The Two Baltimores."

25. Olson, *Baltimore,* p. 23.

26. In response to the persistence of the problem, Baltimore public health officials have begun offering Norplant (the surgically implanted contraceptive) in city schools. See T. Lewin, "Baltimore School Clinics to Offer Birth Control by Surgical Implant," *New York Times,* December 4, 1992.

27. *The Report of the Governor's Commission on School Funding* (Annapolis, MD, January 1994), pp. 36 and 5.

28. Wilson, *When Work Disappears,* p. 136.

29. Kurt L. Schmoke, "The Why and How of Making Baltimore 'The City That Reads,'" *Sun,* January 7, 1990.

30. See Kasarda, "Urban Industrial Transition and the Underclass."

31. Peter Szanton, *Baltimore 2000* (Baltimore: Morris Goldseker Foundation, 1986).

32. Ibid., p. 34.

33. Ibid., p. 10.

34. Associated Black Charities, *A Study of the Management of the Baltimore City Public Schools* (Baltimore: ABC, 1992).

35. David R. Mayhew, *Placing Parties in American Politics* (Princeton: Princeton University Press, 1986), pp. 84–89, provides a brief yet informative discussion of Democratic party politics in Maryland.

36. On machine politics in Baltimore, see Henry Bain, "Five Kinds of Politics: A Historical and Comparative Study of the Making of Legislators in Five Maryland Constituencies" (Ph.D diss., Harvard University, 1970); Marion Orr, "The Struggle for Black Empowerment in Baltimore: Electoral Control and Governing Coalitions," in *Racial Politics in American Cities*, ed. Rufus P. Browning, Dale Rogers Marshall, and David H. Tabb, 2d ed. (New York: Longman Press, 1997), pp. 201–19; Joseph Arnold, "The Last of the Good Old Days: Politics in Baltimore," *Maryland Historical Magazine* 7 (spring 1976): 443–48; and Harvey Wheeler, "Yesterday's Robin Hood: The Rise and Fall of the Trenton Democratic Club," *American Quarterly* (winter 1955): 332–44.

37. Howard Schneider, "D.C. Suburbs Eclipsing Baltimore's Domination," *Washington Post*, January 6, 1991.

38. William F. Zorzi Jr., "Governor Sees His Future in City Vote," *Sun*, September 19, 1995.

39. Thomas Byrne Edsall, *Power and Money: Writings About Politics, 1971–1987* (New York: Norton, 1988), p. 31.

40. Vernon S. Vavrina, "The History of Public Education in the City of Baltimore, 1829–1956" (Ph.D. diss., Catholic University of America, 1958).

41. U.S. Commission on Civil Rights, *Racial Isolation in the Public Schools*, 2 vols. (Washington, DC: U.S. Printing Office, 1967), 1:28.

42. Abell Foundation, "A Growing Inequality: A Report on the Financial Condition of the Baltimore City Public Schools," January 1989, p. 12.

43. U.S. Commission on Civil Rights, *Racial Isolation in the Public Schools*, p. 28.

44. The trend of state governments' increasing contributions to education budgets is not confined to Maryland and Baltimore City. In 1971 and 1972, state governments contributed about 38 percent of all revenues for public elementary and secondary schools; from 1986 to 1987, this increased to nearly 50 percent. In actual dollars, state governments were spending four times as much in 1986 and 1987 than they were in 1971 and 1972. Although total state expenditures have continued to grow, the state percentage declined to about 46 percent as of 1991 and 1992.

45. *Hornbeck v. Somerset* 458 A2d 758 (Md.1983).

46. *1983 Report of the Task Force to Study the Funding of Public Education*, Annapolis, MD, December 1, 1983.

47. Susan P. Leviton and Matthew H. Joseph, "An Adequate Education for all Maryland's Children: Morally Right, Economically Necessary, and Constitutionally Required," *Maryland Law Review* 52 (1993): 1137–91.

48. For a good discussion of some of the recent challenges Montgomery County public schools face, see Susan E. Eaton, "Slipping Toward Segregation: Local Control and Eroding Desegregation in Montgomery County," in *Dismantling Desegregation: The Quiet Reversal of Brown v. Board of Education*, ed. Gary Orfield and Susan E. Eaton (New York: New Press, 1996), pp. 207–39, and Cheryl Jones and Connie Hill, "Strategy and Tactics in Subsystem Protection: The Politics of Education Reform in Montgomery County, Maryland," in *Changing Urban Education*, ed. Clarence N. Stone (Lawrence: University Press of Kansas, 1998), pp. 139–57.

49. Olson, *Baltimore: The Building of An American City*, p. 396.

50. Eric Garland, "The End of Baltimore As a Blue-Collar Town," *Baltimore Magazine* (December 1980): p. 53.

51. Levine, "A Critical Appraisal of the Baltimore Renaissance," p. 113.

52. David Rusk, *Baltimore Unbound, A Strategy for Regional Renewal* (Baltimore: Abell Foundation, 1996), pp. xv and xxiv.

53. Edward Berkowitz, "Baltimore's Public Schools in a Time of Transition," *Maryland Historical Magazine* 92 (winter 1997): 417.

54. This is not to suggest that black politicians have not reached out to white voters; a few black candidates have gained white support (see chap. 3). Kurt Schmoke, for example, captured white support in his first citywide campaign for state's attorney. During his successful mayoral election in 1987, Schmoke stressed that he wanted to be seen as the candidate of the city as a whole. However, in his 1995 reelection campaign, Schmoke was challenged by white city council president Mary Pat Clarke. The result was a racially polarized election. Local observers criticized Schmoke for making subtle racial appeals to blacks through his campaign posters, with the red, black, and green colors of African nationalism. In the weeks before the election "Schmoke made a heavy pitch to black pride, presenting himself as an example of black success." See Eric Siegel, "Schmoke Sees Need for 'Healing' After Campaign," *Sun,* September 14, 1995; Roger Simon, "The Race Equation Adds Up to a Schmoke Victory," *Sun,* March 13, 1994; and Paul W. Valentine, "Schmoke Victory Reveals Baltimore's Racial Polarization," *Washington Post,* September 15, 1995.

5. SCHOOL REFORM THROUGH SITE-BASED MANAGEMENT

1. Marion Orr, "Urban Regimes and Human Capital Policies: A Study of Baltimore," *Journal of Urban Affairs* 14 (1992): 182.

2. Harry Boyte, *Commonwealth: A Return to Citizen Politics* (New York: Free Press, 1989), p. 123.

3. Betty Malen, Rodney Ogawa, and Jennifer Kranz, "What Do We Know About School-Based Management? A Case Study of the Literature," in *Choice and Control in American Education,* Vol. 2, *The Practice of Choice, Decentralization, and Restructuring,* ed. William Clune and John Witte (Philadelphia: Falmer Press, 1990).

4. Anthony S. Bryk, David Kerbow, and Sharon Rollow, "Chicago School Reforem," in *New Schools for a New Century,* ed. Diane Ravitch and Joseph P. Viteritti (New Haven: Yale University Press, 1997), p. 169.

5. Council of Great City Schools, *National Urban Education Goals, 1992–1993 Indicators Report* (Washington, DC: Council of Great City Schools, 1994).

6. Interview with author, December 4, 1990, Baltimore.

7. Mike Bowler, *The Lessons of Change: Baltimore Schools in the Modern Era,* a report for the Fund for Educational Excellence, Baltimore, MD, 1991, p. 37.

8. Veronica D. Diconti, *Interest Groups and Education Reform: The Latest Crusade to Restructure the Schools* (Lanham, MD: University Press of America, 1996) p. 130.

9. Ibid.

10. Ibid.

11. Ibid.

12. Sandra Crockett, "Pinderhughes Says Quiet Goodbye," *Sun,* June 18, 1988.

13. DiConti, *Interest Groups and Education Reform,* p. 137.

14. Before coming to Baltimore, Richard Hunter served eleven years as superintendent in Richmond, Virginia, where he compiled an impressive record. He implemented a mas-

sive busing plan with minimal controversy, raised reading and math scores, upgraded the teaching of basic subjects, and instituted early-childhood-education programs. Hunter then accepted the superintendency for the Dayton, Ohio, public schools. But he left there after nine months, to the considerable anger of Dayton's school board. Hunter's abrupt departure from Dayton to the University of North Carolina influenced the Baltimore school board so that initially he lost a majority vote to be hired there.

15. Marilyn Gittell and T. Edward Hollander, *Six Urban School Districts* (New York: Praeger Press, 1968), p. 181.

16. DiConti, *Interest Groups and Education Reform*, p. 143.

17. Ibid.

18. Ibid., p. 121.

19. City records show that 42 percent of Baltimore's teachers do not live in the city. Nevertheless, BTU is vocal, and its large membership means that hundreds of volunteers can canvass neighborhoods, operate telephone banks, and stuff envelopes. During the 1987 mayoral primary, hundreds of teachers volunteered on election day to help Schmoke's campaign.

20. Malen, Ogagwa, and Kranz, "What Do We Know About School-Based Management?"

21. DiConti, *Interest Groups and Education Reform*, p. 150.

22. Ibid., p. 151.

23. Will Englund, "Home Rule Plan Draws Fire from Parents, Groups," *Sun*, September 17, 1990.

24. Ibid.

25. Editorial, "School Plan Rates a D-Minus," *Sun*, October 10, 1990.

26. Ibid.

27. Will Englund, "Home Rule Plan Offered for Baltimore Schools," *Sun*, August 19, 1996.

28. DiConti, *Interest Groups and Education Reform*, p. 155.

29. Gelareh Asayesh, "City Schools Reluctant on Pilot Plan," *Sun*, February 13, 1991.

30. DiConti, *Interest Groups and Education Reform*, p. 156.

31. Ibid., pp. 153–54.

32. Ibid, p. 157.

33. Jeffrey Pressman and Aaron Wildavsky, *Implementation* (Berkeley: University of California Press, 1984).

34. Interview with author, Baltimore, August 13, 1992.

35. Will Englund, "Hunter Relinquishes Roles to Mayor," *Sun*, January 7, 1990.

36. Editorial, "Schmoke's Worst Grade," *Sun*, March 21, 1990.

37. Kathy Lally, "Schmoke Says School Chief Will Keep Job," *Sun*, April 12, 1990.

38. Ibid.

39. Ibid.

40. Peter Bachrach and Morton S. Baratz, "Two Faces of Power," *American Political Science Review* 56 (December 1962): 947–52.

41. Lally, "Schmoke Says School Chief Will Keep Job."

42. Editorial, "$125,000-a-Year Cheerleader," *Sun*, April 12, 1990.

43. Will Englund, "Schmoke Tells City School Board to Get Rid of Hunter," *Sun*, December 20, 1990.

44. Bowler, *Lessons of Change*, p. 26.

45. Will Englund and Kathy Lally, "City Principals Told Jobs Depend on Performance," *Sun,* August 7, 1990. While many business leaders applauded, Mayor Schmoke asked Andrews to "back off" from the principals. Schmoke was concerned about the political ramifications of many principals being reassigned or losing their jobs.

46. Mike Bowler, "History," in *The State of Baltimore Schools,* ed. Christopher S. Lambert and Jennean E. Reynolds (Baltimore: Advocates for Children and Youth, June 1997), p. H–17.

47. Along with Amprey's appointment, the board announced that two other candidates for the superintendency, Lillian Gonzalez and Patsy Baker Blackshear, would be hired as Amprey's top deputies. Many observers noted that the "troika" experiment was not only unusual but also a disaster. Several respondents pointed out that Gonzalez had the support of school board president Phillip Farfel and a minority of board members for the top position. Patsy Blackshear, then an associate superintendent in the BCPS, is said to have been the preferred candidate of Baltimore delegate Howard "Pete" Rawlings. At the time, Rawlings was becoming an influential member of the Maryland legislature and later became chair of the House of Delegates Committee on Appropriations, making him a central player in Baltimore's school reform at the state level.

48. Gelareh Asayesh, "Search for a School Superintendent: Walter G. Amprey," *Sun,* April 28, 1991.

49. Associated Black Charities, *A Study of the Management of the Baltimore City Public Schools* (Baltimore: ABC, 1992), p. I-1.

50. Baltimore City Public Schools, *Enterprise Schools Task Force Report* (May 1993).

51. Ibid., p. 8.

52. Joan Jacobson, "Amprey Divides Budget," *Sun,* March 22, 1994.

53. MGT of America, *A Report on Monitoring and Evaluating Implementation of Management Study Recommendations in Baltimore City Public Schools* (Tallahassee, FL, 1995).

54. Ibid., p. vi.

55. For an innovative program designed to prepare and develop public school leaders with the assistance of the Greater Baltimore Committee, see Lawrence E. Leak, Wesley O. Petersen, and Lyle R. Patzkowsky, "Developing Leaders for Urban Schools: The Baltimore Experience," *Urban Education* 31 (January 1997): 510–28.

56. Gary Gately, "Shift to School-Based Management Is Faulted in Report as Poorly Planned," *Sun,* January 13, 1995.

57. Wilbur C. Rich, *Black Mayors and School Politics: The Failure of School Reform in Detroit, Gary and Newark* (New York: Garland, 1996).

6. NEIGHBORHOOD MOBILIZATION

1. Sam Stringfield, *Fourth Year Evaluation of the Calvert School Program at Barclay School* (Baltimore: Center for the Social Organization of Schools, Johns Hopkins University, 1994), p. 2.

2. Ibid., p. 4.

3. Mike Bowler, "At Calvert School, the Curriculum Is Traditional, but Some of the Techniques Aren't," *Sun,* January 22, 1996.

4. Millicent Lawton, "Borrowing from the Basics," *Education Week* (April 20, 1994): 32.

5. Legend has it that Calvert's home-study department was founded in 1906 by Virgil M. Hillyer, the school's headmaster at the time, when a contagious disease (probably whooping cough) raged through the city, confining to bed children enrolled in the school. Today, Calvert's worldwide home-study course reaches about 2,000 children, mostly in remote locations such as ranches, missionary homes, military outposts, and ships at sea.

6. Lawton, "Borrowing from the Basics," p. 32.

7. Marion Orr, "Urban Politics and School Reform: The Case of Baltimore," *Urban Affairs Review* 31 (January 1996): 314–45.

8. Alex Friend, "The Kingdom and the Power: Inside the Abell Foundation, a Bastion of Wealth and Change," *Warfield's Business Record* 7 (December 18, 1992): 1.

9. Orr, "Urban Politics and School Reform," p. 330.

10. Quoted in Robert Barnes, "Schmoke Tilts Scales in Baltimore," *Washington Post,* January 22, 1987.

11. Veronica D. DiConti, *Interest Groups and School Reform* (Lanham, MD: University Press of America, 1996), p. 139.

12. Interview with author, Baltimore, December 4, 1990.

13. Peter Marris and Martin Rein, *Dilemmas of Social Reform: Poverty and Community Action in the United States,* 2d ed. (Chicago: Aldine, 1973).

14. DiConti, *Interest Groups,* p. 146.

15. Ibid.

16. Will Englund, "Barclay Parents Call Schools' Action Unfair," *Sun,* March 17, 1989; Lavinia Edmonds, "The Woman Who Battled the Bureaucrats," *Reader's Digest* 143 (December 1993): 142–47.

17. Gelareh Asayesh, "Barclay Weathers Battle and Flourishes," *Sun,* March 20, 1992.

18. Kathy Lally, "Schmoke Tells City School Board to Get Rid of Hunter, *Sun,* December 20, 1990.

19. DiConti, *Interest Groups,* p. 146.

20. Edmunds, "The Woman Who Battled the Bureaucrats," p. 144.

21. Editorial, "Dr. No," *Sun,* March 11, 1989; see also, editorial, "Hunter in Wonderland," *Sun,* March 16, 1989.

22. Edmunds, "The Woman Who Battled the Bureaucrats."

23. Will Englund, "Mayor Backs Hunter in Rejecting Barclay School Plan," *Sun,* March 11, 1989.

24. Orr, "Urban Politics and School Reform."

25. Friend, "The Kingdom and the Power," p. 1.

26. Clarence N. Stone, "Systemic Power in Community Decision Making," *American Political Science Review* 74 (December 1980): 978–90.

27. Will Englund, "Barclay Wins Curriculum Fight with Mayor's Aid," *Sun,* March 23, 1990.

28. Will Englund, "Hunter Says He Will Stay on the Job," *Sun,* March 21, 1990.

29. Stringfield, *Fourth Year Evaluation.*

30. *Economist* (December 2–8, 1995): 23.

31. See Joe Nathan, ed., *Public Schools by Choice: Expanding Opportunities for Parents, Students, and Teachers* (Minneapolis: Free Spirit Publishing, 1989), and Joe Nathan and James Ysseldyke, "What Minnesota Has Learned About School Choice," *Phi Delta Kappan* 75 (May 1994): 682–88.

32. *Proposal for a Public, Teacher-Directed Community School in the Memorial Stadium Area* (Baltimore, 1993), p. 35 (author's file).

33. Ibid., p. 3.

34. Gary Gately, "Parents Ask to Open School of Their Own," *Sun,* March 4, 1994.

35. Ibid.

36. Ibid.

37. Ibid.

38. Editorial, "Give the Stadium School a Chance," *Evening Sun,* March 10, 1994.

39. Baltimore City Public Schools Stadium School Meeting, "Minutes" (March 28, 1994) (author's file).

40. Ibid. (April 20, 1994) (author's file).

41. "The Stadium School Project: Why K–12?" (Baltimore, n.d) (author's file).

42. *Proposal for a Public, Teacher-Directed Community School in the Memorial Stadium Area,* p. 35.

43. Mary R. Nicholsome to Phillip Farfel, May 27, 1994, CPHA files, Baltimore.

44. Gary Gately, "Board Angers Leaders of Proposed School," *Sun,* June 10,1994.

45. Phillip Farfel to Hathaway Ferebee, June 16, 1994, CPHA files, Baltimore.

46. Quoted in Gary Gately, "New School Shut out of Memorial Stadium," *Sun,* September 3, 1994.

47. Lenora Heilig Nast, Laurence N. Krause, and R. C. Monk, eds., *Baltimore: A Living Renaissance* (Baltimore: Historic Baltimore Society, 1982), p. 28.

48. Katharine Lyall, "A Bicycle Built-for-Two: Public-Private Partnership in Baltimore," *National Civic Review* 72 (November 1983): 540.

49. Sam Stringfield, *Fourth Year Evaluation.*

50. Kathy Lally, "Educators' Four-Day Meeting Puts the Issues on the Board," *Sun,* March 24, 1997.

7. CIVIC ELITES AND THE BALTIMORE COMMONWEALTH

1. Robert D. Putnam, "Tuning In, Tuning Out: The Strange Disappearance of Social Capital in America," *PS: Political Science and Politics* 28 (December 1995): 664–83.

2. On the Boston Compact, see Sandra Waddock, *The National Alliance of Business Compact Project: Business Involvement in Public Education* (Boston: Carroll School of Management, Boston College, 1991); Peter Dreier, "Economic Growth and Economic Justice in Boston: Populist Housing and Jobs Policies," in *Unequal Partnerships,* ed. Gregory Squires (New Brunswick, NJ: Rutgers University Press, 1989); and Eleanor Farrar and Colleen Connolly, *Improving Middle Schools: The Boston Compact Initiative* (Buffalo, NY: Graduate School of Education Publications, 1990).

3. Quoted in Kevin O'Keeffe, *Baltimore Politics, 1971–1986: The Schaefer Years and the Struggle for Succession* (Washington, DC: Georgetown University Press, 1986), p. 91.

4. Harry C. Boyte, *Commonwealth: A Return to Citizen Politics* (New York: Free Press, 1989), p. 119.

5. Quoted in Veronica D. DiConti, *Interest Groups and Education Reform* (University Press of America: Lanham, MD, 1996), pp. 122–23.

6. U.S. Commission on Civil Rights, *Urban Minority Economic Development,* hear-

ings held in Baltimore, Maryland, November 17–18, 1981 (Washington, DC: U.S. Printing Office).

7. Ibid., p. 22.

8. U.S. Commission on Civil Rights, *A Greater Baltimore Commitment: A Study of Urban Minority Economic Development* (Washington, DC: U.S. Printing Office, 1983), p. 21.

9. Ibid., pp. 21 and 95.

10. Marion Orr, "Urban Regimes and School Compacts: The Development of the Detroit Compact," *Urban Review* 25 (June 1993): 105–22.

11. Boyte, *Commonwealth*, p. 120.

12. Quoted in Marion Orr, "Urban Regimes and Human Capital Policies: A Study of Baltimore," *Journal of Urban Affairs* 14 (1992): 179.

13. Robert Crain, *The Politics of Desegregation* (Chicago: National Opinion Research Center, 1968), p. 78.

14. Sharon P. Krefetz, *Welfare Policy-Making and City Politics* (New York: Praeger, 1976), and Peter Bachrach and Morton Baratz, *Power and Poverty* (New York: Oxford University Press, 1970).

15. Quoted in Orr, "Urban Regimes and Human Capital Policies," p. 178.

16. Marilyn Gittell and T. Edward Hollander, *Six Urban School Districts: A Comparative Study of Institutional Response* (New York: Praeger Press, 1968), p. 180.

17. John Crew, E. Nolan, G. Eugene, and R. Newton, *Effective Public Education: The Baltimore Story* (New York: New Dimensions, 1982), p. 42.

18. Quoted in Orr, "Urban Regimes and Human Capital Policies," p. 175.

19. Clarence Stone, *Regime Politics* (Lawrence: University Press of Kansas, 1989), p. 9.

20. Boyte, *Commonwealth*, p. 120.

21. Wiley A. Hall III, "Ballots and Blessings," *Sun Magazine* (August 23, 1987): 8–9, 20–22.

22. Subsequent analyses supported these findings. A 1987 Baltimore Urban League report concludes: "There exists significant evidence which suggests that discrimination in the workplace continues to be a major hurdle to black employment advances, particularly in the Baltimore metropolitan area." A 1991 study conducted by the Joint Center for Political and Economic Studies expressed concern for what it called "the apparent absence of blacks in senior management of most Baltimore companies." The report observed that "very few of these corporations were doing anything to increase the number of black executives." See Dewayne Wickham, *Destiny 2000: The State of Black Baltimore* (Baltimore: Baltimore Urban League, 1987), and Joint Center for Political and Economic Studies, *Moving Up with Baltimore: Creating Career Ladders for Blacks in the Private Sector* (Washington, DC: JCPES, 1991).

23. David Rosenthal and Will Englund, "Who's Got the Clout?" *Sun Magazine* (February 17, 1991): 11.

24. Boyte, *Commonwealth*, p. 120.

25. Ibid.

26. Ibid., pp. 120–21.

27. U.S. Commission on Civil Rights, *Greater Baltimore Commitment*, p. 20.

28. *Time Magazine* (August 24, 1984): 47.

29. Quoted in Marion Orr, "Black Political Incorporation—Phase Two: Baltimore and Detroit" (Ph.D. diss., University of Maryland, 1992), p. 350.

30. Quoted in Orr, "Urban Regimes and Human Capital Policies," p. 179.

31. Quoted in Orr, "Black Political Incorporation—Phase Two," p. 351.

32. Ibid.

33. Ibid., p. 352.

34. Harold A. McDougall, *Black Baltimore: A New Theory of Community* (Philadelphia: Temple University Press, 1993), p. 179.

35. Ibid., p. 352.

36. Quoted in Lynda Gorov, "Baltimore, BUILD Battle Decline in Public Education," *Chicago Reporter* (February 1989): 9.

37. Carol F. Steinbach, "Investing Early," *National Journal* (September 3, 1988): 2193.

38. Quoted in Boyte, *Commonwealth,* p. 121.

39. Ibid., p. 197.

40. Ibid., p. 111.

41. Quoted in Orr, "Black Political Incorporation—Phase Two," p. 347.

42. Kweisi Mfume, *No Free Ride: From the Mean Streets to the Mainstream* (New York: Ballantine Books, 1996), p. 241.

43. Martin Evans, "Baptist Ministers Announces Support for Judge Murphy," *Baltimore Afro-American,* May 10, 1983.

44. O'Keeffe, *Baltimore Politics, 1971–1986,* p. 98.

45. Lisa Leff, "Schaefer, Coalition Square Off," *Washington Post,* November 17, 1986.

46. Quoted in Orr, "Black Political Incorporation—Phase Two," p. 352.

47. Kenneth Wong, *City Choices* (Albany: State University of New York Press, 1990), p. 114.

48. Marion Orr, "Urban Politics and School Reform: The Case of Baltimore," *Urban Affairs Review* 31 (January 1996): 314–45.

49. Leff, "Schaefer, Coalition Square Off," p. B1.

50. Hall, "Ballots and Blessings," p. 8.

51. Quoted in Orr, "Urban Regimes and Human Capital Policies," p. 181.

52. Sandy Banisky and Michael Ollove, "With Schmoke on Record Favoring It, Campaigning Burns Also Backs BUILD," *Sun,* July 1, 1987.

53. Sandra Crockett, "BUILD's Social-Action Goals Praised by Schmoke at Its 10th Anniversary," *Sun,* November 9, 1987.

54. Quoted in Orr, "Black Political Incorporation—Phase Two," p. 360.

55. Ibid., p. 362.

56. City of Baltimore, "Job Description: Baltimore Commonwealth Coordinator," Office of the Mayor, Baltimore, 1990.

57. Steinbach, "Investing Early," p. 2193.

58. To help bolster the level of participation in the Commonwealth, in spring 1988 BUILD volunteers organized a telephone campaign, contacted thousands of parents of high school students, and held dozens of meetings on the program.

59. Peter Szanton, *Baltimore 2000: A Choice of Futures* (Baltimore: Morris Goldseker Foundation, 1986), p. 15.

60. Amy Goldstein, "BUILD Coalition Opens College Doors to City Students, with Mixed Results," *Sun,* September 27, 1987.

61. BUILD leaders pointed to the case of a Patterson High School graduate: a B-plus student, he enrolled at Johns Hopkins in 1987 with the help of scholarships and loans that covered all but $500 of his $17,500 bill for tuition, dormitory room, and meals.

62. John D. Kasarda, "Urban Industrial Transition and the Underclass," *Annals of the American Academy of Political and Social Science* 501 (January 1989): 26–47.

63. Lawrence N. Bailis, Andrew Hahn, Paul Aaron, Jennifer Nahas, and Tom Leavitt, *The Baltimore CollegeBound Foundation: Lessons from an External Evaluation,* report prepared for the Baltimore Community Foundation, Baltimore, Maryland, June 1995, p. 14.

64. Ibid., p. 13.

65. Baltimore's high schools resemble a pyramid. At the apex are four citywide exam schools, Baltimore City College, Western High School, Baltimore Polytechnic Institute, and Baltimore School for the Arts. Nearly 80 percent of these students go on to college. At the base of the pyramid are the zone/neighborhood high schools, where dropout rates are high, SAT scores low, and college attendance is rare.

66. Bailis et al., *Baltimore CollegeBound Foundation,* pp. 19–20.

67. Ibid., p. 19.

68. Rosenthal and Englund, "Who's Got the Clout?" p. 9.

69. William J. Wilson, *The Truly Disadvantaged* (Chicago: University of Chicago Press, 1987).

70. Mark S. Granovetter, "The Strength of Weak Ties," *American Journal of Sociology* 78 (May 1973): 1360–80.

71. Boyte, *Commonwealth,* p. 125.

72. In 1994 William Jews, president and CEO of Blue Cross/Blue Shield of Maryland, was named the first African-American chair of GBC's board.

8. THE DEFEAT OF PRIVATE MANAGEMENT

1. Paul T. Hill, "Contracting in Public Education," in *New Schools for a New Century,* ed. Diane Ravitch and Joseph P. Viteritti (New Haven: Yale University Press, 1997), p. 61.

2. Interview with author, Baltimore, August 28, 1992.

3. Kenneth Eskey, "Public Schools, Private Contractors: Firm Hopes to Earn Profit from Rejuvenating Education," *Houston Chronicle,* August 30, 1992.

4. Paul W. Valentine, "Private Firm May Run Nine Maryland Schools," *Washington Post,* June 10, 1992.

5. For a detailed discussion of EAI's corporate structure and of John Golle, see Craig E. Richards, Rima Shore, and Max B. Sawicky, *Risky Business: Private Management of Public Schools* (Washington, DC: Economic Policy Institute, 1996).

6. Education Alternatives, Inc., *Schools That Work* (Minneapolis: EAI, n.d.), p. 1.

7. Ibid.

8. Quoted in Richards, Shore, and Sawicky, *Risky Business,* p. 22.

9. Ibid.

10. Amy Virshup, "John Golle's Hard Lessons," *Washington Post Magazine,* April 7, 1996, p. 15.

11. Robert C. Embry Jr. to Marion Orr, September 9, 1994 (in author's file).

12. Norman J. Walsh, "Public Schools, Inc.: Baltimore's Risky Enterprise," *Education and Urban Society* 27 (February 1995): 202. Walsh served as associate superintendent when the decision was made to contract with EAI.

13. Minutes of the Meeting of the Board of School Commissioners, Baltimore City Public Schools (May 16, 1991), Legislative Reference Library, City Hall, Baltimore, p. 6.

14. Gelareh Asayesh, "Baltimore Board Weighs Private School Operation," *Sun,* May 17, 1991.

15. Minutes of the Meeting of the Board of School Commissioners, May 16, 1991, p. 7.

16. Interview with author, Baltimore, August 28, 1992.

17. Mike Bowler, "Other Areas Have Dropped School Boards," *Sun,* November 11, 1995.

18. Mark Bomster, "Minneapolis Firm to Run Nine Schools," *Sun,* June 10, 1992.

19. Ibid.

20. Donna M. Owens, "Nine Public Schools to Undergo Change," *Baltimore Afro-American,* June 13, 1992.

21. Editorial, "Schools in Another Dimension," *Sun,* June 11, 1992.

22. Thomas W. Waldron, "Teaching Firm Bound for Baltimore Gets Rave Reviews," *Sun,* June 14, 1992.

23. Arnold Graf, "Seeing No Value in 'Privatized' Public Education," *Sun,* July 20, 1992.

24. Michael A. Fletcher, "Schmoke: No School Moratorium," *Sun,* July 21, 1992.

25. Mark Bomster, "Schmoke Facing Challenge Tonight on School Reform," *Sun,* July 20, 1992, and Fletcher, "Schmoke: No School Moratorium."

26. Fletcher, "Schmoke."

27. Ibid.

28. Interview with author, Baltimore, August 28, 1992.

29. Marion Orr, "The Challenge of School Reform in Baltimore: Race, Jobs, and Politics," in *Changing Urban Education,* ed. Clarence N. Stone (Lawrence: University Press of Kansas, 1998), pp. 93–117.

30. Employment discrimination in Baltimore's private-sector economy is documented in Joint Center for Political and Economic Studies, *Moving Up with Baltimore: Creating Career Ladders for Blacks in the Private Sector* (Washington, DC: JCPES, 1991); Dewayne Wickham, *Destiny 2000: The State of Black Baltimore,* report from the Baltimore Urban League, 1987; and U.S. Commission on Civil Rights, *Greater Baltimore Commitment: A Study of Urban Minority Economic Development* (Washington, DC: U.S. Printing Office, 1983).

31. Sara Horowitz, "A Public Defeat on Privatization," *Washington Post,* March 3, 1994; Charles Mahtesian, "The Precarious Politics of Privatizing Schools," *Governing* 12 (June 1994): 46–51.

32. Mike Bowler, "EAI Taps Xerox Executive to Take Over in Baltimore," *Sun,* May 6, 1995.

33. Mitchell, "Pastors Review Plan."

34. Interview with author, Baltimore, August 28, 1992.

35. It is also the case that a number of persons knew Schmoke and Amprey were considering private management before the formal public announcement. The matter came before the school board in May 1991. As an education reporter put it: "It's something that shouldn't have taken a lot of people by surprise. In fact, they should have known this was taking place."

36. William Trombley, "For-Profit Public Schools Test Is Off to a Mixed Start," *Los Angeles Times,* December 22, 1992.

37. Interview with author, Baltimore, July 28, 1993.

38. Editorial, "The Future of Our Schools," *Baltimore Afro-American,* June 13, 1992.

39. The growing split between Schmoke and BUILD was the subject of much discussion in the local press. See, for example, editorial, "Stop the Bickering," *Baltimore Afro-American,* July 25, 1992; editorial, "Let the Mayor Be Mayor," *Sun,* July 23, 1992; and the Reverend Sidney Daniels, "Baltimore Must Strive to Keep Her Priorities in Place," *Baltimore Afro-American,* August 8, 1992.

40. Baltimore City Public Schools, *Professional Services Agreement—Educational Alternatives, Inc.* (Baltimore: City of Baltimore, 1992).

41. Quoted in Walsh, "Public Schools, Inc.," p. 196.

42. Lois C. Williams and Lawrence E. Leak, "School Privatization's First Big Test: EAI in Baltimore," *Educational Leadership* 24 (October 1996): 57.

43. Richards, Shore, and Sawicky, *Risky Business,* especially chapter 3.

44. Former superintendent Richard C. Hunter, who became an education professor, discusses the problems this arrangement creates for Baltimore's school superintendent; see "The Mayor Versus the School Superintendent: Political Incursions into Metropolitan School Politics," *Education and Urban Society* 29 (February 1997): 217–32.

45. Mark Bomster, "Contract Passed with Firm to Run City Schools," *Sun,* July 23, 1992.

46. Ibid.

47. Gary Cohn, JoAnna Daemmrich, and Kim Clark, "McLean Telephoned Speculator Before EAI Stock Dropped," *Sun,* January 6, 1994.

48. Bomster, "Contract Passed with Firm to Run City Schools."

49. Ibid.

50. John Doxey, "Baltimore School Experiment Could Fail amid Squabbling," *City and State,* November 16, 1992.

51. Trombley, "For-Profit Public Schools Test Is Off to a Mixed Start."

52. Mark Bomster, "Minnesota Firm Tells Baltimore Parents How It Can Teach Kids and Make Money," *Sun,* June 26, 1992.

53. Mike Bowler, *Lessons of Change; Baltimore Schools in the Modern Era,* report commissioned by the Fund for Educational Excellence, Baltimore, 1991, p. 12.

54. Mark Bomster, "Nine Schools Start to Mend," *Sun,* November 15, 1992.

55. Gary Putka, "Baltimore Test of Privatization Gets a Bad Start," *Wall Street Journal,* September 23, 1992.

56. Mark Bomster, "City Teachers Divided on Takeover of Schools," *Sun,* August 26, 1992.

57. Gary Gately, "250 Protest Impending Layoffs, Moves for School Workers," *Sun,* June 7, 1994.

58. The American Federation of Teachers, BTU's parent organization, targeted EAI in its opposition to private management of public schools. At its annual convention in 1994, AFT delegates called for a moratorium on contracts with EAI, claiming it poorly managed the nine Baltimore schools. In March 1994, the AFT asked the U.S. Department of Education to investigate whether EAI violated federal law by cutting services to students with learning disabilities. The AFT also released a scathing report that raised "grave questions" about EAI's performance. Moreover, Albert Shanker, then-president of the AFT, used his national newspaper column to criticize EAI. See Associated Press, "Teachers Union Calls for Moratorium on EAI," *Sun,* July 18, 1994; American Federation of Teachers, *The Private Management of Public Schools: An Analysis of the EAI Experience in Balti-*

more (Washington, DC: AFT, n.d.); Gary Gately, "Teachers' Union Asks for Federal EAI Investigation," *Sun*, March 31, 1994; and Albert Shanker, "Striking a Good Bargain," *New York Times*, June 5, 1994, and "What Are We Selling?" *New York Times*, June 18, 1995.

59. Norris P. West and JoAnna Daemmrich, "Teacher Union Seeks Amprey's Resignation," *Sun*, June 1, 1994.

60. Lois C. Williams and Lawrence E. Leak, *The UMBC Evaluation of the Tesseract Program in Baltimore City* (Center for Educational Research: University of Maryland, Baltimore County, 1995), p. 118.

61. Early in 1966 Superintendent Laurence Paquin (1965–1967) proposed a reorganization of city high schools, calling for an end to tracking. However, his plan "ran into a wall of resistance at City College, which would have lost its identity as an exclusive college-preparatory school." Politically influential parents and alumni complained to members of the city council. Then-city councillor, William Donald Schaefer, an alumnus of City College, held hearings on the issue. City College was not changed; the Paquin plan died. See Bowler, *Lessons Of Change*, p. 10.

62. Will Englund, "System Tolerates Poor Teachers, Foundering Pupils," *Sun*, May 2, 1988.

63. Laura Lippman, "The City Is Her Stage," *Sun*, August 25, 1995; JoAnna Daemmrich, "Clarke's Loss Ends an Era," *Sun*, September 17, 1995.

64. Joanna Daemmrich, "'95 Campaign Has Already Begun: Can Mary Pat Clarke Beat Mayor Schmoke?" *Sun*, November 27, 1994.

65. Gary Gately, "Give All Schools as Much Funding as Those EAI Runs, Clarke Urges," *Sun*, March 4, 1994.

66. Gary Gately, "Public Can Speak Tonight on School Privatization," *Sun*, May 25, 1994.

67. Gary Gately, "Council Members Call for a Delay on EAI Expansion," *Sun*, May 26, 1994.

68. JoAnna Daemmrich, "Council Seeks to Oversee Privatization Effort," *Sun*, May 17, 1994.

69. Mayor Kurt L. Schmoke to Mary Pat Clarke and members of the city council, "Veto Message of Bill 727," June 16, 1994, Legislative Reference Library, City Hall, Baltimore.

70. Gately, "250 Protest Impending Layoffs."

71. Walter G. Amprey, "An Open Letter to Teachers," *Baltimore Afro-American*, July 2, 1994.

72. Gary Gately, "Amprey Won't Spend More to Expand EAI," *Sun*, June 11, 1994.

73. Mike Bowler and Gary Gately, "Inquiry into Tests Launched," *Sun*, November 19, 1994.

74. Gary Gately and JoAnna Daemmrich, "Pressure Grows to Terminate EAI Experiment," *Sun*, October 19, 1994.

75. Gary Gately and JoAnna Daemmrich, "Mayor Links Future of EAI to Test Scores," *Sun*, October 21, 1994.

76. Williams and Leak, *UMBC Evaluation*.

77. Using a different technique, Richards, Shore, and Sawicky found larger disparities. Their analysis showed that EAI's eight elementary schools' per pupil allowance was 26 percent above the district cost for elementary school students. Harlem Park, the only middle school run by EAI, had a per pupil allowance 36 percent above other middle schools; see *Risky Business*, pp. 108–9.

78. Williams and Leak, *UMBC Evaluation*, p. 115.

79. Williams and Leak, "School Privatization's First Big Test, p. 57.

80. Jean Thompson, "City School Board Ends Effort to Privatize," *Sun,* December 1, 1995.

81. Alex Molnar, "Education for Profit: A Yellow Brick Road to Nowhere," *Educational Leadership* 52 (September 1994): 72–75.

82. Clarence N. Stone, "Civic Capacity and Urban School Reform," in Stone, ed., *Changing Urban Education,* p. 268.

83. Marilyn McCraven, "Black Voters Sensed a 'Crisis' and Turned Out," *Sun,* September 17, 1995.

9. SCHOOL REFORM AND THE CITY-STATE CONNECTION

1. Daniel Elazar, *American Federalism: A View from the States* (New York: Harper and Row, 1984).

2. Frederick Wirt and Michael W. Kirst, *Schools in Conflict* (Berkeley, CA: McCutchen, 1992), pp. 257–58.

3. Kathy Lally, "Clash Over Fate of Minds," *Sun,* February 18, 1996.

4. *The Report of the Governor's Commission on School Performance,* Maryland State Dept. of Education, August 1989, Annapolis.

5. David R. Berman, "Takeovers of Local Governments: An Overview and Evaluation of State Policies," *Publius: The Journal of Federalism* 25 (summer 1995): 55–70.

6. Jean Anyon, *Ghetto Schooling: Political Economy of Urban Educational Reform* (New York: Teachers College Press, 1997), and Wilbur C. Rich, *Black Mayors and School Politics: The Failure of Reform in Detroit, Gary, and Newark* (New York: Garland Press, 1996).

7. Jean Thompson, "Parents Join Forces Against MSPAP Test," *Sun,* May 4, 1997.

8. Gary Gately and Mike Bowler, "Make the Grade: Maryland Demands That Local Districts Improve Schools, or Risk State Takeover," *Sun,* August 28, 1994.

9. Greater Baltimore Committee, *The Strength of Maryland Depends on the State of Baltimore* (Baltimore: GBC, 1991), p. 10.

10. Gary Gately, "Two Schools Targeted for State Takeover," *Sun,* January 18, 1994.

11. Ivy D. Jernigan, "Friends of Douglass High School Try to Derail State Takeover," *Baltimore Afro-American,* February 26, 1994.

12. Ivy D. Jernigan, "Douglass Supporters Prepare for Future Threats of Takeover," *Baltimore Afro-American,* April 23, 1994.

13. Melody Simmons and Gary Gately, "Patterson Students Walk Out," *Sun,* June 8, 1994.

14. Jean Thompson, "Reform Ordered at Three Schools in Baltimore," *Sun,* February 2, 1998.

15. Jean Thompson, "City Presses State to Let It Mend Its Own Schools," *Sun,* January 28, 1995.

16. Veronica D. DiConti, *Interest Groups and Education Reform* (Lanham, MD: University Press of America, 1996), pp. 143–44.

17. Michael A. Fletcher, "City to Sue Maryland over Funding for Education," *Sun,* May 15, 1992.

18. Richard Tapscott, "Sparks Fly over Schmoke's Aid Fight," *Washington Post,* May 26, 1992.

19. Editorial, "Equal Educational Opportunity," *Sun*, May 17, 1992.

20. John W. Frece, "Mayor's Threat of Lawsuit Draws Fire from Legislature and Governor," *Sun*, May 16, 1992.

21. Letter from Delegate Timothy F. Maloney to the Hon. Mayor Kurt L. Schmoke, May 26, 1992 (on file with author).

22. Michael A. Fletcher, "Schmoke Decides Against Suing State to Get More Money for Poorer Schools," *Sun*, June 11, 1993.

23. John S. Ward to the Hon. Kurt L. Schmoke, January 4, 1993 (in author's file).

24. *The Report of the Governor's Commission on School Funding*, Maryland State Dept. of Education, January 1994, Baltimore.

25. Montgomery County's liberalism dates back to the 1950s when middle-class reformers wrested control of the county from E. Brooke Lee, leader of the "country club conservatives" who held sway from the 1920s until 1946. During the 1960s Montgomery's influence in Annapolis and in statewide elections was consistently in favor of civil rights, welfare, consumer, and environmentalist legislation. For the past decade the county has been represented in the U.S. Congress by Connie Morella, a liberal-to-moderate Republican.

26. See Cheryl L. Jones and Connie Hill, "Strategy and Tactics in Subsystem Protection: The Politics of Education Reform in Montgomery County, Maryland," in *Changing Urban Education*, ed. Clarence N. Stone (Lawrence: University Press of Kansas, 1998), pp. 139–57.

27. Quoted in Lanny J. Davis, "Montgomery and Baltimore: Tale of Two Jurisdictions," *Sun*, December 6, 1992.

28. Editorial, "Mr. Heller's Question," *Silver Spring Gazette*, September 8, 1993.

29. *Report, Governor's Commission on School Funding*, pp. 24–31.

30. Dennis E. Gale, *Washington, D.C.: Inner-City Revitalization and Minority Suburbanization* (Philadelphia: Temple University Press, 1987), and Valerie C. Johnson, "The Political Consequences of Black Suburbanization: Prince George's County, Maryland, 1971–1994" (Ph.D. diss., University of Maryland, 1995).

31. Susan E. Eaton and Elizabeth Crutcher, "Magnets, Media, and Mirages: Prince George's County's 'Miracle' Cure," in *Dismantling Desegregation*, ed. Gary Orfield and Susan E. Eaton (New York: New Press, 1996), pp. 265–89.

32. Richard Tapscott, "Baltimore Official Rips Legislative Criticism," *Washington Post*, December 5, 1992.

33. Catherine Marshall, Douglas Mitchell, and Frederick Wirt, *Culture and Education Policy in American States* (New York: Falmer Press, 1989), pp. 17–18.

34. John W. Frece, "Rawlings Now Has the Power to Help His Hometown, but . . . ," *Sun*, November 17, 1992.

35. Letter from Delegate Howard P. Rawlings to the Hon. Kurt L. Schmoke, May 22, 1990 (author's file).

36. Ibid.

37. Peter Jensen, "Rawlings Undeterred by Flak over School Aid," *Sun*, February 17, 1996.

38. In an effort to "ensure sensitivity" to the issues facing the largely African-American school population and central office administrators, two senior African Americans from the consultant firm's staff "played major roles throughout the study process." Further, an external review committee of prominent black and white civic and business leaders (among them Mayor Schmoke's personal minister, the Reverend Marion C. Bascom; Carol Reckling

of BUILD; McDonald's franchise owner Osborne Payne; and civic leader Walter Sondheim) oversaw the study process.

39. Associated Black Charities, *A Report of a Management Study of the Baltimore City Public Schools,* June 26, 1992.

40. Ibid., p. 3–24.

41. Ibid., p. 3–23.

42. Ibid., p. 3–32.

43. Ibid., p. 3–36.

44. Ibid., p. 3–35.

45. Ibid., p. 1–4.

46. Ibid., p. 1–6.

47. Gary Gately and Mike Bowler, "Baltimore to Sue State for More School Dollars," *Sun,* December 2, 1994.

48. ACLU Foundation of Maryland, *Education Casenotes* 1, 1 (January 1996): 2.

49. Eric Siegel, "Schmoke to Delay Lawsuit," *Sun,* January 20, 1995.

50. MGT of America, *A Report on the Monitoring and Evaluating Implementation of Management Study Recommendations in Baltimore City Public Schools,* January 12, 1995.

51. Gary Gately, "Shift to School-Based Management Is Faulted in Reports as Poorly Planned," *Sun,* January 13, 1995.

52. Letter from Howard P. Rawlings to Community Leaders in Baltimore City, January 24, 1995 (author's file).

53. *Mayor and City Council of Baltimore vs. State of Maryland* (Circuit Court for Baltimore City, September 15, 1995).

54. Letter from Gov. Parris N. Glendening to the Hon. Casper R. Taylor Jr., May 28, 1996 (in author's file).

55. Letter from Gov. Parris N. Glendening to the Hon. Kurt Schmoke, May 28, 1996 (in author's file).

56. Letter from Mayor Kurt L. Schmoke to the Hon. Parris Glendening, June 14, 1996 (in author's file).

57. Letter from Mayor Kurt L. Schmoke to the Hon. Parris Glendening, June 20, 1996 (in author's file).

58. Henry W. Bogdan, "Letter to the Editor," *Sun,* May 23, 1996.

59. A study prepared by the Council of the Great City Schools also estimated that Baltimore would need approximately $577.6 million more a year if it were to provide educational services comparable to the state's six wealthiest school districts. See Michael Casserly, "State Funding of the Baltimore City Public Schools: An Analysis of Adequacy," report for the Council of Great City Schools, Washington DC, October 1996.

60. Editorial, "Schools: The Mayor's Money Pot," *Sun,* August 8, 1996.

61. Ronnell M. Maybank, "Clergy, Educators Blast State Plan to Take Over City Schools," *Baltimore Afro-American,* August 10, 1996.

62. Fern Shen and Charles Babington, "Maryland, Baltimore Plan Overhaul of City Schools," *Washington Post,* November 22, 1996.

63. "School Board Lashes Out at Restructuring Proposal," *Sun,* February 16, 1996.

64. Jean Thompson and Eric Siegel, "City, State Sign Deal for Schools," *Sun,* November 7, 1996.

65. Ibid.

66. *Bradford v. Maryland State Board of Education,* "Consent Decree," November 26, 1996 (in author's files).

67. Margie Hyslop, "Prince George's, Montgomery Counties Unite in School Bucks War," *Montgomery Journal,* February 6, 1997.

68. Thomas W. Waldron and William F. Zorzi Jr., "House Passes Measure on City Schools," *Sun,* April 6, 1997.

69. "Baltimore Aid Critics Called 'Hogs,'" *Montgomery Journal,* March 20, 1997.

70. Terry Neal and Manuel Perez-Rivas, "Heated Rhetoric Roils Maryland Assembly," *Washington Post,* January 12, 1997.

71. Quoted in Mark Bomster, "Leaner Schools Yet to Shake Pudgy Image," *Sun,* January 17, 1993.

72. Josh Kurtz, "Unions Fight Baltimore School Deal," *Silver Spring Gazette,* February 19, 1997.

73. For interesting local commentary and analysis on this point, see Gregory Kane, "City Should Rethink Selling Control of Schools Cheaply," *Sun,* March 22, 1997, and William F. Zorzi Jr., "Power and City Schools Bill," *Sun,* April 8, 1997.

74. Jean Thompson, "Ministers Join PTA Group in Opposition to Giving Up Control of Baltimore Schools," *Sun,* March 26, 1997.

75. "Two Ministers Join Effort to Defeat City Schools Deal," *Sun,* April 1, 1997.

76. The open letter was published in the *Sun,* April 1, 1997.

77. Tony White, "Community Leaders Oppose School Settlement," *Baltimore Afro-American,* April 5, 1997.

10. LESSONS FROM THE BALTIMORE EXPERIENCE

1. Floyd Hunter, *Community Power Structure* (Chapel Hill: University of North Carolina Press, 1953).

2. See Stokely Carmichael and Charles V. Hamilton, *Black Power: The Politics of Liberation in America* (New York: Vintage Books, 1967), especially pp. 2–32.

3. Robert D. Putnam, "Tuning In, Tuning Out: The Strange Disappearance of Social Capital in America," *PS: Political Science and Politics* 28 (December 1995): 664–83.

4. John Portz, Lana Stein, and Robin R. Jones, *City Schools and City Politics* (Lawrence: University Press of Kansas, 1999), p. 35.

5. Among the many provisions of the legislation is a requirement that at least four of the nine members of the Baltimore school board have experience working in a high-level management position within a large business or with a nonprofit or government entity. When the new board was appointed in May 1997, it was composed of leaders from the corporate community, top administrators from area universities, and volunteers with high-caliber experience as managers.

6. Wilbur C. Rich, *Black Mayors and School Politics: The Failure of Reform in Detroit, Gary, and Newark* (New York: Garland Press, 1996), p. 211.

7. Robert Guy Matthews, "Mayor's Focus Is Back on Downtown," *Sun,* January 23, 1998.

8. Sam Stringfield, *Fourth Year Evaluation of the Calvert School Program at Barclay School* (Baltimore: Johns Hopkins University, Center for the Social Organizations of Schools, n.d), p. 4 (emphasis in original).

9. U.S. General Accounting Office, *School Finance: State and Federal Efforts to Target Poor Students* (Washington, DC: U.S. Printing Office, 1998).

10. Robert D. Putnam, *Making Democracy Work* (Princeton: Princeton University Press, 1993), p. 167 (emphasis added).

11. See Francis Fukuyama, *Trust: The Social Virtues and the Creation of Prosperity* (New York: Free Press, 1996).

12. Adolph Reed Jr., "Demobilization in the New Black Political Regime," in *The Bubbling Cauldron: Race, Ethnicity, and the Urban Crisis,* ed. Michael Peter Smith and Joe R. Feagin (Minneapolis: University of Minnesota Press, 1995), p. 189.

13. Barbara Ferman, *Challenging the Growth Machine: Neighborhood Politics in Chicago and Pittsburgh* (Lawrence: University Press of Kansas, 1996).

14. Steven P. Erie, *Rainbow's End: Irish-Americans and the Dilemmas of Urban Machine Politics, 1840–1985* (Berkeley: University of California Press, 1988).

15. Robert D. Putnam, *Making Democracy Work,* p. 181.

16. See Russell Hardin, *One for All: The Logic of Group Conflict* (Princeton: Princeton University Press, 1995).

17. See Clarence N. Stone, "Civic Capacity and Urban School Reform," in *Changing Urban Education,* ed. Clarence N. Stone (Lawrence: University Press of Kansas, 1998), pp. 250–73.

18. Richard Edward DeLeon, *Left Coast City: Progressive Politics in San Francisco, 1975–1991* (Lawrence: University Press of Kansas, 1992).

19. Richard E. DeLeon, "Progressive Politics in the Left Coast City: San Francisco," in *Racial Politics in American Cities,* ed. Rufus P. Browning, Dale Rogers Marshall, and David H. Tabb, 2d ed. (New York: Longman Press, 1997), p. 140.

20. For an insightful discussion of issues concerning the movement from biracial coalition-building to the much more difficult multiracial coalitions, see the essays in *The Politics of Minority Coalitions: Race, Ethnicity, and Shared Uncertainties,* ed. Wilbur C. Rich (Westport, CT: Praeger Publishers, 1996).

21. Rich, *Black Mayors and School Politics,* p. 31.

22. Gary Orfield and Susan Eaton, *Dismantling Desegregation* (New York: New Press, 1996), p. xv.

23. Mark Granovetter, "The Strength of Weak Ties," *American Journal of Sociology* 78 (May 1973): 1360–80.

24. Mark Schneider, Paul Teske, Melissa Marschall, Michael Mintrom, and Christine Roch, "Institutional Arrangements and the Creation of Social Capital: The Effects of Public School Choice," *American Political Science Review* 91 (March 1997): 82–93.

25. Louann A. Bierlein, "The Charter School Movement," in *New Schools for a New Century: The Redesign of Urban Education,* ed. Diane Ravitch and Joseph Viteritti (New Haven: Yale University Press, 1997), pp. 37–60.

26. Tim Simmons, "Charter Schools' Diversity Is Challenge for Board," *Raleigh News and Observer,* June 4, 1998.

27. Gunnar Myrdal, *An American Dilemma,* 2d ed. (New York: Harper and Row, 1962), p. 952.

Index

CPSIA information can be obtained
at www.ICGtesting.com
Printed in the USA
FSHW020923221221
87025FS